Investment Demand

and U. S. Economic Growth

Investment Demand and U. S. Economic Growth

Bert G. Hickman

The Brookings Institution *Washington D.C.*

[1965]

Published February 1965

Library of Congress Catalogue Card Number 65-16626

THE BROOKINGS INSTITUTION is an independent organization devoted to nonpartisan research, education, and publication in economics, government, foreign policy, and the social sciences generally. Its principal purposes are to aid in the development of sound public policies and to promote public understanding of issues of national importance.

The Institution was founded December 8, 1927, to merge the activities of the Institute for Government Research, founded in 1916, the Institute of Economics, founded in 1922, and the Robert Brookings Graduate School of Economics and Government, founded in 1924.

The general administration of the Institution is the responsibility of a self-perpetuating Board of Trustees. The Trustees are likewise charged with maintaining the independence of the staff and fostering the most favorable conditions for creative research and education. The immediate direction of the policies, program, and staff of the Institution is vested in the President, assisted by the division directors and an advisory council, chosen from the professional staff of the Institution.

In publishing a study, the Institution presents it as a competent treatment of a subject worthy of public consideration. The interpretations and conclusions in such publications are those of the author or authors and do not purport to represent the views of the other staff members, officers, or trustees of the Brookings Institution.

Foreword

THE INABILITY of the United States to achieve full employment since 1957 has caused widespread concern about the viability of the economy and the chances of following a full employment growth path in the future. In this study, Bert G. Hickman, a member of the senior economics staff of the Brookings Institution, seeks to provide a better understanding of the causes of the recent slowdown of growth and of the prospects for maintaining a satisfactory growth rate in the future. He analyzes the key role played by the demand of business firms for investment in plant and equipment and applies the results to an analysis of recent and prospective trends of potential investment demand at full employment.

The author wishes to express his thanks for the constructive comments and suggestions of the Reading Committee, which consisted of R. A. Gordon, Dale W. Jorgenson, and Arthur M. Okun. He is also indebted to Jack Alterman, W. Locke Anderson, Edward Denison, and Robert Eisner for reading the manuscript and offering many helpful comments. The project has benefited greatly from the assistance of Sheau-eng Lau in data collection, preparation, and processing. Mrs. Lau also drew the charts. Use was made of the excellent program for data processing and multiple regression prepared by Rudolf Rhomberg and Lorette Boissonneault. Frank deLeeuw and Ann Walka provided helpful statistical advice and programming assistance. Virginia Haaga edited the manuscript and prepared the index. The study was prepared in the Economic Studies Division, which is under the direction of Joseph A. Pechman.

The research for this study was financed by a grant from the Ford Foundation. The Institution is grateful for this support.

The opinions and interpretations are those of the author and do not purport to represent the views of other staff members, officers, or trustees of the Brookings Institution, or of the Ford Foundation.

ROBERT D. CALKINS
President

November 1964
The Brookings Institution
1775 Massachusetts Ave., N.W.
Washington, D.C.

Contents

Tables

Charts

PART I

1 / *Introduction and Summary*

SINCE 1957 THE UNITED STATES economy has failed to achieve full employment even at business cycle peaks. The gap that opened between the nation's growing productive potential and the total demand for goods and services during the 1958 recession was narrowed but never eliminated during the ensuing business expansions of 1958–60 and 1961–64. Thus a deficient growth rate of aggregate demand was the proximate cause of the persistent economic slack, and the primary purpose of this study is to demonstrate the key role of business fixed investment demand in the aggregate demand lag and to form a judgment about probable trends in fixed investment demand during the remainder of the 1960's.

Investment is both a source of demand for current output and a determinant of the growth of capital stock and potential output. This simple truism is at the heart of the modern growth theory that was nurtured in the writings of Roy F. Harrod and Evsey D. Domar and has been extensively developed by Robert M. Solow and others in recent years. This study is more in the spirit of Harrod and Domar than of Solow, since it takes the growth path of potential output as given and asks whether business demand for plant and equipment can rise fast enough to keep the economy moving along that path—instead of investigating the effect that realized investment has on the potential growth rate itself.[1] This distinction will be elaborated on as the analysis proceeds.

My research procedure was to estimate statistical investment demand functions from time series for nineteen industrial sectors and for the entire business economy by multiple regression techniques and then to apply the results to an analysis of recent and prospective trends of potential fixed investment demand at full employment. The study falls naturally into two main divisions. The investment functions are described and their basic

[1] The best empirical study of the determinants of potential economic growth in the United States is that of Edward F. Denison, *The Sources of Economic Growth in the United States* (Committee for Economic Development, 1962).

properties analyzed in Chapters 2–5. Some of the material in these chapters is necessarily technical and may be skipped by the general reader who is more interested in the substantive conclusions than in the assumptions on which they rest. Those substantive conclusions are developed in Chapters 6–9, in which the investment equations are applied to the analysis of investment trends. Finally, the sensitivity of the principal conclusions to certain crucial assumptions is investigated in Appendix A.

Principal Characteristics of the Investment Functions

The investment model underlying the demand equations is set forth in Chapter 2. It is a capital stock adjustment model, in which net investment, or the change in net (depreciated) capital stock during year t, is assumed to depend on the gap between the existing capital stock and the stock that would be desired in long-term equilibrium (under the conditions prevailing in year t). It is *not* assumed, however, that the entire gap will actually be eliminated and long-term equilibrium established during year t, owing to lags in the adjustment process. Thus in order to implement the theory empirically, it is necessary to specify both the determinants of desired stock and the general form of the adjustment process.

Desired capital stock is assumed to depend on (a) output, (b) relative prices, and (c) time. Both lagged and current outputs are included in the equations for most sectors on the hypothesis that businessmen rely on past as well as on current experience when estimating expected long-term or normal output levels in order to make investment decisions. Similar treatment is accorded the relative price variables although significant price relationships were obtained in only seven industries. A time trend is included in all equations to allow for the effects of technical progress on the average productivity or output capacity of the stock of plant and equipment.

In addition to the expectational lag implied by the inclusion of lagged terms for output and prices in the function for desired stock, a lag is also assumed in the speed of adjustment of desired to actual stock. This adjustment or reaction lag is due partly to uncertainty and partly to technical and institutional delays in financing, ordering, producing, and installing plant and equipment. The specific magnitudes of the expectational and reaction lags can be inferred from the investment regression. In combination, the two lags imply that the investment response to a once-for-all increase of output or relative prices will typically take the form of a distributed lag in which net investment rises to a peak in the second or third year following the change and declines progressively thereafter.

The stock-adjustment model directly concerns only net investment. Replacement investment is not neglected, however, since it is assumed to equal current depreciation. Since depreciation is measured gross of obsolescence, this concept of replacement demand allows for effective partial retirement of old assets through functional downgrading and less intensive utilization, as well as for the direct substitution of a new asset for one that is being permanently retired. Because the depreciation estimates underlying the capital stock data are based on an exponential or declining-balance formula, depreciation is functionally related to net capital stock. Thus the net investment regression can be used to predict gross as well as net investment if an exogenous estimate of the depreciation rate is supplied. This is the procedure followed in estimating gross investment demand for alternative paths of actual or potential output in the later chapters.

The process by which a single investment regression was selected for each industry to best "explain" the postwar behavior of net investment within the confines of the basic theoretical model is detailed in Chapter 3. The equations were fitted by ordinary least squares to annual data for 1949–60, although many of them also contain lagged explanatory variables going back to 1948 or 1947. The final set of regressions includes equations for aggregate business fixed investment and for investment in seven major sectors—manufacturing, railroads, nonrail transportation, public utilities, communications, commercial and other enterprises, and farming—and thirteen manufacturing sub-industries. On the whole, the equations are reasonably satisfactory as judged by the usual statistical criteria, although their quality naturally varies and the results are much better for some industries than for others. In particular the equations for major sectors are generally superior to those for the manufacturing sub-industries, so less weight is given the latter group in the subsequent analysis of investment trends. Fortunately excellent results were obtained for the important aggregative equation. Full details on the statistical properties of the regressions are given in Chapter 3, including a test of their forecasting ability during 1961–62, or two years beyond the original period of fit.

As for the economic implications of the equations, the following points should be stressed. First, the aggregative equation and those for all individual industries except railroads and public utilities assume constant returns to scale. As is explained in Chapter 3, it was found that better statistical results could generally be obtained by imposing an a priori value of unity on the long-term elasticity of capital stock with respect to output, and this amounts to assuming constant returns to scale. It is likely that slightly increasing returns to scale do in fact prevail for the economy as a whole, but the regression equation obtained by permitting the value of the long-term output elasticity of capital stock to be determined by the data would lead to virtually the same conclusions as the present aggregative equation with its imposed unitary elasticity.

Second, meaningful price coefficients were obtained in only seven industries—stone, clay, and glass, textiles, and miscellaneous nondurable manufactures, and nonrail transportation, communications, farming, and the commercial and other sector. These coefficients refer to relative price variables formed from a combination of capital goods prices, interest rates, depreciation rates, and either wage rates or product prices. These compound variables were chosen because it is relative prices which theoretically influence investment decisions (Chapter 2). Additional regressions were nevertheless run to test whether the compound variables were covering up offsetting influences among the component prices. These experiments failed to produce meaningful coefficients for the separate prices where none had been found for the compound variables. These negative findings may establish a presumption that apart from a cyclical timing effect, to be discussed later, aggregate business fixed investment is influenced only weakly or not at all by changes in interest rates, construction costs, wage-price ratios, and the like. But it is merely a presumption, for reasons discussed below in connection with the policy implications of the findings.

Third, the equations for the entire business sector and most individual industries contain negative trend terms, indicating a steady decrease over time in the amount of capital desired per unit of output. As is explained in Chapter 2, the downtrend of unit capital requirements is primarily a reflection of technical progress. This is because the capital stock is measured in constant-cost rather than constant-quality units, so improvements in the productivity of successive vintages of capital goods show up as increases in output per constant-dollar unit of capital stock rather than as increases in the quantity of capital in constant-quality units.

Fourth, the short-term investment response to a change in output or relative prices is much smaller than the long-term response, owing to the expectational and adjustment lags. For instance, the aggregative equation implies that only 12.5 percent of the total long-term increase of capital stock induced by a once-for-all increase of output would occur during the first year of output increase, and that it would take three years to complete half of the total adjustment. The implications of the investment lags are fully developed in Chapter 4, which presents measures for each industry of (1) the time profile of the distributed investment lag resulting from an output or price change during the five years following the change; (2) marginal capital-output ratios for periods of up to five years of investment response; (3) the stabilizing effect of the lags on the investment response to output fluctuations.

Fifth, the timing and magnitude of the investment response to an output change differs from industry to industry. The differences are sufficiently pronounced for compositional shifts to affect significantly the volume of aggregate investment demand at a given level of national output. Annual estimates of the quantitative influence of output shifts on aggregate net and gross business fixed investment demand were accordingly prepared, as described in Chapter 4. The calculations indicate that for the period 1949–62 as a whole, output shifts augmented net investment by 13.7 percent and gross investment by 5.5 percent, as compared with the amounts that would have been forthcoming had national output followed the same path but with an unchanged composition.

Sixth, my formulation of the investment function implies a precise relationship between capital stock and capacity, where the latter is defined as the output at which average total cost is a minimum for the given techniques, factor prices, and physical plant.[2] Annual estimates of capacity and capacity utilization are developed from this relationship for nineteen industries and the entire business economy in Chapter 5, which also contains an analysis of their properties and a comparison of these new estimates for manufacturing with those made by other investigators. To my knowledge, the new capacity estimates are the most comprehensive of any presently available.

It is important in this connection to distinguish beween plant capacity and potential output. Whereas the concept of potential output relates to full employment of the labor force, that of capacity refers to optimum utilization of the fixed capital stock. Given the existing stock of productive facilities, potential gross national product is defined as the output that

[2] This concept of optimum short-term capacity is to be distinguished from the idea of peak capacity, which underlies most other empirical estimates of capacity growth and utilization, and which is presumably meant to approximate the output at which marginal cost becomes prohibitively high under normal conditions of production.

would be produced if 96 percent of the labor force were employed, whereas capacity is defined as the output that would be produced if no more labor were used than was necessary to operate all plants at minimum average cost. In the past, investigators have usually depended on the civilian unemployment rate or on closely related estimates of the ratio of actual to potential output for indicators of economy-wide resource utilization, but these are poor measures to use in analyzing investment demand. Rates of capacity utilization can differ, and have differed, substantially from labor force utilization over the postwar years, and it is the former rather than the latter that are relevant for investment demand.

Investment and Aggregate Demand in the Postwar Economy

Chapter 6 sets the stage for the analysis of the role of business fixed investment demand in the deceleration of the rate of growth in recent years. It is first shown that the deceleration of aggregate output growth since the Korean War was due primarily to a slowdown in the growth rate of aggregate demand. The rate of growth of potential GNP, or the nation's output capability at full employment, also decreased after 1953, but the expansion of aggregate demand slowed even more markedly, with the result that unemployment rose from 3.1 percent of the labor force in 1951–53 to 4.3 percent in 1955–57 and 5.6 percent in 1960 and 1962–63. The estimates of aggregate plant capacity prepared for this study also provide evidence of a substantial decrease in demand pressures during recent years, since they indicate that capital facilities have been utilized much less intensively since 1957 than before despite a sharp deceleration in their rate of growth.

A brief survey of the proximate causes of the aggregate demand lag is presented in the last half of Chapter 6. The post-Korean slash in defense expenditure was a powerful autonomous depressant during 1953–54. The initial adjustment to the defense cutback went smoothly, nevertheless, and the subsequent expansion of private demand carried the economy nearly to full employment during 1955–57. Unfortunately, however, this favorable initial adjustment involved an unsustainable shift in the composition of aggregate demand. In particular, the share of business fixed investment in GNP (current prices) rose from 9.9 percent in 1953 to 10.7 percent in 1957, but it dropped thereafter to 9.4 percent in 1960 and 9.0 percent in 1963. A review of the principal components of aggregate demand strongly suggests that the sluggishness of business fixed investment was at the heart of the demand lag after 1957, given the fiscal and monetary policies of the period.

The last qualification is necessary, of course, because the demand shortfall might have been offset by appropriate fiscal or monetary actions, as will be discussed more fully below. For the present it is enough to note that full employment cannot be maintained in the face of a falling rate of potential business fixed investment demand unless there is an offsetting increase in some other investment category or a decrease in private or government saving rates. No such adjustment occurred during 1957–63.

Notice, however, that it is the behavior of potential investment demand that is in question. May not the recent sluggishness of business fixed investment demand be the result rather than the cause of the shortfall of actual GNP below potential? After all, since investment demand is importantly affected by the level of output, the fact that the latter is below potential certainly means that the former is smaller in dollar terms than it would be at potential, and perhaps it is smaller also in relation to GNP. In view of the interaction between investment demand and national output, it is clearly necessary to estimate potential investment demand at full employment before drawing any firm conclusions about cause and effect.

Given the aggregative investment equation, it is a simple arithmetic operation to estimate the path of real business fixed investment demand corresponding to any specified path of potential output. This is done for 1956–63 in Chapter 7, under the assumption that potential GNP was equal to actual GNP in 1955 and increased at a rate of 3.5 percent a year thereafter. This potential path is the same as that assumed by the Council of Economic Advisers.

According to the estimates, the real business fixed investment share would have fallen steadily during 1956–63 even if actual GNP had equaled potential throughout the period. Thus the potential share would have decreased under the stipulated assumptions from 10.2 percent in 1956 to 8.8 percent in 1963 (in 1954 prices). The corresponding shares based on current prices are estimated at 10.7 percent in 1956 and 9.8 percent in 1963.[3] The downtrend of the current-price shares is slower than that of the

[3] Arthur M. Okun has presented similar estimates for a single year in "Investment Demand at Full Employment," in *Proceedings of the Business and Economic Statistics Section*, American Statistical Association (1963), pp. 232–36. His estimates place the current-dollar full-employment business fixed investment share between 9.1 and 10.9

constant-price shares because of my assumption that capital goods prices would have risen relative to the over-all price level at an annual rate of 0.75 percent if the economy had continued to operate at potential after 1957 (see Chapter 7). Even after this allowance for a possible relative price increase for capital goods along the full-employment path, however, the current-dollar estimates confirm the active role of business fixed investment demand in the growth deceleration since the mid-fifties, since they indicate that it would have fallen substantially as a share of potential GNP and hence that it was a steadily weakening demand offset to full employment saving.

The remainder of Chapter 7 probes more deeply into the causes of the downtrend in the investment-output ratio, which in turn is due proximately to a downtrend in the amount of capital desired per unit of output. In terms of the investment model, unit capital requirements are affected by scale economies, relative factor prices, and technical change. The equations for the entire business economy and most individual industries contain negative time trends, implying that the strongest and most pervasive source of declining unit capital requirements is technical change. With regard to scale economies, the regressions for railroads and public utilities imply increasing returns, a factor which reinforces the downtrend of unit capital requirements due to technical change in those industries. Finally, it appears that economies in the use of capital have been encouraged by relative price trends in four other industries. However, it is not claimed that the attempt to distinguish among the effects of relative prices, scale economies, and technical change was completely successful, for reasons considered at length in Chapter 3.

Aggregate capital requirements are also affected by shifts in the composition of output. It is shown in the concluding section of Chapter 7 that compositional shifts retarded the fall of the over-all business fixed capital-output ratio by 15 percent during 1949–62. The time pattern and industrial distribution of gains and losses from output shifts is also examined. It is found that investment demand was favored by compositional shifts during the few post-Korean years relatively more than before, but that this has not been true since 1959. Thus the adverse effects of over-all output growth

---

percent of potential GNP in 1962, depending on the particular investment equation chosen for the calculations. He regards 9.8 percent as "a realistic target—it would be hard to argue that it was decidedly too high or too low." My estimate for 1962 is also 9.8 percent, based on a potential real GNP virtually identical to his and assuming a relative increase of investment goods prices of 0.75 percent a year after 1957.

retardation on investment demand were partly offset by an enlarged shift effect during 1953–57, but compositional shifts exerted a debilitating influence on the growth of aggregate investment demand in subsequent years.

Looking Ahead

Conditional projections of aggregate investment demand are presented for a variety of output paths in Chapter 8. These projections do *not* refer to the investment quotas necessary to support alternative growth rates of output for a given growth rate of labor input. It is assumed instead that each potential growth rate corresponds to a different growth rate of the labor force, so that the projections show how much investment is necessary to supply the same average complement of plant and equipment per worker along each alternative output path. This is the only procedure consistent with the investment regression on which the projections are based, because extrapolation of the trend term implies a continuation of the same rate and factor-bias of technical change as in the period of fit, and because the absence of a relative price term precludes dealing with price-induced changes in the ratio of labor to capital.

The first set of projections gives the calculated annual real gross investment shares corresponding to potential growth rates of 3.0, 3.5, and 4.0 percent during 1956–70. On a 1954 price basis, the estimated share for a 3.5 percent growth rate falls from 10.2 percent of GNP in 1956 to 8.8 percent in 1963 and 8.1 percent in 1970. For the reasons given in Chapter 7, the downtrend in the investment share would be faster for a 3.0 percent growth rate and slower for a 4.0 percent rate, so that the estimated 1970 shares for those cases would be respectively 7.8 and 8.4 percent.

Thus the slow-growth assumption is the most pessimistic of the three as regards the implied contribution of business fixed investment demand to the attainment of a full-employment level of aggregate demand. On the other hand, the small range of the investment shares for alternative growth rates carries the more optimistic corollary that it would require only a small diversion of resources into business fixed investment to sustain a markedly higher growth rate, provided there was a complementary acceleration of labor force growth.

Estimates are also presented of the development of capacity and capacity utilization along each of the assumed growth paths of potential output. It is shown that an equilibrium rate of capacity utilization would be achieved in the closing years along any one of the paths. Hence it is unrealistic to expect the postwar downtrend in utilization rates to be prolonged indefinitely unless there is a continuous deceleration of output growth. At the same time, it must be stressed that a constant utilization rate does *not* imply a constant share of real gross investment in output. On the contrary, a constant capacity utilization rate implies a falling real investment share, owing to the continuous improvements in capital productivity resulting from technical progress.

The foregoing projections have served to draw out the implications of the aggregative equation concerning investment behavior under conditions of steady growth at full employment. Since the projections assumed steady growth along the potential path throughout 1956–70, however, they are not realistic estimates of the investment demand to be expected upon a return to full employment during the mid- or late 1960's. This is because the level of potential investment demand in a given year depends not only on the level of potential GNP in that year but also on the path by which it is approached. Past departures from the potential path are reflected in a cumulative lag of actual capital stock relative to what it would have been under continuous full-employment growth, and the level of desired stock depends on lagged as well as on current output. It is interesting, therefore, to explore the investment implications of four alternative paths from actual GNP in 1962 to potential GNP in 1970.

The paths were chosen to represent a wide range of possible approaches to potential GNP, as defined in the medium or 3.5 percent projection. They range from an assumption that full employment is reached in 1963 (included for illustrative purposes only) to another that the potential path is not regained before 1970. The largest current-dollar potential investment share attained along the most optimistic path is 10 percent, whereas a more realistic approach to full employment implies a maximum share ranging from 9.9 down to 9.3 percent, depending on the particular assumption made about relative price increases for capital goods during the projection period. These figures are notably lower than the 10.7 percent share actually attained in 1957, the latest year of approximately full employment.

A comparison of the terminal positions under the four growth paths shows how full-employment investment demand in 1970 would be affected by the alternative approaches. The differences are smaller than might be expected, with the estimated constant-dollar investment shares for 1970 ranging from 8.2 to 8.6 percent. Nor would the final level of plant capacity be greatly affected by the path to full employment in 1970; the most pessimistic approach implies a capacity increase of 33.9 percent between 1962 and 1970, as compared with one of 38.4 percent for the most optimistic path.

The forward projections of aggregate investment demand just discussed can be no more accurate than the assumptions on which they are based. Experience will provide the only conclusive test of their validity, and then only if the postulated conditions are met. It is possible, however, to examine the reasonableness of some of the basic assumptions and in some cases to measure the consequences of varying them within certain limits. This was done with respect to the postulated path of GNP, for example, by presenting investment estimates for alternative paths to full employment by 1970 or before. Moreover, current-dollar shares were estimated for each path on the basis of three alternative assumptions about relative price increases for investment goods, as is discussed in Chapter 8.

A different kind of problem concerning the projections is investigated in Chapter 9. It was shown in Chapter 4 that shifts in the composition of output augmented aggregate investment demand during 1949–62 by favoring the growth of industries with above-average unit capital requirements. And Chapter 7 demonstrated that this favorable influence of compositional shifts on the aggregate investment-output relationship is implicitly reflected in the parameters of the aggregative regression. If there are grounds for believing that output shifts will lose their potency as an investment stimulus in the years ahead, the projections of aggregate investment demand must be considered overly optimistic. Does the evidence cited earlier that compositional shifts favored investment demand relatively less after 1957 than before imply such a loss of potency?

Probably not, to judge from the analysis in Chapter 9. Basically, output shifts that are themselves induced by changes of aggregate demand must be distinguished from those that are determined independently by differential changes in tastes or costs. Thus the shift index contains an induced component reflecting the wide swings of product demand in cyclically-sensitive industries as well as an income-autonomous component relating to longer-run changes in output composition. To the extent that the low level of investment demand during recent years reflects the dampening effect on the cyclically-sensitive industries of inadequate aggregate demand, an increase of aggregate demand relative to potential would itself augment total investment demand substantially by stimulating these temporarily depressed industries.

A systematic structural analysis of the factors determining the path of output in each industry could not be attempted in this study. A crude separation of the induced and income-autonomous components of output change was achieved, however, by regressing the output of each of the 19 industries on GNP and time during 1947–62. The results are in line with expectations, indicating especially large output responses to aggregate demand fluctuations in the manufacturing and transportation industries. The regressions were then used to predict the individual output increases corresponding respectively to a 3.5 percent and 4.5 percent increase in GNP. When weighted by appropriate investment factors, these output calculations confirm the proposition that an acceleration of aggregate demand would enhance the contribution of output shifts to investment demand by inducing large output increases in the cyclically sensitive industries.

A somewhat more refined analysis was undertaken for the seven major sectors distinguished in the study. The output regressions for these sectors were used to project the industry paths corresponding to a recovery of GNP from its actual level in 1962 to full employment in 1966. The investment regressions were then used to project the corresponding annual investment streams in the several sectors. This experiment also leads to the conclusion that the earlier aggregative projection is consistent with the implications of the individual output and investment relationships and that output shifts cannot be said to have lost their investment potency merely on the basis of experience since 1957.

These findings are subject to an important qualification, however. It has not been proven that income-autonomous compositional shifts will favor investment demand as much in the near future as they did in 1949–62. This question was actually begged in the sectoral investment projections for 1963–66, since they were based on the assumption that the autonomous growth trends in the output regressions for 1949–62 would continue at undiminished rates during 1963–66. If instead the strong growth trend in a key investment sector, such as public utilities or communications, should weaken substantially, much of the income-autonomous support for aggregate investment demand would be lost unless or until some other fast-growing and capital-intensive sector took its place.

So much for the role of compositional factors in the investment projections. The principal finding of this study about recent experience is that the failure of aggregate demand to grow along a full-employment path since the mid-fifties is traceable largely to a downtrend in the share of business fixed investment at potential GNP, and the principal implication of the forward projections is that the downtrend in the investment share will continue into the future. Both conclusions hinge on the twofold assumption that the downtrend in the desired capital-output ratio has been correctly estimated and is likely to continue at the same rate as in the recent past. This crucial assumption is examined from several viewpoints in Appendix A.

It is first shown that the recent downtrends in the desired capital-output ratio and the investment-output ratio are prolongations of secular declines that have been under way since World War I or earlier. Hence one can be more confident in projecting a continuing decline than if the tendency had been manifest for no more than ten or fifteen years.

The next question is whether the investment-output and capital-output ratios should be measured in current or in constant dollars. This may appear at first to be an important issue, since the constant-dollar ratios decline much more rapidly than the current-dollar ratios owing to a rise of capital goods prices relative to other prices as conventionally measured, and since the price indexes for capital goods are incompletely adjusted for quality improvements. It is shown in fact to be an unimportant issue, provided the implications of the deflation procedure are properly understood. Those implications concern the method of allowing for improvements in the productivity of successive vintages of capital goods and for the effects on saving-investment relationships of differential price trends of consumers' and producers' goods.

The final subject for investigation in Appendix A is the extent to which the results of the study are sensitive to the particular measure of capital stock developed and used here. Would the conclusions be substantially altered, for example, by varying the assumptions about useful lives or depreciation formulas? What would be the effect of substituting capital stock estimates prepared by other investigators using different data sources?

The Office of Business Economics of the United States Department of Commerce has recently published six variants of aggregate business fixed capital stock obtained by altering the assumptions about useful lives and depreciation methods. All six series were derived by the perpetual inventory method, and all six are based on the same underlying estimates of gross business fixed investment. Two of the series are estimates of gross capital stock based on different assumptions about useful lives, whereas the others are net stock concepts employing different combinations of useful lives and depreciation formulas. An inspection of the six variants shows that they differ substantially in level but had rather similar trends during 1948–61. This last is significant, since it implies similar trends in the capital-output ratios based on the various concepts.

A direct test of the influence of alternative stock concepts on the analysis of postwar investment demand was made by running new investment regressions for the six OBE variants. These regressions are of exactly the same form and are fitted to the same output data and for the same time span as the aggregative equation based on my own stock estimates. The poorest regression results were obtained for the two gross stock series. This finding tends to confirm the a priori reasoning of Chapter 2 that net stock is the better concept for a stock-adjustment model of investment decisions, since depreciation accounting provides an implicit vintage-adjustment for quality change. Because the four OBE net stock series differ primarily in level, the resulting regressions have similar slope coefficients even though their constant terms differ substantially. None of the regressions based on the OBE data is as good as my original equation.

Next the new regressions are used to project gross business fixed investment demand at potential output during 1956–70, using the same procedures as before. The projections were not carried past 1961 for the two gross stock concepts, however, for reasons given in Appendix A. But this is no great loss since the gross stock regressions are conceptually and statistically inadequate, and their projections for 1956–61 yield implausible results.

With regard to the four OBE net stock variants, the estimated potential investment shares are similar in level and trend during 1956–70 despite substantial variation in the underlying assumptions about useful lives and depreciation methods. This is because altering the depreciation assumptions affected the level of net stock much more than its growth rate, and similar growth rates mean similar investment regressions. Whereas it is true that the same growth rate implies a smaller absolute amount of net investment the lower the level of the stock series, this difference is compensated by the higher depreciation rate underlying a lower stock estimate. Thus the principal result of varying the depreciation assumptions is to produce a different division of predicted gross investment between net and replacement expenditure without markedly affecting the total.

Finally, it is found that there is an increasing discrepancy between the potential investment shares as projected by the OBE net stock variants and my own series during the mid- and late 1960's. The projected decline is greater for my series, so that by 1970 the estimated real investment share is about 6 percent lower than under any of the OBE variants, for reasons discussed in Appendix A. Thus the substitution of one of the OBE net stock variants for my capital series would lead to somewhat less pessimistic conclusions about the probable strength of business fixed investment demand in the years ahead, but the difference would be one of degree rather than kind.

Policy Implications

As has already been noted, the conditional investment projections presented in Chapter 8 for alternative full-employment approaches during 1963–70 imply a considerable reduction of potential investment demand from the level last observed under full-employment conditions in 1957. Extrapolations of this sort can obviously go awry for a number of reasons, but it would be unwise to discount them completely in view of the sluggishness of investment demand during 1958–63 and the long-standing downtrend in the business fixed investment share. Whether full employment is likely to be achieved and maintained during the next few years and beyond cannot be determined merely from an analysis of prospective trends in business fixed investment demand, however, even if the projections are taken at face value.

Assuming a balanced government budget, the condition for the achievement of full employment is that private domestic and foreign investment demand be large enough to absorb the private saving that would be forthcoming with the economy operating at its potential. Since the share of gross private saving has shown marked stability at about 15 percent of GNP in high-employment years, investment demand must be at least this large at potential GNP unless tax rates are set to yield a deficit at full employment. And it must be even larger than 15 percent of potential GNP if the government budget implies a full-employment surplus, as it did throughout 1956–63.

Thus there are several possible offsets to a reduction of potential business fixed investment demand. These include an increase in some other category of investment demand, a reduction in the private saving rate, and a reduction in the (potential or implicit) government surplus.

With regard to other investment demands, it is found that residential construction, net foreign investment, and inventory investment accounted respectively for 4.3, 0.5, and 0.8 percent of realized GNP in 1963. The shares of residential construction and net foreign investment would probably have been a little smaller at full employment, but the three categories together would probably still have totaled at least 5.2 percent of potential GNP. The actual share of business fixed investment in 1963 was 9.0 percent, and the full-employment share is estimated at 9.8 percent. Hence total investment demand at full employment in 1963 would have been about 15 percent of potential GNP, or about enough to offset the probable rate of gross private saving. Similar calculations for 1960 also indicate a potential investment share from all sources of about 15 percent.

It appears then that full employment would have been achieved or closely approached during recent periods of cyclical expansion, despite the downtrend of potential business fixed investment demand, if only government expenditures or taxes had been adjusted to yield a balanced full-employment budget instead of an implicit surplus ranging from 1 to 2 percent of potential GNP (Chapter 6).

Achieving full employment is one thing, however, and maintaining it is another. The difficulty may be illustrated with one of the conditional projections from Chapter 8, in which it is assumed that GNP will rise steadily until full employment is reached in 1966 and move along the potential path thereafter and that capital goods prices will rise relative to the over-all price level by 0.75 percent each year. The estimated current-dollar business fixed investment shares under these assumptions are as follows (in percent):

1963	9.0	1967	9.6
1964	9.3	1968	9.5
1965	9.5	1969	9.3
1966	9.5	1970	9.2

These are percentages of assumed actual GNP until 1965 and of assumed potential GNP in 1966 and later years.

The reader will observe that the investment share rises during the approach to full employment but soon declines again as expansion proceeds along the full-employment path. This is partly because the approach to full employment necessarily requires a faster expansion of GNP than can be sustained after full employment is reached, and the business fixed investment share varies positively with the rate of increase of GNP at any given time, as is explained in Chapter 7. Also as explained in Chapter 7, however, steady expansion at any given growth rate implies a falling real investment share owing to technical progress, so that the projected constant-dollar share continues to fall even after the transition has been made to a slower rate of expansion. The downtrend in the real share is partly offset by the assumed relative price increase for investment goods, but it would imply an implausibly high rate of relative price increase to keep the current-dollar share from falling along with the real share (see Chapter 8). There is thus an unmistakable implication in the investment relationships estimated for this study that the future maintenance of a full-employment rate of growth of aggregate demand will require more than a once-for-all adjustment to a once-for-all reduction of potential business fixed investment demand. This does not refer to the brief cyclical lapses that are to be expected in any event, but rather to the possibility of regularly reaching full employment during business expansions.

An appraisal of probable trends in net foreign investment, inventory investment, or housing demand is outside the scope of this study. But the reader should be reminded that foreign demand or residential construction could conceivably increase enough to offset, or more than offset, the projected down-trend of business fixed investment—just as they could conceivably reinforce its effects by decreasing. Nor is it possible to appraise herein the likelihood of significantly affecting any of these alternative investment sources by fiscal or monetary means. What *can* be discussed is the feasibility of stimulating business fixed investment itself by such means, should it prove necessary or desirable.

The empirical results in this study lead to pessimistic conclusions about the probable response of business fixed investment demand to an easy money policy. Meaningful relative price coefficients were obtained in only seven of nineteen industries, despite the numerous statistical attempts to improve on these results that are described in Chapter 3. This finding would be unlikely if interest rates and other prices did in fact exert a strong and continuous influence over investment decisions, although even then it might be difficult to measure their separate influence because of high intercorrelations among the various explanatory variables.

In view of the large risk discounts, which appear to be typical of business investment decisions, moderate changes in the level of long-term interest rates may be presumed to exert only a weak influence on the desired level of capital stock.[4] This probably explains why such influences are so difficult to detect in a capital stock adjustment model fitted to annual data.

[4] William H. White argues, however, that the weight given to uncertainty in investment decisions has "greatly diminished since the depression-dominated prewar and early

On the other hand, it is quite conceivable that interest rates may affect the short-term timing of investment decisions in situations where they do not significantly influence the level of desired stock. Thus in discussing the failure of the expansion of investment during a business upswing to continue more or less indefinitely, Burns argues that:

> In thinking of the investment process, it is essential to keep in mind that a "decision to invest" is one thing and a "decision to invest *now*" is quite another. . . . In reaching a "decision to invest," [investors] may have given little or no conscious attention to the protracted increase that has already occurred in construction and financing costs. But this decision must be followed by another, whether to carry out the project now or later. At this stage investors are likely to consider very carefully the economic outlook in the months immediately ahead.[5]

This line of reasoning is corroborated by the recently published empirical findings of Meyer and Glauber, based on an econometric analysis of quarterly time series for a number of manufacturing industries during 1948–58:

> In general, it appears that if the interest rate rises to a relatively high level, as it did during early 1953 and late 1957, an adverse impact occurs on investment approximately three quarters later that cannot be accounted for by capacity utilization, fund flow, or other variables commonly included in investment models. Furthermore, there is some evidence that these interest rate influences are most likely to be felt near the very end of a general period of cyclical improvement, like 1953, or during the early phases of a general cyclical downturn, such as the first part of 1958. . . . In short, there is evidence that monetary policy has exerted at least a negative influence on investment when applied very vigorously and under certain cyclical conditions.[6]

Perhaps this sort of timing effect is responsible for the recent successes of several investigators in detecting statistically significant interest rate influences over manufacturing investment decisions in quarterly models.[7]

---

postwar periods" and that "the evidence of the lowness of individual large companies' required rates of return on new investment, reinforced by the payoff period evidence that was found to connote fairly low required rates of return, rules out the presumption of return requirements so high that risk was predominant, the immediate future the only concern, or cost of capital ignored." See his "The Changing Criteria in Investment Planning," in *Variability of Private Investment in Plant and Equipment*, materials submitted to the U. S. Congress, Joint Economic Committee, 87 Cong. 2 sess., Pt. II (1962).

[5] Arthur F. Burns, "Hicks and the Real Cycle," *Journal of Political Economy* (February 1952), p. 21.

[6] John R. Meyer and Robert R. Glauber, *Investment Decisions, Economic Forecasting, and Public Policy* (Harvard University Press, 1964), p. 170.

[7] Franz Gehrels and Suzanne Wiggins, "Interest Rates and Manufacturers' Fixed

The investment theory underlying my regressions emphasizes the influence of relative prices on the equilibrium demand for capital stock and abstracts from the possibility that short-term interest rate or price expectations may critically affect the rate of adjustment of desired to actual stock at certain stages of the business cycle. Conceivably this omission could be a serious deficiency in a study of changes in investment over the course of the business cycle; but it is probably an unimportant consideration in analyzing potential investment trends at full employment.

What can be said about fiscal measures to augment business fixed investment demand? It is necessary first to distinguish between the direct and indirect effects of tax reductions on investment demand. A cut in personal income tax rates, for example, may be expected to raise consumption expenditure directly and thereby to stimulate investment demand indirectly by raising capacity utilization rates. Nor may such an investment stimulus be assumed to be unimportant merely because it is indirect, as will be seen. For the moment, however, attention will be focussed on the direct impact of corporate tax reductions on investment expenditure.

The work of other investigators must be looked to for information concerning these direct effects, since my model abstracts from them. One of the principal hypotheses about investment behavior that has been tested in recent years, for example, is that it is independently influenced by the flow of gross retained earnings, usually defined as current depreciation charges plus profits after taxes and dividends. Investment decisions are thought to be influenced by the flow of internal funds, because their imputed cost is presumed to be smaller than that of external funds. Therefore, the cost-of-funds rises for amounts of investment expenditure in excess of the current rate of internal saving. Thus investment expenditure may be affected not only by shifts in the schedule of prospective returns to additional capital owing to changes in the ratio of output to capital stock or capacity, but also by shifts in the supply-of-funds schedule in response to changes in the flow of gross retained earnings.[8]

Notice that what is basically at issue is the relative importance of internal

---

Investment," *American Economic Review* (March 1957), pp. 79–92; Frank de Leeuw, "The Demand for Capital Goods by Manufacturers: A Study of Quarterly Time Series," *Econometrica* (July 1962), pp. 407–23; Albert Ando, E. Cary Brown, Robert M. Solow, and John Kareken, "Lags in Fiscal and Monetary Policy," Commission on Money and Credit, *Stabilization Policies*, Research Study No. 1 (Prentice-Hall, 1963).

[8] The theoretical rationale for this formulation of the investment decision is developed most completely in James S. Duesenberry, *Business Cycles and Economic Growth* (McGraw-Hill, 1958).

funds and capacity utilization as determinants of investment expenditure. This question has been the subject of intensive study by several investigators in recent years, and the consensus that has emerged is that the elasticity of investment with respect to changes in profits or retained earnings is substantially smaller than that with respect to changes in capacity utilization. Meyer and Glauber estimate the short-term elasticity of gross investment with respect to gross internal funds and capacity utilization at respectively 0.26 and 0.68 for manufacturing firms.[9] Kuh places the typical elasticity with respect to sales (for given capacity) at 1.0 and that with respect to internal funds at 0.10–0.15.[10] Eisner does not give his results in elasticity form, but he clearly would place that for profits close to zero.[11] Thus the unanimous verdict of these empirical findings is that a moderate reduction in the corporate income tax rate or liberalization of depreciation allowances for tax purposes cannot be expected to increase gross investment demand substantially at a given level of national income.

Jorgenson has approached this same general question by another route which makes no distinction between internal and external sources of finance.[12] Instead he introduces explicit policy parameters into his investment function, including the corporate income tax rate, the proportion of "true" depreciation chargeable against income for tax purposes, and the proportion of interest chargeable against income (see page 60 below). Provided that at least one of the latter proportions differs from unity, changes in the corporate tax rate will affect the "user cost of capital," and hence the desired stock of capital, in this model. Similarly a change in either of the proportions will affect the user cost of capital at a given tax rate.

Jorgenson estimates that gross fixed investment in manufacturing has a long-term elasticity of *minus* 0.42 with respect to the corporate income tax rate and of *minus* 0.38 as regards the market rate of interest. These values are neither markedly out of line with other studies nor implausible a priori.

[9] *Op. cit.*, p. 157.

[10] Edwin Kuh, "Theory and Institutions in the Study of Investment Behavior," *American Economic Review* (May 1963), p. 266. He selected these values from a range of alternative estimates given in his *Capital Stock Growth: A Micro-Econometric Approach* (Amsterdam: North-Holland Press, 1963), pp. 221–30.

[11] Robert Eisner, "Capital Expenditures, Profits and the Acceleration Principle," *Models of Income Determination*, Studies in Income and Wealth, Vol. 28 (Princeton University Press, 1964), pp. 137–65. Eisner's variable is profits, either before or after tax, but not including depreciation, which is used elsewhere in the model in a measure of capital durability.

[12] Dale W. Jorgenson, "Capital Theory and Investment Behavior," *American Economic Review* (May 1963), pp. 247–59.

It is impossible to judge their statistical significance, however, since each of them is deduced from a complex variable involving all price and output influences that bear on the investment decision rather than being independently estimated from the data as a net regression coefficient.

In summary, it appears that the elasticity of business fixed investment with respect to interest rates and direct taxes is small enough that a substantial reduction of either type would be required to increase the investment share of GNP from, say, 9.0 to 9.5 percent. This would require an investment increase of 5.5 percent and would imply a percentage reduction in interest rates or taxes of several times that amount.

In contrast, most studies, including my own, place the long-term elasticity of gross investment demand with respect to output at approximately unity.[13] Thus if the economy is at an underemployment level and taxes are reduced to stimulate consumption demand, as in 1964, the induced output increase will itself cause the absolute volume of investment demand to rise substantially over a period of several years under *ceteris paribus* conditions. It is important to recognize, however, that any such favorable output effects are already included in the forward projections of business fixed investment and that those estimates do not suggest either a large or a permanent increase in the potential investment *share* at full employment. They imply instead that if full employment is in fact achieved in future years under the stimulus of tax cuts, it will be less because investment demand was raised than because the consumption share was augmented by the reduction in government saving. Alternatively, of course, the implicit surplus could be reduced, or, if need be, converted to an implicit deficit, by a sufficiently rapid expansion of government expenditures at given tax rates.

[13] This elasticity would be exactly unity in my model for an increase of output between two stationary states. This is because net investment would be zero in the long run at either output level. But capital stock, and hence replacement demand, would increase in the same proportion as output between the two levels, given the unitary long-term elasticity of capital stock with respect to output assumed in the aggregative equation. In a dynamic setting, and for a finite time period, however, the elasticity of gross investment with respect to a marginal output increase depends on the degree of output acceleration and the speed of adjustment of capital stock to output. Hence, it can vary over a wide range.

PART II

PART II

2 / *The Investment Model*

THE PURPOSE OF this chapter is to derive and explain the investment model that underlies the analysis which follows of recent and prospective trends in business fixed investment demand. The same model is used for nineteen major sectors of the economy. It is hoped thus to establish the relative importance of each determinant in the several sectors by a uniform comparative analysis. A structural analysis of this sort should contribute to a better understanding of the determinants of aggregate investment demand.

Net investment is the dependent variable in the investment regressions which form the backbone of the study. This does not mean, however, that replacement demand is neglected. Instead, current replacement demand is equated with current depreciation on the capital stock except in those years when a decrease in capital stock occurs. When net investment is negative, replacement investment is equal to depreciation minus the amount of the net decline in capital stock. Since depreciation is measured gross of obsolescence, this concept of replacement demand allows for the effective partial retirement of old assets through functional downgrading and less intensive use instead of being restricted to the direct substitution of a new asset for one that is being permanently retired.

Annual estimates of replacement investment are a direct by-product of the estimates of net capital stock, which provide the dependent variable for the net investment regressions, and it is sufficient to note here that they are based on an exponential or declining-balance depreciation model. For the present the focus will be on the determinants of net fixed investment, defined as the excess of gross investment over depreciation.

Net fixed investment by definition is equal to the change in the stock of net fixed assets during a given period. It is positive when the capital stock demanded exceeds the capital stock on hand at the beginning of the period and negative when the reverse is true. Net investment during a given period, therefore, depends on (1) the size of the gap between desired and actual stock and (2) the speed with which businessmen attempt to adjust the actual stock to the desired level.

The Demand for Fixed Capital

The demand for fixed capital is a long-run concept. In the short run the stock of plant and equipment is given, and it may be over- or under-utilized owing to seasonal or cyclical variations in product demand or resource supplies. The process of adjusting the capital stock to a new long-term equilibrium position, moreover, may take several years. Thus even in the absence of seasonal, cyclical, or sporadic disturbances, the actual stock may never become fully adjusted to the desired level, especially since the latter itself tends to change over time. The influence of lags in the adjustment process will have to be allowed for at a later point, but first this analysis will concentrate on the determinants of the desired (long-run equilibrium) stock of fixed plant and equipment. The basic hypothesis to be tested and applied in the subsequent empirical analysis is that the desired stock at a given time is a function of (1) expected output, (2) expected prices, and (3) the level of technology.

1. The demand for capital stock varies positively with expected long-term output whether factor proportions are fixed or variable under given techniques of production. If factor proportions are fixed, capital stock must necessarily vary proportionally with output. Even under the more realistic assumption of variable factor proportions, an increase of output increases the marginal physical productivity of any given stock of capital (since it increases the proportion of other inputs to capital) and hence implies a larger desired stock than would be associated with a lower output in long-term equilibrium.

2. Two forms of relative price variable have been tried in the multiple regressions. The first assumes full profit-maximization, whereas the second depends only on cost-minimization for its rationale.

According to the conventional theory of the firm, the demand for inputs and the supply of output will be so chosen as to maximize profits within the constraints set by product demand, factor supplies, and the technical relationship between inputs and outputs embodied in the production function. Assuming that the firm takes product and factor prices as given and assuming that each input is subject to diminishing returns as it increases relatively to the others, if profits are to be maximized, each factor of production must be used in such quantity that the value of the marginal physical product is equal to its price.[1] This means that the demand for real capital stock will vary positively with product price and inversely with the price of capital, just as the quantity of labor demanded varies positively with product price and inversely with the money wage.

In this context, the "price of capital" is analogous to money wages, which are the price of labor, and hence it is a complex variable combining the several factors which together determine the cost per annum of the use of a unit of real capital in production.[2] The sum of the interest and depreciation rates gives the cost per annum in real terms of the use of a unit of capital stock. The money cost per unit is the product of this real cost and the current price of capital goods. The interest and depreciation charges on physical capital are valued at current (replacement) prices because it is the price for the use of a unit of new real capital that affects the investment decision.

In symbols, the price of capital is given by $P_k(d+r)$, where P_k is an index of the price of capital goods and d and r represent respectively the annual depreciation and interest rates. Thus the price of capital varies positively with the interest rate, the depreciation rate, and the price of new capital goods. In the empirical work the several price influences will be combined in one relative-price variable $P_k(d+r)/P$, representing the ratio of the price of capital and the price of the product. This ratio may be called the real price of capital, by analogy with the real wage.

The reader may wonder whether the component P_k/P of the real price of capital is capable of much variation over time. As regards an individual industry, it is clear that product price can move differently from the price

[1] If there are imperfections in either the product market or the factor market, this condition must be modified by substituting marginal revenue for product price and marginal outlay for factor price. Marginal revenue and marginal outlay are usually positively correlated with product and factor prices at a given level of output, however.

[2] My attention was first directed to this price concept by Dale W. Jorgenson, who calls it "the user cost of capital." See his "Capital Theory and Investment Behavior," *American Economic Review* (May 1963), pp. 247–59, for a rigorous derivation of the concept. (See also the closely related concept of W. E. G. Salter in *Productivity and Technical Change* [Cambridge, England: Cambridge University Press, 1960], pp. 18–20.) I have adopted a simpler index of user cost than Jorgenson's own variable, however, since he allows for the taxation of corporate income in computing his measure. This point is discussed further in Chapter 3.

paid for capital goods, owing to a faster or slower rate of productivity advance or to a relative demand shift as compared with the capital goods sector. This fact does not give much scope for movement in the ratio of P_k/P for manufacturing industries heavily engaged in capital goods production, however. On the aggregative level, P_k/P may change over time if the rate of productivity advance in the capital goods sector as a whole differs from that in the consumer goods sector, and the weight of evidence suggests that this is indeed the case.[3] For further discussion of the causes and implications of differential trends in capital goods and other prices, see Appendix A.

In an alternative formulation of the investment function it is assumed that the demand for capital at any given level of output depends on the relative prices of labor and capital, as measured by the ratio of the money wage and the money price of capital, $w/P_k(d+r)$. The principle of cost minimization is sufficient to justify this formulation of the factor substitution effect independently of any assumptions about profit-maximization or pricing policies.

It may be argued that a rise in wage rates will result in an equal relative increase of capital goods prices, since capital goods are produced with labor, and hence that no change in w/P_k is possible under competitive market conditions. As Salter points out, however, "even though the wage rate and the interest rate may be constant, the cheapening of capital goods which originates in technical progress reduces the capital costs of real investment and so induces substitution of capital equipment for labour."[4]

3. In static analysis it is customary to assume given techniques of production, but for present purposes the effects of technical progress on the demand for capital must be allowed for. The particular way in which this is done depends in part on how capital stock is defined and measured. According to the model, a net increase in the stock of capital goods will be undertaken whenever the desired stock, as established by marginal productivity conditions, exceeds the existing stock (although it is not assumed that the entire discrepancy will be removed in a single year). Therefore the stock of capital must be measured in some way that permits direct comparison of the productivity of existing assets with that of new assets to be added.

Thus it is not enough simply to add up the physical or constant-dollar units of all surviving capital goods irrespective of their ages. The reason is that the stream of service values from a given asset typically declines over

[3] Robert A. Gordon, "Differential Changes in the Prices of Consumers' and Capital Goods," *American Economic Review* (December 1961), pp. 937–57.

[4] *Op. cit.*, p. 36.

time, owing both to physical deterioration and to obsolescence.[5] Thus the productivity of an old unit of physical capital is smaller than that of a new unit of equal real cost.[6] The capital goods of each vintage should therefore enter the capital stock with a weight that varies inversely with their age, and one way to do this is to measure all capital at its net depreciated value, where the depreciation rate reflects the loss of value of assets due to obsolescence as well as to deterioration. This is the procedure I have followed in measuring capital stock for this study. Depreciation is measured on a declining-balance model, for reasons described in Appendix B. The net capital stock as just defined incorporates one method of allowing for improvements in the productivity of capital goods owing to technical progress.[7] An alternative procedure, proposed by Solow, is to weight the capital goods of each vintage by a "productivity improvement factor" that increases over time.[8] The same constant-cost gross investment stream underlies both methods. Under the first method, however, each unit of old capital is "written down" each year—counted as the equivalent of less physical capital than before—in order to make it comparable with a unit of new capital, so that the entire stock is expressed in *equivalent units of capital of*

[5] *Cf.* George Terborgh, *Realistic Depreciation Policy* (Machinery and Allied Products Institute, 1954), Chaps. 4–5.

[6] The reduced productivity of old assets because of obsolescence is reflected in lower rates of utilization than those of new assets—including at the extreme the placing of old assets in stand-by status for occasional use to meet peak demands—and by functional downgrading of the old assets. Simon Kuznets, in particular, has emphasized the need to allow for differences in the rate of utilization of modern and obsolescent equipment in the measurement of capital stock. See, for example, his comment on Edward Denison's paper in *Problems of Capital Formation*, Studies in Income and Wealth, Vol. 19 (Princeton Univ. Press, 1957), especially pp. 277–78.

[7] For a critique of this method, see Edward Denison's penetrating discussion of the "Theoretical Aspects of Quality Change, Capital Consumption, and Net Capital Formation" in *ibid.*, especially pp. 242–43.

[8] Robert M. Solow, "Investment and Technical Progress," in K. J. Arrow, S. Karlin, and P. Suppes (eds.), *Mathematical Methods in the Social Sciences* (Stanford Univ. Press, 1959); and "Technical Progress, Capital Formation, and Economic Growth," *American Economic Review* (May 1962), pp. 76–86. A third alternative, closely related to the Solow approach, is to deflate the gross investment expenditure of each year by a price index that takes into account those quality changes that are not reflected in the costs of capital goods, and hence are not captured in the conventional price indexes, and then to cumulate the survivors from each year to arrive at the capital stock. If this last procedure is followed, however, it appears appropriate also to alter the measure of aggregate output so as to include the augmented, quality-adjusted flow of investment goods instead of the quality-unadjusted flow. Obviously the behavior of the capital-output ratio will differ according to whether the adjustment for productivity improvement is confined to capital stock, as under Solow's method and my method, or is also extended to output.

current vintage at constant cost. Under the Solow method, the capital of each vintage is multiplied by a productivity improvement index which equals unity in some base year and increases at a constant rate over time, so that the entire stock is expressed in *equivalent units of capital of base year quality or productivity.*

The two methods are equivalent in the sense that the relative weights applied to successive vintages of capital are the same under both (see the technical note at the end of this chapter). There is one important difference between them, however. The Solow method incorporates investment-linked technical improvements directly into the stock of capital and attributes the resulting output increase to an increase of capital measured in constant-quality units. In contrast, improvements in the productivity of successive new vintages of capital show up as increases in output per constant-cost unit of capital stock under the depreciation method of vintage weighting.

This last is the reason why a time trend is included in my regression equations to reflect the influence of technical progress on the efficiency of the capital stock. As a general rule, the trend term will be negative, indicating that less real capital in constant dollars is needed to produce a unit of output in year $t+1$ than in year t. If technical change in a particular industry or for a particular period is biased in the direction of increasing the capital-labor ratio with a constant ratio of factor prices, however, and if the bias is sufficiently large to offset the general tendency for innovation to reduce unit capital requirements as well as unit labor requirements, a positive trend may appear in the capital-output ratio.[9]

In summary, for the purpose of regression analysis the stock of capital desired under long-term equilibrium conditions is assumed to depend upon output, relative prices, and time. The exact form assumed for the empirical relationship is specified in the next section.

The Adjustment Process

Assume that an industry is initially in long-term equilibrium, so that the stock of plant and equipment is fully adjusted to the given conditions of

[9] See Salter, *op. cit.*, Chap. III, for an excellent discussion of the characteristics of technical advance as they affect factor requirements.

demand and supply in product and factor markets and the given state of technical knowledge. Then let the desired stock increase for some reason—perhaps because product demand increases or the interest rate falls. It does not follow that the entire gap thereby opened between the desired and the actual stock will be eliminated during one time period. On the contrary, it is likely that only part of the gap existing at the beginning of a year will be filled by investment during that year. It takes time to design new installations, arrange for financing, let construction contracts and order equipment, build or manufacture the ordered items, and put the facilities in place. Apart from these technical lags, in an uncertain world businessmen often are reluctant to adjust production facilities immediately and fully to the new demand or cost conditions. They prefer to make a partial initial adjustment and wait to see if the new conditions persist before undertaking further expansion.

Thus current investment expenditure is dependent not only on the relationship between desired and actual stock but also on the time pattern and speed of adjustment of desired to actual stock. A great deal of evidence has accumulated recently to indicate that the investment response to a change in the demand for capital stock is typically distributed over several years.[10]

This idea can be clarified by a simple hypothesis concerning the adjustment process, which has met with considerable success in empirical applications.[11] Let K^*_t be the "desired" (long-term equilibrium) capital stock in year t and K_{t-1} be the actual stock at the end of the previous year. Now assume that the increase of capital stock undertaken during year t is some fixed proportion b of the difference between desired and actual stock. In symbols:

$$K_t - K_{t-1} = b(K^*_t - K_{t-1}); \qquad 0 < b \leq 1. \tag{2.1}$$

If b is equal to one, the entire gap between desired and actual stock will be eliminated within year t, but if b is less than one, only a fraction of the adjustment will be completed during the year. In the latter case, a once-for-

[10] For direct evidence on the time shape of the investment stream associated with capital projects of different types, see Thomas Mayer, "The Inflexibility of Monetary Policy," *Review of Economics and Statistics* (November 1958), pp. 359–74. Mayer's study is based on engineering and questionnaire information. The econometric studies cited in note 12 establish typical lag patterns by statistical methods rather than direct information, but they are broadly consistent with Mayer's results.

[11] For example, see Hollis B. Chenery, "Overcapacity and the Acceleration Principle," *Econometrica* (January 1952), pp. 1–28; L. M. Koyck, *Distributed Lags and Investment Analysis* (Amsterdam: North-Holland Press, 1954); and Arnold C. Harberger (ed.), *The Demand for Durable Goods* (Univ. of Chicago Press, 1960).

all increase in desired stock will result in a gradual approach of actual stock to the new long-term equilibrium level. That is, the investment response will be distributed over a number of years, with the distributed lag taking the form of a geometric progression in which the investment of each year is a constant fraction, $1-b$, of that of the preceding year. For example, if the initial gap between desired and actual stock were 10 and b were 0.4, the net investment of the first year would be 4, that of the second year 2.4 (0.4 times [10 minus 4], or 0.6 times 4), and so on.

As an alternative to (2.1), it may be assumed that the adjustment equation is

$$\frac{K_t}{K_{t-1}} = \left(\frac{K_t^*}{K_{t-1}}\right)^b; \quad 0 < b \leq 1,$$

which upon being converted to logarithmic form becomes:

$$\text{(2.1a)} \qquad \log K_t - \log K_{t-1} = b(\log K^*_t - \log K_{t-1});\ 0 < b \leq 1.$$

In this formulation, the adjustment constant b now represents (approximately) the proportion of the *percentage* gap between desired and actual stock which is eliminated during year t. For example, if K^*_t were 110 and K_{t-1} were 100, implying a percentage gap of 10 percent, and if b were 0.4, then according to equation (2.1a), (K_t/K_{t-1}) would be 1.039, implying a percentage increase of capital stock of 3.9 percent during the year.

To apply equation (2.1) or (2.1a) empirically the determinants of desired stock must be specified. According to the theory of demand for capital set forth above, the desired stock is a function of the expected long-term or "normal" levels of output Y^* and relative prices P^* in year t, plus a time trend T. The simplest assumption would be to postulate the linear relationship:

$$\text{(2.2)} \qquad K^*_t = a_1 + a_2 Y^*_t + a_3 P^*_t + a_4 T.$$

An alternative formulation would be to assume that the equation for desired stock is:

$$K^*_t = a_1 (Y^*_t)^{a_2} (P^*_t)^{a_3} e^{a_4 T},$$

which can be transformed to the logarithmic form:

$$\text{(2.2a)} \qquad \log K^*_t = \log a_1 + a_2 \log Y^*_t + a_3 \log P^*_t + a_4 T.$$

The logarithmic form is convenient because the coefficients a_2 and a_3 then provide direct estimates of the long-term elasticity of capital stock with respect to the output and relative price variables. Similarly, a_4 is a measure of the net trend of capital stock in exponential or compound interest terms. Equation (2.2a) has therefore been chosen as the basic hypothesis about desired stock.

The coefficient of log Y^*_t is required to be positive. The expected sign of the coefficient of log P^*_t is negative when the real price of capital is the variable and positive in the alternative formulation, where the relative prices of labor and capital are used. The trend coefficient will usually be negative, but a positive value is not ruled out a priori, for reasons already discussed.

It should be reiterated that the equation for desired stock defines a moving equilibrium, owing to the inclusion of a time trend. It differs in that respect from the long-term equilibrium concept of conventional price theory, which abstracts from technical change. The equation must be interpreted as defining that capital stock which would enable the "normal" output of period t to be produced at minimum cost, given the prevailing prices and technology. The equilibrium capital stock changes over time as techniques improve even if output and relative prices are constant. Since the effect of technical change is usually to reduce the capital-output ratio, net investment is usually negative under stationary output and price conditions; that is, a constant productive capacity can be maintained with a declining capital stock of increasing quality. Conversely, zero net investment does not signify zero capacity increase in the present model. It means merely that the capacity increase is limited to the amount made possible by "replacing" part of the old stock with capital of current vintage, either by eliminating obsolete equipment entirely or by utilizing it less intensively than new equipment.

Since (2.2a) has been chosen as the equation for desired stock, it is natural to choose (2.1a) as the adjustment hypothesis. Substitution of (2.2a) into (2.1a) yields:

$$(2.3)\quad \log K_t - \log K_{t-1} = (b) \log a_1 + (ba_2) \log Y^*_t + (ba_3) \log P^*_t + (ba_4)T - (b) \log K_{t-1}.$$

The dependent variable, or rather its antilogarithm (K_t/K_{t-1}), will be called the capital expansion ratio. To give a numerical illustration of its meaning, the capital expansion ratio will be 1.05 if net investment during the year is positive and equal to 5 per cent of the capital stock existing at the beginning of the year.

Although equation (2.3) shows the general form of the basic investment hypothesis, it is not possible to fit the regression until the determinants of normal output and relative prices are specified. The simplest assumption is that businessmen expect the current levels to persist indefinitely into the future. In that case, the desired stock depends on current output and relative prices, and (2.3) may be fitted directly to the current data. There are two serious objections to this simple procedure, however.

First, it implies a distributed lag, with the largest fraction of the total long-term adjustment to an increase of, say, output taking place in the same year as the output increase. Koyck discovered in his pathbreaking study, however, that better results were generally obtained by allowing the investment response of the first year after the increase to be determined independently of the geometrically distributed lag, which was begun with the second year instead of the first. This is because typically investment rises for a time before it falls, so that investment during the second year of adjustment is usually larger than in the first year.[12]

Second, it is probably unrealistic to assume that businessmen automatically accept the current level of output as the best estimate of expected long-term output. If output drops during a brief recession, for instance, businessmen are likely to discount much of the drop insofar as fixed investment plans are concerned; but if the recession drags on, they will revise downward their estimate of expected output. Similar considerations hold for output increases.

I have allowed for these difficulties by modifying Koyck's procedure. The assumption of a constant annual speed of adjustment of desired to actual stock is retained, but the estimate of expected long-term or normal output (and price) is a weighted average of current and recent outputs (and prices).[13] This has been done by trying lagged as well as current outputs

[12] Koyck, *op. cit.* This general pattern is confirmed on the aggregative level in the excellent recent studies by Frank de Leeuw ("The Demand for Capital Goods by Manufacturers: A Study of Quarterly Time Series," *Econometrica* [July 1962], pp. 407–23); Robert Eisner ("Investment: Fact and Fancy," *American Economic Review* [May 1963], pp. 237–46); and Jorgenson (*op. cit.*). For additional evidence and industry detail, see Eisner's earlier articles, "A Distributed Lag Investment Function," *Econometrica* (January 1960), pp. 1–29, and "Capital Expenditures, Profits, and the Acceleration Principle," in *Models of Income Determination*, Studies in Income and Wealth, Vol. 28 (Princeton Univ. Press, 1964), pp. 137–65. In the present study, the peak annual investment response to an increase in demand for capital stock occurs in the second year following the demand increase in 14 of 19 industrial sectors, including 12 of the 13 manufacturing industries (see Chapter 4). Moreover, two of the five remaining industries do not reach the peak response until the third year.

[13] The analogy with Milton Friedman's concept of permanent income (*A Theory of the Consumption Function* [National Bureau of Economic Research and Princeton Univ. Press, 1957]) will be apparent, although at most three years of output is included here in the average, and the weights are determined by the investment regression. Both

(and prices) in regressions of the general form of (2.3). Alternative regressions were fitted including one, two, or three output (and price) terms, and the equation was then selected which yielded the best over-all results for each industry, as judged by statistical criteria and certain a priori constraints to be discussed in the next chapter.

To illustrate the interpretation of such an equation, suppose that the best regression for a particular industry includes output and price terms for the current and the preceding year:

$$(2.4)\quad \log K_t - \log K_{t-1} = (b) \log a_1 + (ba_{21}) \log Y_t + (ba_{22}) \log Y_{t-1} + (ba_{31}) \log P_t + (ba_{32}) \log P_{t-1} + (ba_4)T - (b) \log K_{t-1}.$$

A comparison of (2.3) and (2.4) shows that

$$(2.5)\quad (a_2) \log Y^*_t = (a_{21}) \log Y_t + (a_{22}) \log Y_{t-1},$$

and similarly for the relationship between the price variables. If output is stationary for two successive years, $Y^*_t = Y_t = Y_{t-1}$ and the long-term elasticity of capital stock with respect to output a_2 is seen to equal $a_{21}+a_{22}$. It follows directly that normal output is a weighted (geometric) average of the outputs of the current year and the preceding year, with weights respectively of $a_{21}/a_{21}+a_{22}$ and $a_{22}/a_{21}+a_{22}$. Similar relationships hold for the price variables and for regressions involving more output or price lags.

Although equation (2.4) combines a complex hypothesis about the determinants of desired stock with another about the adjustment process, it is a simple matter to disentangle the several influences. The annual rate of adjustment of desired to actual stock is given by the coefficient b of $\log K_{t-1}$. Dividing the other regression coefficients by b yields the various a's. The long-term elasticities of capital stock with respect to output and relative prices are then found by summing the appropriate a coefficients. Finally, the expected long-term or normal output Y^*_t and relative price P^*_t are derived as weighted averages of the output and price terms, with weights determined by the a coefficients. This last step makes it possible to write the equation for desired stock as a function of normal output and

---

Eisner (*op. cit.*) and Charles Schultze ("Uses of Capacity Measures for Short-run Economic Analysis," *American Economic Review* [May 1963], pp. 293–308) have recently emphasized the importance of using some concept of permanent or normal sales or output in analyzing fixed investment. The present formulation was developed independently of theirs. Koyck included lagged as well as current output in his regressions, but the following interpretation of the coefficients derived from such regressions, based on a distinction between output expectations and adjustment rates, is my own.

price, as in (2.2a) above, and hence to derive the relationship between capital stock and capacity discussed in Chapter 5.

The time shape of the investment response to an output increase implied by equation (2.4) may readily be illustrated by dropping the price and time variables[14] and rewriting the equation as follows:

$$(2.6)\quad \log K_t - \log K_{t-1} = b[(\log a_1 + a_{21} \log Y_t + a_{22} \log Y_{t-1}) - \log K_{t-1}].$$

The expression in parentheses is the simplified equation for desired stock, and that in square brackets is the gap between desired and actual stock.

Assume that the industry is initially in long-term equilibrium with capital stock fully adjusted to output. Now let there be a once-for-all increase of output of 1 percent beginning in year t. The immediate result is to create a gap between desired and actual stock equal to a_{21} percent. However, only a fraction b of the gap is filled by investment in year t, so that the investment of the first year is equal to ba_{21}.

The situation is changed in two respects during the second year of adjustment. Since the new level of output has proven to be more than temporary, the level of expected or normal output, and with it the desired stock, is again revised upward. Both output terms of equation (2.6) are now up by one unit, and hence the gap between the desired and the initial actual stock has been increased to $a_{21}+a_{22}$ instead of a_{21}, as it was in the first year. Meanwhile, however, the gap has been narrowed in the amount ba_{21} owing to the investment of the first year. Thus the gap in the second year is given by $a_{21}+a_{22}-ba_{21}$. The investment of the second year is therefore equal to $b(a_{22}+[1-b]a_{21})$.

Since only two output terms are included in equation (2.6), the desired stock fully reflects the once-for-all output increase by the second year.The desired stock remains unchanged thereafter, and the investment of each succeeding year becomes progressively smaller as actual stock approaches the equilibrium level. It is easily shown that beginning in the third year, the investment of each successive year is $1-b$ times that of the preceding year.

Appropriate modifications in the calculations are made for equations containing one or three output terms. The progressive investment decline in proportion $1-b$ begins in the second year for regressions of the first type, whereas it is delayed until the fourth year for regressions including three output terms.

[14] These variables are dropped for expositional convenience only since they do not affect in any way the calculation of the time path of the response to an output increase.

TECHNICAL NOTE ON VINTAGE WEIGHTING OF CAPITAL STOCK

The purpose of this brief note is to show how vintage weighting by alternative methods affects the measurement of capital stock. The note is based on unpublished derivations I made in the spring of 1962. For more general treatments of the subject and its implications for investment and growth models, the reader is referred to the work of Jorgenson and Brown.[15]

Solow built his first vintage model on the assumption that "all technical progress is uniform and approximately exponential over time, and that capital goods at their moment of construction embody all the latest knowledge but share not at all in any further improvements in technology. If $Qv(t)$ stands for the output produced at time t using equipment of vintage v, then

$$Qv(t) = Be^{\lambda v}Lv(t)^{\alpha}Kv(t)^{1-\alpha}. \tag{2.7}$$

Thus the Cobb-Douglas function applies for output produced with capital of given vintage, but it is also evident that the multiplicative improvement factor turns itself off the moment that capital goods take shape."[16] In this function, λ is the rate of technical progress, $Kv(t)$ represents the number of machines or units of capital of vintage v still in existence at time $t \geq v$, and $Lv(t)$ is the labor to be allocated to vintage v capital.

Solow then goes on to show by an elegant aggregation process that the corresponding aggregative production function is

$$Q(t) = Be^{-\delta(1-\alpha)t}L(t)^{\alpha}J(t)^{1-\alpha}, \tag{2.8}$$

where

$$J(t) = \int_{-\infty}^{t} e^{[\delta+\lambda/(1-\alpha)]v}I(v)dv. \tag{2.9}$$

In the "equivalent stock of capital" $J(t)$, the gross investment of vintage v, $I(v)$, is weighted by the factor $e^{[\delta+\lambda/(1-\alpha)]v}$, in which δ stands for the rate of (physical) depreciation of capital stock.

It is easy to understand why λ appears in the weighting function, since the purpose of weighting is to allow for improvements in the productivity of successive vintages of capital goods owing to technical progress; but why is the physical depreciation rate also included in the weighting factor? The answer is found

[15] Dale W. Jorgenson, "Capital Theory and Investment Behavior, Part I: Theory," Working Paper No. 26, Committee on Econometrics and Mathematical Economics, Institute of Business and Economic Research, University of California, Berkeley (Sept. 1, 1962); Murray Brown, "An Iconoclastic View of the New View of Investment," Report 6402, Econometric Institute, Netherlands School of Economics (Jan. 3, 1964).

[16] Robert M. Solow, "Investment and Technical Progress," *Mathematical Methods in the Social Sciences* (Stanford Univ. Press, 1959), K. J. Arrow, S. Karlin, and P. Suppes (eds.), pp. 91–92.

most easily by making a slight revision of the capital stock concept. Notice that (2.8) can be re-written as:

$$Q(t) = BL(t)^{\alpha}[e^{-\delta t}J(t)]^{1-\alpha}, \tag{2.10}$$

where

$$e^{-\delta t}J(t) = \int_{-\infty}^{t} e^{-\delta(t-v)}e^{[\lambda/(1-\alpha)]v}I(v)\,dv. \tag{2.11}$$

Solow had taken $e^{-\delta t}$ outside the capital stock integral in (2.8), since it did not affect the integration over v, but δ obviously attaches to the concept of capital stock, and its role is much clearer when it is included as a negative factor in the definition of the equivalent stock of capital, as in (2.10) and (2.11), a procedure which Solow himself followed in his next article on the subject.[17]

The interpretation of the two exponential terms in (2.11) is straightforward. The first one is a negative factor measuring the cumulative loss of vintage v capital by year t because of physical deterioration, whereas the second is the productivity weight to be given the remaining amount of vintage v capital still surviving in the year t. Thus the "equivalent stock of capital adds up the survivors of each vintage after weighting them by the appropriate productivity improvement factor."[18]

Given the slight modification represented by the substitution of (2.10) and (2.11) for (2.8) and (2.9), then, Solow's original production function with vintage weighted capital stock is:

$$Q(t) = BL(t)^{\alpha}\left[\int_{-\infty}^{t} e^{-\delta(t-v)}e^{[\lambda/(1-\alpha)]v}I(v)\,dv\right]^{1-\alpha}. \tag{2.12}$$

The next thing to notice is that (2.12) is equal to:

$$\begin{aligned} Q(t) &= BL(t)^{\alpha}\left[e^{[\lambda/(1-\alpha)]t}\int_{-\infty}^{t} e^{-\delta(t-v)}e^{-[\lambda/(1-\alpha)](t-v)}I(v)\,dv\right]^{1-\alpha} \\ &= Be^{\lambda t}L(t)^{\alpha}\left[\int_{-\infty}^{t} e^{-[\delta+\lambda/(1-\alpha)](t-v)}I(v)\,dv\right]^{1-\alpha}. \end{aligned} \tag{2.13}$$

The expression in brackets in (2.13) is the formula for the net depreciated stock of capital, where the depreciation rate $[\delta+\lambda/(1-\alpha)]$ reflects both physical deterioration δ and obsolescence $[\lambda/(1-\alpha)]$. Thus the production function (2.13) is the direct equivalent of (2.10) or (2.8), as Solow himself showed via another route in sections 7 and 8 of his 1959 article. When capital stock is measured by its net depreciated value as in (2.13), however, it is necessary to include a time trend in the production (or investment) function to allow for technical progress, as (2.13) clearly reveals. The reason is simply that in (2.13) capital is always measured in equivalent units of current vintage at constant cost, and the productivity

[17] "Technical Progress, Capital Formation, and Economic Growth," *American Economic Review* (May 1962), p. 77.

[18] *Ibid.*

of a unit of real capital of current vintage increases each year at the rate λ by assumption (2.7).

That the relative weights applied to successive vintages of capital are the same under both methods is easily demonstrated. The expansion of the capital stock integral in (2.12) is:

$$e^{[\lambda/(1-\alpha)]t}I_t + e^{-\delta}e^{[\lambda/(1-\alpha)](t-1)}I_{t-1} + e^{-2\delta}e^{[\lambda/(1-\alpha)](t-2)}I_{t-2} + \cdots, \tag{2.14}$$

whereas that for (2.13) is:

$$I_t + e^{-[\delta+\lambda/(1-\alpha)]}I_{t-1} + e^{-2[\delta+\lambda/(1-\alpha)]}I_{t-2} + \cdots. \tag{2.15}$$

If the common term in (2.14) is factored out, the result is:

$$e^{[\lambda/(1-\alpha)]t}[I_t + e^{-[\delta+\lambda/(1-\alpha)]}I_{t-1} + e^{-2[\delta+\lambda/(1-\alpha)]}I_{t+2} + \cdots]. \tag{2.16}$$

Thus the relative weights applied to successive vintages of capital at time t are the same in (2.16) as in (2.15), since the factor outside the brackets in (2.16) is common to all vintages and cancels out of the ratios between vintages.

Finally a comparison of (2.12) and (2.13) shows that Solow's equivalent stock of capital (K^s) has the following relationship to the depreciated net stock concept (K^d):

$$K^s{}_t = e^{[\lambda/(1-\alpha)]t}K^d{}_t.$$

Thus K^s rises more rapidly than K^d over time, at the rate $[\lambda/(1-\alpha)]$. This rapid relative rise compensates, of course, for the absence of a specific trend term for technical progress in (2.12), since technical progress has been incorporated directly into the capital stock and treated as an increase in the quantity of capital as measured in constant-quality units of the vintage which serves as the base year for the productivity improvement index.

3 / *The Basic Regressions*

THIS CHAPTER PRESENTS the investment regressions that form the backbone of the entire study. First, the underlying data will be described and then the regressions themselves.

The Data

The basic data needed for the regressions consist of annual estimates for each industry of net capital stock, output, product price, interest and depreciation rates, capital goods prices, and the wage rates. All data are reproduced in Appendixes B and C, but a brief description of sources and methods is given here.

The estimates of net capital stock were developed in this study from data on real gross investment expenditures and useful lives, using the perpetual inventory method. Net investment during any given year was derived by subtracting depreciation from gross investment for that year, and net capital stock at the end of the year was obtained by adding net investment to the value of the net capital stock at the beginning of the year.

The estimates of gross investment were taken primarily from the annual surveys of business expenditures for new plant and equipment conducted jointly by the Office of Business Economics of the United States Department of Commerce and the Securities and Exchange Commission and published periodically in the *Survey of Current Business*. The estimates were corrected for changes in prices of capital goods and were expressed in 1954 dollars.

For the most part, prewar acquisitions were depreciated at a slower rate than were postwar purchases. The estimates therefore allow for a gradual decline in average useful lives during the postwar years in most industries, owing to the increasing importance of postwar acquisitions in the total stock. The estimates of useful lives of capital stock for prewar manufacturing industries were prepared by Patrick Huntley from data on asset values and depreciation allowances, as reported in corporate income tax records published in *Statistics of Income*. I estimated the postwar lives from the same source. The useful lives implied in the income tax records for the years 1954–55 were taken as representative of all postwar acquisitions, since by that time the influence of prewar acquisitions on depreciation allowances and gross asset values was minor; yet the reported allowances were still largely free from the effects of curvilinear depreciation and hence could be used to infer the composite useful life from a straight-line depreciation formula. Determination of useful lives in nonmanufacturing industries is based largely on the work of Melville Ulmer and Frederick Schadrack cited in Appendix B.

The reciprocal of the useful life gives the straight-line depreciation rate for each industry, and this rate was increased by amounts ranging from one and one-half to two times the rate to provide the declining-balance depreciation rates used in the study. The estimate of depreciation for a given year was then derived by applying the depreciation rate to the real net capital stock at the end of the preceding year and to one-half the real gross investment of the same year.

Estimates of net investment in constant dollars were computed for the postwar years by subtracting depreciation from gross investment. Benchmark estimates of net capital stock were prepared for 1945 or were obtained from other sources for that or some other year. Given the benchmark estimate, it was necessary only to carry it forward by the annual data on net investment to obtain the final series on net capital stock in 1954 dollars.

The data on output refer to the real gross product originating in each industry. Output is measured net of the value of materials and services purchased from other industries but gross of depreciation and indirect business taxes in the given industry. If all industries were included in our study, the individual outputs would add up to gross national product in 1954 dollars. As it is, the aggregate output of the covered sectors amounted to 78 percent of gross national product in 1954.[1] The estimates for nonmanufacturing

[1] The omitted sectors are general government, households, rest of the world, mining except petroleum, and real estate.

industries were prepared in the Office of Business Economics[2] and those for manufacturing industries, by Charles Schultze and Joseph Tryon.[3]

The real price of capital is a compound variable formed from indexes of product and capital goods prices and data on interest and depreciation rates. The product price indexes are those implicit in the current and constant-dollar estimates of gross product originating in each industry, as given in the sources cited. Similarly the indexes of capital goods prices are those implicit in the current and deflated estimates of gross investment given in Appendix B. The derivation of the estimates of depreciation rates has already been described. Moody's estimates of yields on corporate bonds were used to measure the interest rate.

The money wage rate used in the other formulation of the relative price variable represents employee compensation per man-hour, including both production and nonproduction workers. The unpublished estimates were supplied by Charles Schultze.

Mining is not distinguished as a separate activity in the industrial breakdown used in this study. However, petroleum mining has been consolidated with petroleum refining and included in the manufacturing sector for the purposes of the investment analysis, for reasons explained in Appendix B. The small amount of investment activity in the remainder of the mining classification has been ignored.

The Regressions

To accomplish the analytical objectives of this study it was necessary to select the one regression for each industry and for the aggregate that best "explained" the behavior of net investment within the confines of the theoretical model described in Chapter 2. The final set of regressions was chosen from among hundreds of candidates, since several lag patterns were tried for each of several variants of the basic model in each industry. In general those regressions were selected which had the best combination of characteristics, judged by (1) the economic criteria of consistency with a

[2] Martin L. Marimont, "GNP by Major Industries," *Survey of Current Business* (October 1962), pp. 6–18.

[3] Described in *Prices and Costs in Manufacturing Industries*, Study Paper No. 17, U. S. Congress, Joint Economic Committee, *Study of Employment, Growth, and Price Levels*, 86 Cong. 2 sess. (Jan. 25, 1960).

priori constraints on the signs of the variables and the implied elasticity values and (2) the statistical criteria of goodness of fit and significance of coefficients. The primary purpose of this chapter is to describe the principal characteristics of the final regressions, with considerable attention to the statistical difficulties encountered in developing them.

All regressions were fitted by the least-squares method to annual data for 1949–60, and are of the general form illustrated for the case of two lags in equation (2.4). The best preliminary equations for the major industrial sectors are shown in Table 1. According to the underlying model, net investment, or more strictly, the net capital expansion ratio, depends on output, relative prices, time, and capital stock at the end of the previous year, with all variables except time expressed in logarithms. Output and relative prices may enter the regressions with lags of up to two years. Five of the eight preliminary regressions contain two or more output terms, implying a distributed lag in which the current investment response to an output change tends to be smaller than that occurring in one or more subsequent years. The lag patterns will be discussed in detail in the next chapter. It is also noteworthy that price terms are missing from half of the regressions, including those for the aggregate of all industries and for total manufacturing. The failure to obtain meaningful price coefficients in many of the industries will also be discussed at a later point. Finally, it should be observed that squared terms are included in the trends for two of the sectors, producing nonlinear exponential trends.

These initial regressions are fairly satisfactory by the usual statistical tests, although most of them can and will be improved by subsequent modifications. The coefficients of multiple correlation R range from 0.926 to 0.989. As measured by $\overline{R}^2$, the coefficient of multiple determination (the squared multiple correlation coefficient corrected for degrees of freedom), the regressions "explain" between 77.6 percent and 96.6 percent of the variance in net investment. The Durbin-Watson serial correlation test statistic, *SCT*, indicates little cause for concern about serial correlation in the residuals.[4]

The regression coefficients may be examined with regard to both sign

[4] The critical values of *SCT* for an equation with 6 explanatory variables (including the constant term) and 15 observations are 0.48 and 2.09 for a one-tailed test against positive serial correlation (the type suspected in time series analysis) at the 0.025 significance level. If *SCT* is greater than 2.09, the hypothesis of serial correlation is rejected; if it is less than 0.48, the hypothesis is accepted; and if it falls between these limits, the test is inconclusive. The available tables do not give critical values of *SCT* for the present number of observations (12) or for those of the present equations that contain more than 6 explanatory variables.

TABLE 1. *Regression Results for Major Sectors, Variable Elasticities*

Sector	Regression coefficients									R^2	R	SCT
	$\log K_{t-1}$	T	T^2	$\log Y_t$	$\log Y_{t-1}$	$\log Y_{t-2}$	$\log P_t$	$\log P_{t-1}$	Constant term			
All industries	−.2594** (.0484)	−.0016** (.0004)		.1235** (.0149)	.1157** (.0168)				.0833 (.0970)	.966	.989	2.57
Manufacturing	−.2731* (.1286)	−.0035 (.0053)	−.0000 (.0002)	.1896** (.0523)	.2311** (.0346)				−.2999 (.3454)	.951	.987	2.71
Railroads	−.2473** (.0602)	−.0011** (.0001)		.0404** (.0104)	.0388** (.0095)				.3337** (.0933)	.928	.977	2.78
Nonrail transportation	−.1380 (.1726)	−.0027** (.0006)		.2097** (.0421)			.1511*[a] (.0682)		.0759 (.2203)	.776	.926	2.25
Public utilities	−.5022** (.1419)	−.0040 (.0041)		.0763 (.1016)	.1070 (.0871)	.1631 (.1003)			.5370* (.1237)	.883	.968	1.89
Communications	−.6669** (.0945)	−.0025 (.0031)		.2009* (.0908)	.6187** (.0825)			.0656*[a] (.0260)	.1158 (.0749)	.951	.987	3.14
Commercial and other	−.1927 (.2549)	−.0029 (.0016)	.0001 (.0000)	.2064** (.0453)			.0957*[a] (.0462)		.0286 (.4886)	.782	.939	2.92
Farming	−.2056** (.0396)	.0004 (.0005)		.0178 (.0653)			−.0278[b] (.0301)		.3079* (.1235)	.957	.986	2.18

Note: The dependent variable in the regressions is ($\log K_t - \log K_{t-1}$). See equation (2.4) for the general form of the regressions. The standard error of each variable is in parentheses below the variable.

* Coefficient significant at .05 level. ** Coefficient significant at .01 level.

Two-tail test for constant term and time coefficient and one-tail test for all other variables.

[a] Relative price variable is in form $w/P_k(d+r)$ with expected sign positive. [b] Relative price variable is in form $P_k(d+r)/P$ with expected sign negative.

and statistical significance. All 8 coefficients of lagged capital stock are of the required negative sign, but only 6 of them are significantly different from zero at the 0.05 level or better by the standard *t* test (see Table 1). The 14 output terms carry the correct positive sign, and 10 of them are statistically significant. The 4 price terms also show the correct sign (positive or negative according to the form of the price variable), and 3 of them are significant. Most of the trends are negative, as expected, but not required, a priori; however, only 3 of the 10 coefficients are significant. Finally, 3 of the 8 constant terms are significant.

The least satisfactory regressions are those for nonrail transportation and commercial and other investment. Both sectors have low coefficients of determination and capital-stock coefficients that are smaller than their standard errors. The situation is not much better for the manufacturing and farming equations, each of which contains several regression coefficients that are unreliable in terms of their standard errors. The results for these four industries will be substantially improved by subsequent modification of the equations. Unfortunately the same cannot be said of the equation for public utilities, which will be retained as the final regression despite its lack of statistically significant output and trend terms.

The Long-Term Elasticities

Capital stock, output, and the real price of capital all had pronounced uptrends in most sectors during 1949–60, introducing a high degree of intercorrelation among these variables and between each of them and the time trend.[5] One of the principal problems created by this high multicollinearity among the explanatory variables concerns its effect on the reliability of the elasticity estimates.

It will be recalled that the coefficient of lagged capital stock measures the speed of adjustment of actual to desired stock and that the long-term elasticity of capital stock with respect to output (or price) is found by summing the coefficients of the one or more output (or price) terms and dividing by the speed of adjustment. Thus the value of b, the adjustment coefficient, is critical to the estimate of the long-term elasticities. Although multicolline-

[5] An attempt to overcome this problem by transforming the equations to first-difference form was unsuccessful. Not only were the coefficients of multiple determination reduced, as was to be expected, but the proportion of "wrong signs" and large error terms was higher than in the original regressions.

TABLE 2. *Estimated Values of the Long-Term Elasticity of Capital Stock With Respect to Output, Major Sectors*

Sector	Low	Medium	High
All industries	.7771	.9221	1.1336
Manufacturing	1.0473	1.5405	2.9114
Railroads	.2576	.3202	.4233
Nonrail transportation	.6751	1.5196	∞
Public utilities	.5378	.6898	.9614
Communications	1.0764	1.2289	1.4319
Commercial and other	.4611	1.0711	∞
Farming	.0726	.0866	.1072

arity does not tend to bias the net regression coefficients, it often leads to large standard errors and hence to uncertain estimates. The values of the output elasticities implied by the regressions for the major sectors are shown in column 2 of Table 2, together with the higher and lower values that would result if the *b* coefficients were off by only one standard error in either direction from their estimated values.

It is clear from a glance at the table that the elasticity estimates for nonrail transportation and the commercial and other sector are quite unreliable owing to the large standard errors of the *b* coefficients. The range of estimates for other sectors, while not inconsiderable, is less disquieting than in these two cases.

All these ranges would widen still further, however, if allowance were also made for the sampling errors in the output coefficients, which enter the numerator of the elasticity expression. This is especially critical for the farm sector, for which the absurdly low elasticity estimate lacks statistical as well as economic significance because the output coefficient is a small fraction of its standard error. The estimate for public utilities is also rather precarious from the statistical viewpoint, resting as it does on relatively insignificant output coefficients.

One may also ask whether the elasticity estimates are reasonable on economic grounds. The long-term elasticity of capital stock with respect to output reflects the influence of returns to scale. A unitary elasticity implies constant returns to scale. A value of less than one signifies increasing returns to scale, implying, for example, that output can be doubled without doubling capital stock (and other inputs). Values greater than one may be ruled out a priori, since industry output will be expanded by duplicating optimum-sized plants or firms in the long run and natural resource fixities can be overcome by exploration, reclamation, or substitution. By this criterion, the elasticity estimates for manufacturing, nonrail transportation, communications, and the commercial and other sector must be rejected as too high.

In view of these difficulties, it was decided to try new regressions in which a value of one was imposed on the elasticity of capital stock with respect to output, implying constant returns to scale. This was done by assuming the following restriction on the coefficients for output and capital stock:

$$\frac{c_2 + c_3 + c_4}{c_6} = 1, \tag{3.1}$$

where the coefficients are from

$$\log K_t - \log K_{t-1} = \log c_1 + c_2 \log Y_t + c_3 \log Y_{t-1} + c_4 \log Y_{t-2} + c_5 T - c_6 \log K_{t-1}. \tag{3.2}$$

When $(c_2 + c_3 + c_4)$ is substituted for (c_6) in equation (3.2), the result is:

$$\log K_t - \log K_{t-1} = \log c_1 + c_2(\log Y_t - \log K_{t-1}) + c_3(\log Y_{t-1} - \log K_{t-1}) + c_4(\log Y_{t-2} - \log K_{t-1}) + c_5 T. \tag{3.3}$$

The last equation is the form in which the second set of regressions was fitted. A variable like $(\log Y_t - \log K_{t-1})$ will be referred to as a modified output term. Fitting the equation in this form suppresses the strong intercorrelation between lagged capital stock and time.

The speed of adjustment implied by regression (3.3) is found by summing c_2, c_3, and c_4. The form of the regression is the same whether one, two, or three modified output terms are included, since the nature of the restriction is always that the sum of the output coefficients in the underlying equation (3.2) must equal the coefficient of capital stock. No restriction is placed on the coefficients of the price terms when they are included in the regressions.

It should be emphasized that fitting a regression of form (3.3) does not eliminate the influence of lagged capital stock on current investment. It simply constrains the coefficient of capital stock c_6—the speed of adjustment—to equal the sum of the coefficients of output. Once equation (3.3) is fitted, it is a simple matter to rewrite the equation in the familiar version (3.2).

The new set of regressions with unitary output elasticity is shown in Table 3. They are superior to the earlier regressions, with two exceptions. It was decided to retain the original equations for railroads and public utili-

TABLE 3. *Regression Results for Major Sectors, Unitary Elasticities*

Sector	Regression coefficients										
	T	T^2	$(\log Y_t - \log K_{t-1})$	$(\log Y_{t-1} - \log K_{t-1})$	$(\log Y_{t-2} - \log K_{t-1})$	$\log P_t$	$\log P_{t-1}$	Constant term	$\bar{R}^2$	R	SCT
All industries	−.0018** (.0001)		.1236** (.0142)	.1141** (.0157)				.0337** (.0018)	.969	.989	2.48
Manufacturing	.0007 (.0008)	−.0002** (.0001)	.1529** (.0238)	.2173** (.0291)				−.0265** (.0043)	.954	.985	2.72
Railroads	−.0010** (.0001)		.0342* (.0145)	.0374* (.0134)				.0547** (.0147)	.855	.946	1.75
Nonrail transportation	−.0027** (.0005)		.1966** (.0298)			.1547*[a] (.0637)		.1529* (.0560)	.800	.924	2.13
Public utilities	−.0103** (.0027)		.1346 (.1118)	.1374 (.0990)	.2325* (.1076)			.4396* (.1295)	.843	.949	1.22
Communications	.0023** (.0003)		.1126 (.0787)	.6575** (.0876)			.0615*[a] (.2085)	.2306** (.0205)	.941	.981	2.72
Commercial and other	−.0028** (.0007)	.0001* (.0000)	.2051** (.0386)			.0941**[a] (.0309)		.0534 (.0233)	.812	.938	2.89
Farming	.0002 (.0007)		.1604** (.0468)			−.0853**[b] (.0269)		−.0094 (.0269)	.926	.973	2.27

Note: The dependent variable in the regressions is $(\log K_t - \log K_{t-1})$. See equation (3.3) for the general form of the regressions. The standard error of each variable is in parentheses below the variable.

* Coefficient significant at .05 level. ** Coefficient significant at .01 level.

Two-tail test for constant term and time coefficient and one-tail test for all other variables.

[a] Relative price variable is in form $w/P_k(d+r)$ with expected sign positive. [b] Relative price variable is in form $P_k(d+r)/P$ with expected sign negative.

ties, since they had higher coefficients of determination and equally satisfactory regression coefficients, as compared with the unitary elasticity form of the regressions. Moreover, increasing returns to scale are only to be expected in these two industries.

Higher coefficients of determination and more significant explanatory variables were obtained from the unitary elasticity form of the regression for manufacturing, nonrail transportation, and commercial and other investment. Thus the a priori rejection of output elasticities of more than one resulted in superior statistical results for those industries.

The new equations were also selected for communications and farming, despite lower coefficients of determination than in the original regressions. Not only was the original elasticity estimate for farming implausible and statistically unreliable, but the regression coefficients are much improved in the new version. With regard to communications, the a priori rejection of the first regression has led to a great improvement in the significance of the time trend, at the expense of only a slight loss in significance for one of the output variables.

Finally, the unitary elasticity form has also been chosen for the aggregative equation. The regression coefficients are more significant, and the coefficient of determination is higher, for the new version than for the old. Since only slightly increasing returns to scale were indicated by the original equation, however, the imposition of a unitary elasticity has changed very little the regression coefficients for time and output and the (implicit) coefficient for lagged capital stock. This means that the implications to be drawn later from this important equation would be virtually the same if the alternative equation had been chosen for analysis.

As a final comment on this subject, it may be observed that a similar difficulty in isolating the scale factor from technical progress has plagued production-function studies of time series data, owing to "the strong intercorrelation between the time trend for technological progress and the effects of scale."[6] It is also worth noting that such studies usually lead to the conclusion, as does the present one, that returns to scale are approximately constant for the economy as a whole. Of course, the fact that superior statistical results were obtained for most of the investment regressions by imposing a unitary elasticity does not necessarily mean that constant returns to scale prevail in most industries. In view of the evidence from the aggregative regression that the over-all elasticity differs little if at all from one, how-

[6] Robert M. Solow, "Investment and Economic Growth," *Productivity Measurement Review* (November 1959), p. 64.

ever, a unitary elasticity is the most reasonable across-the-board, a priori assumption for these sectors in which scale and technical effects cannot be satisfactorily separated in the free regressions.[7]

The set of final regressions for major sectors then includes six equations with unitary elasticities and two with elasticities of less than one. Including the constant terms, there are 38 regression coefficients in all, of which 29 are statistically significant. Omitting the constant terms, 23 of the 30 slope coefficients are significant. When the variables are classified by type, it is found that 7 of the 10 trend variables are significant, as are 10 of the 14 output or modified output variables and all of the 4 price variables. The capital stock variables in the regressions for railroads and public utilities are also significant.

All coefficients of the equations for aggregate activity and for rail and nonrail transportation are significant, and all coefficients but one are significant for manufacturing, communications, and commercial and other investment. The regressions for public utilities and farming include two insignificant coefficients.

The Manufacturing Industries

Just as in the case of the major sectors, it was necessary to choose the best equation for each manufacturing industry. The final set of manufacturing regressions is shown in Table 4. All of them are in unitary elasticity form. Better statistical results were obtained by imposing a unitary output elasticity in 12 of the 13 industries, which is not surprising since the same was true of the manufacturing aggregate. Only in the case of petroleum and coal was the original regression rejected solely because it implied an output elasticity in excess of one, and even in that industry the final equation with unitary elasticity is only slightly inferior on statistical grounds to the original variant.

On the whole, the set of manufacturing regressions is less satisfactory than that for major sectors. The coefficients of determination range as low as 0.398, although four of them exceed 0.900, and five more are in the 0.800 decile. The test statistics for serial correlation also range lower, and in only six cases can the hypothesis of positive serial correlation be rejected, the test being inconclusive in the remaining instances.

[7] If the separation of scale economies and technical change were the primary research objective, it would be useful to experiment with several regressions for each sector in which alternative elasticity values were imposed before selecting the best variant.

Forty-three of the 67 regression coefficients in the manufacturing equations are significant at the .05 level. This was true of only 1 of the 8 price variables, however. The record is much better for the other variables, with 10 of the 15 trend variables and 23 of the 31 modified output variables passing this test. Finally, 9 of the 13 constant terms are significant.

Perhaps these rather mixed results are all that should realistically have been expected. It would be extraordinary indeed if the wholesale approach of this study yielded excellent results in all industries. It is believed, however, that with the exercise of due caution concerning their shortcomings, the individual relationships are sufficiently reliable to reap the sizable benefits of a comparative analysis of the principal investment determinants and to investigate compositional shift in investment demand.

The complete set of final regressions for major sectors and manufacturing industries is brought together for convenient reference in Table 5. In this table the equations that were fitted in the unitary elasticity form (3.3) have been rewritten in the standard form (3.2) to facilitate comparison of the (implicit) speed-of-adjustment coefficients of lagged capital stock in the various industries. The larger the capital stock coefficient, the faster is the gap between desired and actual stock filled by net investment. The reader is reminded, however, that the time shape of the investment response to an output (or price) change depends in an important way on the number and weight of the lagged output (or price) terms in the desired stock equation as well as on the speed of adjustment of desired to actual stock (Chapter 2). These matters will be discussed at length in Chapter 4.

The Price Variables

The reader will have noted that price variables are missing from 12 of the 19 industry equations and from the aggregative equations for manufacturing and all covered industries. This is because in most sectors the price variables were of the wrong sign, were statistically insignificant, or both. This finding may establish a presumption that price relationships do not regularly influence fixed investment decisions except in a few, albeit large and important, industrial sectors; but it is only a presumption, both because of statistical uncertainties and because the basic model abstracts from the possible effects of changes in interest rates or construction costs on the short-term timing of investment expenditure, as was explained in Chapter 1.

One difficulty in isolating the influence of price changes may be the high intercorrelation between output, time, and the real price of capital (Table 6).

TABLE 4. *Regression Results for Manufacturing Industries, Unitary Elasticities*

Industry	Regression coefficients								R^2	R	SCT
	T	$(\log Y_t - \log K_{t-1})$	$(\log Y_{t-1} - \log K_{t-1})$	$(\log Y_{t-2} - \log K_{t-1})$	$\log P_t$	$\log P_{t-1}$	$\log P_{t-2}$	Constant term			
Primary metals	.0062 (.0027)	.1297* (.0679)	.2383** (.0773)	.1110 (.0947)				.0036 (.0113)	.534	.839	0.86
Machinery	−.0004 (.0005)	.1508** (.0389)	.0975* (.0469)					−.0937** (.0201)	.720	.892	1.54
Motor vehicles	.0226**[c] (.0038)	.1132* (.0415)	.1859** (.0482)					−.1029** (.0230)	.868	.957	2.28
Nonautomotive transportation equipment	−.0214** (.0032)	.2715** (.0669)	.0369 (.0946)	.3232** (.1019)				.0293 (.0131)	.876	.960	2.74
Stone, clay, and glass	.0047* (.0014)	.1837 (.0934)	.0663 (.0596)	.0012 (.0492)	−.0703[b] (.1010)	−.2339[b] (.1390)	−.1367[b] (.1012)	−.4207* (.1052)	.871	.976	2.63
Other durables	−.0032** (.0005)	.2597** (.0391)	.1224* (.0530)					−.1040** (.0200)	.842	.941	1.27
Food and beverages	−.0064** (.0007)	.0029 (.1276)	.3343* (.1239)					−.0414** (.0079)	.924	.972	1.62

Textiles	−.0016 (.0009)	.1577** (.0214)	.1832** (.0177)	.0278 (.0284)	.0448[a] (.0360)	.1222[a] (.0655)	.0985[a] (.0587)	.2538* (.0600)	.986	.997	1.78
Paper	−.0002 (.0006)	.1685 (.0922)	.2321* (.1081)					−.0047 (.0095)	.398	.750	1.11
Chemicals	−.0109**[d] (.0022)	.1317** (.0342)	.3477** (.0417)	.1826* (.0648)				.1244** (.0173)	.933	.982	2.74
Petroleum and coal	−.00002 (.0005)	.1503* (.0503)	.2639** (.0570)					.1598** (.0210)	.918	.970	1.45
Rubber	−.0033** (.0007)	.2085** (.0499)	.2342** (.0616)					−.0574** (.0114)	.738	.899	2.13
Other nondurables	−.0023* (.0007)	.0816* (.0383)	.2488** (.0423)		.2030**[a] (.0396)	.0368[a] (.0435)		.0483 (.0526)	.872	.965	3.27

Note: The dependent variable in the regressions is ($\log K_t - \log K_{t-1}$). See equation (3.3) for the general form of the regressions. The standard error of each variable is in parentheses below the variable.

* Coefficient significant at .05 level. ** Coefficient significant at .01 level.

Two-tail test for constant term and time coefficient and one-tail test for all other variables.

[a] Relative price variable is in form $w/P_k(d+r)$ with expected sign positive.

[b] Relative price variable is in form $P_k(d+r)/P$ with expected sign negative.

[c] Also contains T^2 term of −.0017** with standard error .0003.

[d] Also contains T^2 term of −.0003* with standard error .0001.

TABLE 5. *Final Set of Investment Regressions, All Industries*[a]

Industry or Sector	Regression coefficients										Elasticity
	Constant term	$\log K_{t-1}$	T	T^2	$\log Y_t$	$\log Y_{t-1}$	$\log Y_{t-2}$	$\log P_t$	$\log P_{t-1}$	$\log P_{t-2}$	
All industries	.0337	−.2377	−.0018		.1236	.1141					1
Manufacturing	−.0265	−.3702	.0007	−.0002	.1529	.2173					1
Primary metals	.0036	−.4790	.0062		.1297	.2383	.1110				1
Machinery	−.0937	−.2483	−.0004		.1508	.0975					1
Motor vehicles	−.1029	−.2991	.0226	−.0017	.1132	.1859					1
Nonautomotive transportation equipment	.0293	−.6316	−.0214		.2715	.0369	.3232				1
Stone, clay, and glass	−.4207	−.2512	.0047		.1837	.0663	.0012	−.0703	−.2339	−.1367	1
Other durables	−.1040	−.3821	−.0032		.2597	.1224					1
Food and beverages	−.0414	−.3372	−.0064		.0029	.3343					1
Textiles	.2538	−.3687	−.0016		.1577	.1832	.0278	.0448	.1222	.0985	1
Paper	−.0047	−.4006	−.0002		.1685	.2321					1
Chemicals	.1244	−.6620	−.0109	−.0003	.1317	.3477	.1826				1
Petroleum and coal	.1598	−.4142	−.00002		.1503	.2639					1
Rubber	−.0574	−.4427	−.0033		.2085	.2342					1
Other nondurables	.0483	−.3304	−.0023		.0816	.2488		.2030	.0368		1
Railroads	.3337	−.2473	−.0011		.0404	.0388					.32
Nonrail transportation	.1529	−.1996	−.0027		.1996			.1547			1
Public utilities	.5370	−.5022	−.0040		.0763	.1070	.1631				.69
Communications	.2306	−.7701	.0023		.1126	.6575			.0615		1
Commercial and other	.0534	−.2051	−.0028	.0001	.2051			.0941			1
Farming	−.0094	−.1604	.0002		.1604			−.0853			1

[a] The coefficients of $\log K_{t-1}$ were estimated directly in the regressions for railroads and public utilities (Table 1). For all other industries, the implicit coefficient for $\log K_{t-1}$ was obtained by summing the coefficients of the modified output terms of the regressions in Tables 3 and 4. For equations with unitary elasticity, the coefficients of the output terms in the present table are the same as the coefficients of the modified output terms in the actual regressions.

TABLE 6. *Simple Correlations of Real Price of Capital With Other Variables*

Industry or Sector	Real price of capital correlated with:			
	Output	Modified Output[a]	Time	Change in Output[b]
All industries	.95	.69	.99	.21
Manufacturing	.90	.09	.99	.38
Primary metals	.15	−.65	.85	.40
Machinery	.85	.10	.98	.76
Motor vehicles	.50	−.57	.93	−.02
Nonautomotive transportation equipment	.97	.68	.93	.94
Stone, clay, and glass	.85	.39	.93	.25
Other durables	.86	.57	.98	.01
Food and beverages	.97	.96	.97	−.26
Textiles	.58	.76	.99	−.09
Paper	.90	−.25	.96	−.26
Chemicals	.97	.94	.99	.30
Petroleum and coal	.91	−.66	.93	.18
Rubber	.68	.44	.83	.01
Other nondurables	.98	.97	.98	.48
Railroads	.17	.27	.98	.76
Nonrail transportation	.97	.98	.93	.87
Public utilities	.99	.99	.99	.63
Communications	.85	−.64	.85	.47
Commercial and other	.96	.92	.96	.46
Farming	.96	−.39	.94	.11

[a] Output minus lagged capital stock.
[b] Correlation of first differences of price and output.

One of the worst hazards of multicollinearity is the possibility that it may lead to statistically insignificant results when a new variable is introduced which in fact is a significant factor in the true relationship.[8] That is, when a new variable is added to an equation that already includes one or more explanatory variables with which the new one is correlated, the intercorrelation may so increase the standard error of the added variable as to render it insignificant by the usual statistical tests.

Conceivably the high correlation between time and the real price of capital could be having this effect. New regressions omitting the time trend were therefore run for all industries, but this experiment did not improve the significance of the price coefficients.

[8] Henri Theil, *Economic Forecasts and Policy* (Amsterdam: North-Holland Press, 1958), p. 215.

Output and the real price of capital are also highly correlated in most of our series, and this fact may have affected the reliability of the price coefficients. Much of the correlation between output and the real price of capital is due to pronounced uptrends in the two variables, however, and it is interesting to observe that the significance of the price variables was largely unaffected by alternative formulations of the regressions which reduced the influence of common trends.

One of these alternative formulations involved converting the regressions to first-difference form, in which the annual change in capital stock was related to annual changes in the explanatory variables (with one or two lags) instead of to their absolute levels. First-differencing drastically reduced the correlation between output and the real price of capital in most industries (Table 6, column 4), but the transformed price variables were if anything less significant in the new multiple regressions than in the original ones.

The procedure by which a unitary output elasticity was imposed on most of the final regressions also reduced the intercorrelation between output and the real price of capital in many of the industries. It will be recalled that lagged capital stock was subtracted from each of the output variables in these regressions before the equations were fitted. This procedure substantially reduced the correlation between the real price of capital and the (modified) output variable in a dozen cases (Table 6), but with one or two exceptions there was again no increase in the significance of the price variables in the multiple regressions.

In general the preceding observations apply also to the alternative sets of regressions, in which price influences were represented by the ratio of the price of labor to the price of capital instead of by the real price of capital. Indeed the degree of correlation between the new price variable and either time or output is smaller in most industries than was true of the real price of capital (Table 7). Significant coefficients for the alternative price variable are nonetheless again the exception rather than the rule.

Another possible source of trouble was in the lag specification of the relative price variable. According to the model, the expected long-term levels of output and relative prices are weighted averages of current and recent values. It is certainly conceivable, however, that price expectations are formed on a different basis than are output expectations. Regressions were therefore run for all major sectors in which (1) P_t was tried with Y_t, with Y_t and Y_{t-1}, and with Y_t, Y_{t-1}, and Y_{t-2}, and (2) P_{t-1} was similarly tried with Y_t, with Y_t and Y_{t-1}, and with Y_t, Y_{t-1}, and Y_{t-2}. This was done for both versions of the relative price variable. Again the results were

TABLE 7. *Simple Correlations of Relative Price of Labor and Capital with Other Variables*

Industry or Sector	Relative price correlated with:			
	Output	Modified Output[a]	Time	Change in Output[b]
All industries	.14	.18	.04	.01
Manufacturing	−.48	−.14	−.53	−.43
Primary metals	.27	−.44	.52	−.33
Machinery	−.67	−.08	−.77	−.52
Motor vehicles	−.09	.13	−.15	−.25
Nonautomotive transportation equipment	−.81	−.54	−.72	−.40
Stone, clay, and glass	−.69	−.22	−.76	−.27
Other durables	−.68	−.49	−.80	−.29
Food and beverages	−.49	−.54	−.49	.04
Textiles	−.59	−.76	−.97	−.16
Paper	−.59	.30	−.63	−.15
Chemicals	.19	.08	.21	−.28
Petroleum and coal	−.23	−.23	−.07	−.80
Rubber	−.27	−.16	−.45	.05
Other nondurables	−.90	−.89	−.92	−.15
Railroads	.15	.04	−.74	−.28
Nonrail transportation	−.66	−.67	−.69	−.15
Public utilities	−.72	−.76	−.73	−.28
Communications	−.07	.57	−.08	−.16
Commercial and other	.15	.19	.14	−.03
Farming	−.67	.67	−.66	.42

[a] Output minus lagged capital stock.
[b] Correlation of first differences of price and output.

disappointing except in the single instance of the communications industry. The final regression for communications, in fact, includes two output terms and only one lagged price variable (Table 5).

Another question concerns the form of the relative price variables. Because it is relative prices that theoretically influence investment decisions in either profit-maximization or cost-minimization models, all relevant price relationships have been combined in a single compound variable in the present regressions. This procedure also has the statistical merit of conserving the extremely limited degrees of freedom permitted by a sample of 12 observations. Nevertheless, it was decided to test whether the compound price variables were covering up offsetting influences among the component prices.

This was done by running regressions for the major sectors in which the real price of capital was factored into its two principal components P_k/P and $d+r$. (P and P_k are respectively the indexes of product prices and of capital goods prices, d is the depreciation rate, and r is the long-term interest rate.) A similar procedure was followed for the other form of the relative price variable by factoring the two components w/P_k and $1/d+r$, where the new variable w represents the money wage rate. The regressions also included the usual output and trend terms. These efforts too failed to produce meaningful results in the cases where none had been found for the original compound variables.

Tests were also made for the separate influence of interest rates in all major sectors by omitting all prices except interest rates from one set of regressions and all prices except the sum of depreciation and interest rates from another. Both sets included output and trend terms. Neither experiment produced useful results.

Still another possible source of difficulty concerns the measurement of user cost of capital. In Jorgenson's derivation the formula for user cost, denoted by c, is:

$$c = q\left(\frac{1 - uv}{1 - u}d + \frac{1 - uw}{1 - u}r\right),$$

where q, d, and r are respectively the price of capital goods, the rate of depreciation, and the rate of interest.[9] These are the three variables entering my index of user cost. In Jorgenson's measure, however, the depreciation and interest rates are modified by certain tax parameters. These are u, the rate of direct taxation on corporate income, v, the proportion of depreciation chargeable against income for tax purposes, and w, the proportion of interest chargeable against income. Had I taken these tax parameters into account, some additional variation might have been introduced into the user cost index and might therefore have affected the regressions results for the relative price variable. This does not appear to me to be very likely, however, since I would not expect the tax parameters to show much variability since World War II.

Finally, it is possible that the single-equation methods of estimating used here are partly responsible for the failure to obtain usable price relationships in many of the regressions. That is, each regression has been treated as if it were an investment demand function with all explanatory variables determined independently of the level of current real investment expendi-

[9] See Dale W. Jorgenson "Capital Theory and Investment Behavior," *American Economic Review* (May 1963), p 249.

ture. This means that the coefficients of the current price variables may be biased by simultaneous interaction between current investment demands and supply conditions in the capital goods and credit markets. However, it should be remembered that the lagged price coefficients failed to show improvement when the current price variables were omitted from the regressions for the major sectors.

Interest rates and capital goods prices are determined in national markets, moreover, and may therefore be largely independent of current investment demands in particular sectors, even at the high level of industrial aggregation of the present study.

This last argument does not apply, however, to the aggregative relationship for all covered industries. Nor can the interaction between the investment and output variables be assumed to be of minor importance on the aggregative level. In final defense of the least-squares estimates used in this study despite these elements of simultaneity, it should be observed that the available techniques for dealing with the simultaneous-equations problem are designed for large samples and that the coefficients obtained for small samples seldom deviate significantly from the simple least-squares estimates.[10]

The Time Trends

The trend term in the aggregative equation has a negative sign, indicating a steady decrease over time in the quantity of capital desired per unit of output.[11] Because of this negative trend, and because replacement demand is proportional to capital stock in the model, the equation implies that the share of gross investment in aggregate output would fall continuously under conditions of steady growth. This important implication will be

[10] See, for example, the tests performed on the Klein-Goldberger model by Karl A. Fox reported in "Econometric Models of the United States," *Journal of Political Economy* (April 1956), pp. 128–42.

[11] The estimated trend rate of decline of aggregate desired capital stock is 1.8 percent a year. This rate is found by dividing the coefficient of the trend term in the final investment regression by the coefficient of the capital stock term (see Chapter 2). Because common logarithms were used instead of natural logarithms in fitting the regressions, however, it is also necessary to multiply the trend coefficient by 2.3026 in order to convert it to a compound interest rate. Thus, the aggregate trend rate is calculated as $(-.0018)(2.3026)/.2377 = -.018$. The trend rates for the other sectors may be calculated in the same way from the coefficients shown in Table 5.

investigated in later chapters, but for the present the focus will be on the pervasiveness of the downtrend in unit capital requirements as shown by the industry regressions.

Among the 13 manufacturing industries only primary metals and stone, clay, and glass had positive net trends in desired capital stock throughout the postwar period. The curvilinear trend for motor vehicles implies a rise in the ratio of desired stock to output until 1955 and a decline thereafter. The 10 remaining manufacturing industries show continuously negative net trends, ranging from virtually zero in petroleum and coal to a rate nearly 12 times the national average in nonautomotive transportation equipment. The preponderance of negative trends in the manufacturing industries is reflected in a gradually accelerating downtrend in unit capital requirements in the equation for total manufacturing.

Four of the six equations for nonmanufacturing industries contain pronounced negative trends, whereas the trend term for farming is slightly positive and that for communications decidedly so.

The preponderance of negative trends in unit capital requirements at given factor price ratios is in accord with a priori expectations, as discussed in Chapter 2. This is because capital stock is measured in units of current vintage in the model, and the general effect of technical progress is to increase the productivity of each new vintage of capital goods. As was observed earlier, however, the general tendency for technical change to reduce unit capital requirements may be more than offset in some industries, or for some periods, by capital-using innovations which greatly increase the ratio of capital to labor. Perhaps this is the explanation for the positive trend terms in the equations for primary metals, stone, clay, and glass, and communications. One may also speculate that the period of rising unit capital requirements for motor vehicle production up to 1954–55 was induced by a stream of innovations with a strong capital-using bias and that this trend was reversed thereafter by diminution or elimination of the capital-using bias.

It is not possible to verify such speculations, however, without an intensive study of technical change in particular industries in which outside information or other analytical techniques are brought to bear on the problem. At best the trend terms reflect the net effect of the neutral and factor-biased components of technical change on unit capital requirements, and the two types cannot be disentangled within the present model.

There are at least four reasons, moreover, why the trend terms may be imperfect measures of even the net effects of technical change on unit capital requirements. First, as has already been discussed at length, the attempt made in the original regressions to obtain from the unconstrained data reliable measures of the separate effects of scale economies and technical change on capital requirements was largely unsuccessful. Instead, it was necessary to impose a unitary elasticity of capital stock with respect to output in all but two of the final regressions in order to suppress the strong intercorrelation between time and lagged capital stock. In general this procedure did not reverse the sign of the trend term, but it did alter its value by substantial amounts in some industries. In the case of communications, moreover, the sign of the trend was changed from negative in the original regression to positive in the final one (Tables 1 and 3).[12]

Second, the failure to obtain usable price terms in many of the regressions may mean that the trend variables are picking up the effects, if any, of capital-labor substitution induced by price changes as well as by technical progress.

Third, intra-industry shifts may exert a considerable influence over observed capital-output relationships when the level of aggregation is as high as in this study. In the next chapter it will be shown that inter-industry shifts in the composition of output had a substantial effect on aggregate capital requirements during the postwar years. The same sort of effect can occur within a given "industry" if the level of unit capital requirements differs substantially between two branches that are growing at different rates. In that case the trend term in the industry equation will only partly reflect the pure effects of technical change and will include as well the influence of the intra-industry shifts in capital requirements. For instance, the early uptrend in unit capital requirements in the motor vehicles industry may reflect the shift toward defense production by automobile producers during the Korean War, implying that the subsequent downtrend is due partly to a return to a peacetime composition of output.

Fourth, output is measured by value added instead of total value product in the regressions, whereas capital stock is conceptually related to the latter rather than the former. Any systematic change in the ratio of value added to total value product in a particular industry, as from a vertical integration movement, for example, may be reflected in the trend term.

To sum up, although the trend terms were included in the investment

[12] A positive trend does appear plausible for communications, given the high degree of automation commonly attributed to the telephone industry. Furthermore, the negative trend in the original regression was statistically insignificant in contrast to the positive trend of the final regression.

regressions to allow for the effects of technical change on capital requirements, they are recognizably imperfect measures of those effects and should be interpreted in that light. In addition to technical progress, they may reflect to an unknown extent the effects of scale economies, price-induced factor substitution, compositional shifts in capital requirements, and changes in the ratio of value added to total value product.

Predictive Accuracy of the Equations

The purpose of this section is to compare the actual investment experience of 1961 and 1962 with the values "predicted" by the equations. That is, the predicted capital expansion ratios for 1961 were computed by inserting the actual outputs and prices for 1961 into the original equations as fitted to data for 1949–60, and the process was then repeated for 1962. The computed investment values for 1961 and 1962 are not true forecasts, of course, since they are derived from *ex post* observations of actual output and prices. They do serve, however, to test the accuracy with which the equations can be extrapolated beyond the original range of observation. This question is important both as a test of the investment model—of the stability of the structural relationships presumed to underlie the equations—and because some of the equations will be used to make conditional forward extrapolations of investment demand under alternative growth conditions in Chapters 8 and 9.

The predicted and realized values for 1961 and 1962 are shown in Tables 8 and 9. The investment values are expressed as percentages of capital stock by subtracting unity from the predicted or realized capital expansion ratio K_t/K_{t-1} and multiplying by 100. For example, according to the aggregative equation, the capital expansion ratio should have been 1.012 in 1961 given the actual output of that year. This is merely another way of saying that the net capital stock should have increased by 1.2 percent during the year or that net investment should have been 1.2 percent of the beginning-of-the-year capital stock.

The predicted expansion of aggregate net capital stock of 1.2 percent during 1961 compares with an actually realized expansion of 1.0 percent (Table 8, columns 1 and 2). Is this a good prediction or a bad one? Some error is only to be expected, since the aggregative regression itself is a sto-

TABLE 8. *Predicted and Realized Values of Net Investment, 1961*
(In percent of capital stock)

Industry or Sector	*P* (1)	*R* (2)	*N* (3)	*P–R* (4)	*N–R* (5)
1. All industries	1.2	1.0	1.5	0.2	0.5
2. Manufacturing	0.7	0.2	1.2	0.5	1.0
3. Primary metals	2.0	−0.4	2.8	2.4	3.2
4. Machinery	2.6	2.3	2.9	0.3	0.6
5. Motor vehicles	−4.3	−2.9	−1.3	−1.4	1.6
6. Nonautomotive transportation equipment	−8.1	−2.9	−2.2	−5.2	0.7
7. Stone, clay, and glass	0.8	−0.6	2.5	1.4	3.1
8. Other durables	0.7	−0.1	1.1	0.8	1.2
9. Food and beverages	−1.7	0	−0.8	−1.7	−0.8
10. Textiles	−0.3	−0.7	0	0.4	0.7
11. Paper	4.0	1.8	3.5	2.2	1.7
12. Chemicals	1.1	1.3	1.3	−0.2	0
13. Petroleum and coal	1.7	0.6	0.7	1.1	0.1
14. Rubber	1.9	1.7	3.5	0.2	1.8
15. Other nondurables	2.1	1.7	2.0	0.4	0.3
16. Railroads	−1.2	−1.8	−1.0	0.6	0.8
17. Nonrail transportation	0	−1.3	−0.5	1.3	0.8
18. Public utilities	3.5	3.0	3.6	0.5	0.6
19. Communications	7.3	5.0	6.2	2.3	1.2
20. Commercial and other	2.2	1.9	1.9	0.3	0
21. Farming	0.7	0.5	0.3	0.2	−0.2
Root-Mean-Square					
Manufacturing				1.9	1.6
Nonmanufacturing				1.1	0.7
Total				1.7	1.4

Notes:
1. Column 1: values predicted from the equations.
2. Column 2: actually realized values calculated from Appendix Table B-4.
3. Column 3: naive model prediction, equals actually realized values from year preceding the forecast year.

chastic equation containing a random error component. It is possible to construct a confidence interval for the forecast error, but another approach to the problem has more intuitive appeal. This is to ask whether one could obtain a superior forecast from the "naive model," which predicts no change in net investment from one year to the next.

Since the actual expansion of the aggregate net stock during 1960 was 1.5 percent, this is the value that would be predicted for 1961 under the no-change assumption (Table 8, column 3). Since the naive-model predic-

TABLE 9. *Predicted and Realized Values of Net Investment, 1962*

(In percent of capital stock)

Industry or Sector	*P* (1)	*R* (2)	*N* (3)	*P–R* (4)	*N–R* (5)	*S* (6)
1. All industries	1.3	1.6	1.0	−0.3	−0.6	0.2
2. Manufacturing	0.7	0.8	0.2	−0.1	−0.6	0.5
3. Primary metals	3.8	−0.4	−0.4	4.2	0	2.9
4. Machinery	3.6	3.0	2.3	0.6	−0.7	1.4
5. Motor vehicles	−8.2	−1.7	−2.9	−6.5	−1.2	2.2
6. Nonautomotive transportation equipment	−10.5	−0.9	−2.9	−9.6	−2.0	4.3
7. Stone, clay, and glass	2.4	1.1	−0.6	1.3	−1.7	0.9
8. Other durables	2.1	2.7	−0.1	−0.6	−2.8	0.8
9. Food and beverages	−2.0	−0.2	0	−1.8	0.2	0.5
10. Textiles	1.6	0.9	−0.7	0.7	−1.6	0.3
11. Paper	5.5	2.2	1.8	3.3	−0.4	1.8
12. Chemicals	0.2	0.5	1.3	−0.3	0.8	0.7
13. Petroleum and coal	2.4	0.9	0.6	1.5	−0.3	0.7
14. Rubber	3.3	2.5	1.7	0.8	−0.8	1.2
15. Other nondurables	2.1	1.6	1.7	0.5	0.1	0.3
16. Railroads	−1.0	−1.4	−1.8	0.4	−0.4	0.2
17. Nonrail transportation	2.5	0.5	−1.3	2.0	−1.8	0.6
18. Public utilities	3.3	2.7	3.0	0.6	0.3	0.7
19. Communications	7.5	5.5	5.0	2.0	−0.5	0.5
20. Commercial and other	3.1	2.7	1.9	0.4	−0.8	0.3
21. Farming	1.0	0.8	0.5	0.2	−0.3	0.5
Root-Mean-Square						
Manufacturing				3.6	1.3	
Nonmanufacturing				1.2	0.9	
Total				3.1	1.2	

Notes:

1. Column 1: values predicted from the equations.
2. Column 2: actually realized values calculated from Appendix Table B-4.
3. Column 3: naive model prediction, equals actually realized values from year preceding the forecast year.
4. Column 6: This statistic is based on the standard error of estimate as corrected for degrees of freedom. In conformity with the treatment of the dependent variable in this table the standard error of estimate has been altered by subtracting one from its antilogarithm and multiplying by 100.

tion exceeds the actually realized expansion by 0.5 percentage points (Table 8, column 5), it is clearly inferior to the prediction from the equation, which had an error of only 0.2 percentage points (Table 8, column 4). The superior performance of the equation was repeated for the 1962 prediction, as may be seen by comparing columns 4 and 5 in Table 9.

According to the naive-model test then, the aggregative equation shows good predictive ability. So also does the equation for total manufacturing.

CHART I. *Predicted* versus *Realized Values of Net Investment, 1961*

(In percent of capital stock)

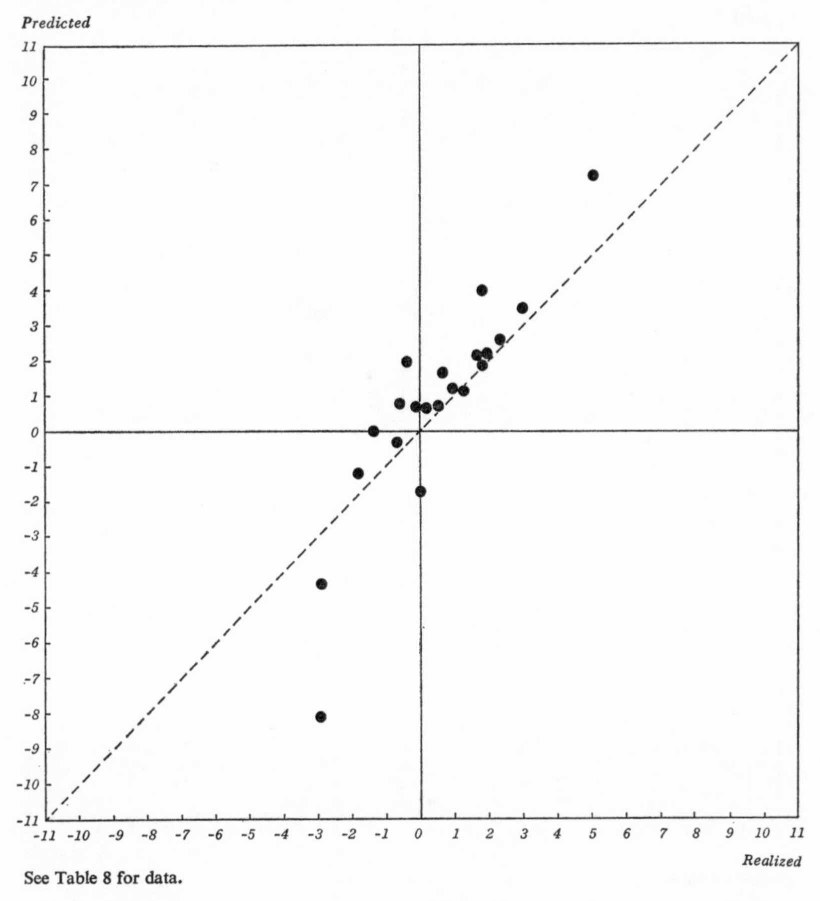

See Table 8 for data.

Unfortunately, however, the results are mixed for the other equations, and some of them are quite unsatisfactory. By way of over-all assessment, it is useful to compare the root-mean-square error of the set of predictions from the individual industry equations with that of the set of naive-model predictions.

As measured by this statistic, the average error of the predictions made for 1961 from the 19 industry equations was 1.7 percentage points. This is somewhat inferior to the corresponding figure of 1.4 for the set of no-change predictions, but not markedly so. The situation is much worse for the 1962 predictions, however, since the root-mean-square errors for that year are respectively 3.1 and 1.2 for the two sets of predictions.

CHART II. *Predicted* versus *Realized Values of Net Investment, 1962*

(In percent of capital stock)

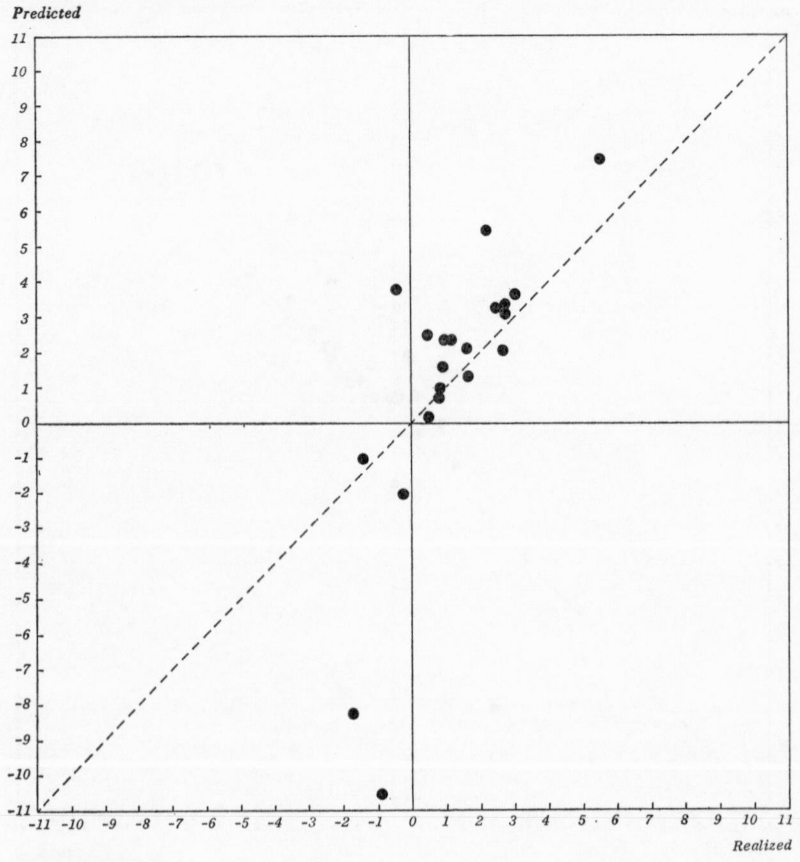

See Table 9 for data.

Inspection of the individual equations reveals that the largest prediction errors are found among the manufacturing industries, and especially in primary metals, motor vehicles, nonautomotive transportation equipment, and paper. The root-mean-square error of the manufacturing predictions was nearly double that for the nonmanufacturing industries in 1961 and more than three times as large in 1962. This is not a surprising outcome in view of the fact that the standard errors of estimate are on the whole much larger for the manufacturing equations (Table 9, column 6). Because of these poor forecasting results, the individual manufacturing equations will not be extrapolated beyond 1962 in the later work.

The predictions for the entire set of 21 equations are plotted against the

TABLE 10. *Predicted and Realized Changes in Net Investment, 1960–61 and 1961–62*

(In percent of capital stock)

Industry or Sector	Change During 1960–61		Change During 1961–62	
	Predicted	Realized	Predicted	Realized
All industries	−0.3	−0.5	0.1	0.6
Manufacturing	−0.8	−1.0	0	0.6
Primary metals	0.4	−3.2	1.8	0
Machinery	−0.5	−0.6	1.0	0.7
Motor vehicles	−2.6	−1.6	−3.9	1.2
Nonautomotive transportation equipment	−1.3	−0.6	−2.4	0.2
Stone, clay, and glass	−1.2	−3.1	1.6	1.7
Other durables	−1.1	−1.2	1.4	2.8
Food and beverages	−0.3	0.8	−0.3	−0.2
Textiles	−0.3	−0.7	1.9	1.6
Paper	−0.3	−1.7	1.5	0.4
Chemicals	0.1	0	−0.9	−0.8
Petroleum and coal	0.1	−0.1	0.7	0.3
Rubber	−2.1	−1.8	1.4	0.8
Other nondurables	0.1	−0.3	0	−0.1
Railroads	−0.1	−0.8	0.2	0.4
Nonrail transportation	0	−0.8	2.5	1.8
Public utilities	0.2	−0.6	−0.2	−0.3
Communications	0.7	−1.2	0.2	0.5
Commercial and other	0.2	0	0.9	0.8
Farming	0.1	0.2	0.3	0.3

Note: These figures represent *changes* in net investment between the specified years. For example, the aggregative equation predicted a net investment percentage of 1.5 in 1960 and 1.2 in 1961, so that the change for 1960–61 is −0.3.

realized values for 1961 and 1962 in Charts I and II. The 45° line represents perfect predictions. Points above this line indicate overestimates of the realized levels of net investment. That is, if realized net investment is negative and predicted investment is either positive or a smaller negative amount than realized, the point will lie above the 45° line, and this will also be true when a larger positive investment is predicted than realized.

It will be seen that the overestimates far outnumber the underestimates in both 1961 and 1962. Why this should be true of so many industries when the aggregative equation yields only a slight overestimate in 1961 and an underestimate in 1962, is far from clear. There is, of course, some offsetting among the individual predictions, especially since the underestimates tend to be large though few in number (column 4 in Tables 8 and 9). Moreover, the overestimates are rather small for railroads, public utilities, farms, and the commercial and other sector, and together these four industries account for 65 percent of aggregate investment. Even so, the consensus of individual predictions exceeds the prediction of the aggregative equation during both years. The sum of the industry predictions for 1961 yields an estimated increase in aggregate capital stock of 1.6 percent instead of the 1.2 percent predicted by the aggregative equation. The corresponding figures for 1962 are 2.1 and 1.3 percent. Notice that although the predictions by industry consensus are poorer than those of the aggregative equation in both years, involving an error of 0.6 in both 1961 and 1962, they are about as good as the aggregative naive-model predictions.

When the naive-model predictions are examined, it is found that only 2 out of a total of 21 were underestimates in 1961 and that only 4 of the 21 were overestimates in 1962 (column 5 in Tables 8 and 9). This pattern is due to the business recession of 1961 and the recovery of 1962. The naive model can never predict turning points, since it assumes no change from one year to the next. The only reason why the naive model predictions were not universally above investment realizations in 1961 and below them in 1962 was that there was a contracyclical movement of investment demand in a few industries.

The equations were reasonably successful in predicting the turning points of net investment during 1960–62. Table 10 compares the predicted and realized *changes* in the net investment rates between 1960 and 1961 and again between 1961 and 1962. With 21 equations in all, 12 turning points were correctly predicted in 1960–61 and 16 in 1961–62.

4 / *Structural Implications of the Equations*

THE PURPOSE OF this chapter is to examine the structural properties of the final set of equations. What do the equations imply about inter-industry differences in the timing and magnitude of investment responses to changes in output or prices? How substantial are the differences between the short- and long-term responses? Are the inter-industry variations sufficiently pronounced to imply that aggregate investment can be substantially affected by shifts in the composition of output?

The Time Shape of the Investment Response

The need to distinguish between the short- and long-term responses of investment to a change in capital requirements was stressed in Chapter 2. Businessmen seldom make a full and immediate adjustment of production facilities to new demand or cost conditions, partly because they are uncertain at first whether the new conditions will persist for a long period and partly because of technical lags involved in the actual execution of investment projects. Chart III pictures the time profile of the investment response to a once-for-all increase of output in each major sector. It shows the net investment that would be undertaken each year during the first five years of adjustment, expressed as a percentage of the total investment needed to bring capital stock into long-term equilibrium. The method by which the profile of the distributed investment lag is calculated was explained in Chapter 2.

It is apparent from the chart that in most sectors the peak annual invest-

CHART III. *Profile of Net Investment Response During First Five Years of Adjustment*

(In percent of total long-term response)

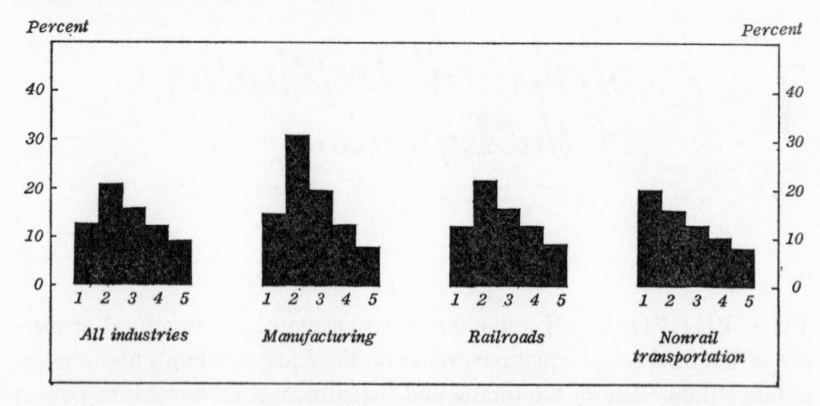

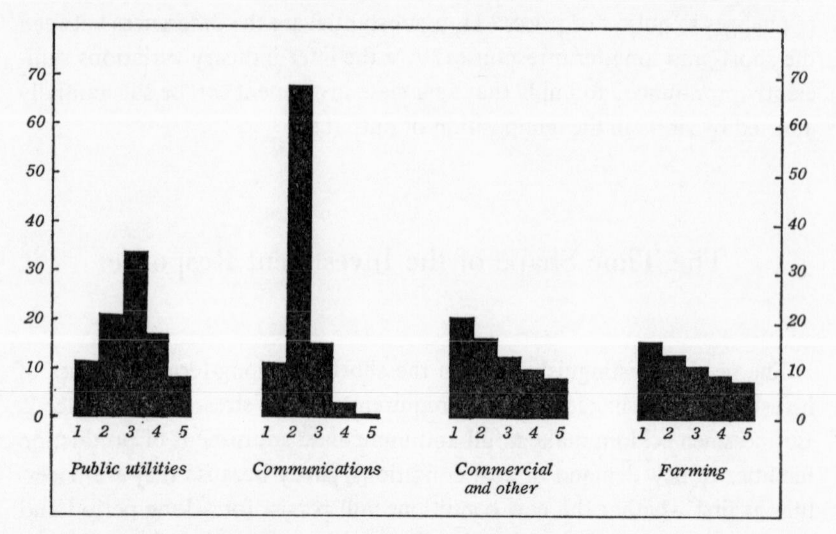

See text for explanatory remarks.

ment response to an increase in demand for capital stock occurs in the second or third year following the increase. A second year peak is found in manufacturing, railroads, and communications, and it is this pattern which dominates the over-all average as reflected in the aggregative equation.

The striking differences between the short- and long-term output-elasticities of fixed investment demand implied by these results is highlighted in Table 11. The table shows the percentage of the long-term response that is completed during the first year, the first two years, and so on

TABLE 11. *Cumulative Proportion of Long-Term Investment Response Completed During First Five Years*

Industry or Sector	Percentage of Total Response Completed by Year:				
	1	2	3	4	5
Aggregates					
All industries	12.4	33.2	49.1	61.2	70.4
Total manufacturing	15.3	46.6	66.4	78.8	86.7
Component industries					
Manufacturing industries:					
Primary metals	13.0	43.6	70.6	84.7	92.0
Machinery	15.1	36.2	52.0	63.9	72.9
Motor vehicles	11.3	37.8	56.4	69.5	78.6
Nonautomotive transportation equipment	27.2	40.8	78.2	92.0	97.0
Stone, clay, and glass	18.4	38.8	54.1	65.7	74.3
Other durables	26.0	54.3	71.7	82.5	89.2
Food and beverages	2.9	33.9	56.2	71.0	80.8
Textiles	15.8	44.0	64.7	77.7	85.9
Paper	16.8	50.2	70.1	82.1	89.3
Chemicals	13.2	52.4	83.9	94.5	98.2
Petroleum and coal	15.0	50.2	70.8	82.9	90.0
Rubber	20.8	55.9	75.4	86.3	92.4
Other nondurables	8.2	38.5	58.8	72.4	81.5
Railroads	12.6	34.2	50.5	62.8	72.0
Nonrail transportation	20.0	35.9	48.7	59.0	67.2
Public utilities	11.1	32.1	66.2	83.1	91.6
Communications	11.3	79.6	95.3	98.9	99.8
Commercial and other	20.5	36.8	49.8	60.1	68.3
Farming	16.0	29.5	40.8	50.3	58.3
Arithmetic mean of component industries	15.5	43.4	63.9	75.8	83.1
Standard deviation	5.7	11.5	13.5	13.0	11.4
RATIO: Standard deviation to mean	0.368	0.265	0.211	0.172	0.137

Note: The method by which these estimates were derived is explained in the text.

up to the first five years. These completion percentages are simply the cumulated annual investment responses for the appropriate number of years.

The average response for the 19 individual industries during the first year is about 16 percent. By the end of the second year 43 percent of the adjustment has been completed on average. Approximately two-thirds is completed in three years and three-fourths in four years. At the end of five years only 17 percent of the total adjustment still remains to be made on the average.

These unweighted average rates of response do not take into account inter-industry differences in the relative importance of investment per unit of output. This will be done later, but for the present it should be noted that the completion percentages computed from the equations for aggregate investment and for total manufacturing are implicitly weighted for inter-industry differences in investment intensities.

The individual completion ratios display considerable variation about the average, especially in the early years. The ratios for the first year, for example, range from 3 percent for food and beverage manufacturing to 27 percent for nonautomotive transportation equipment. A summary measure of the degree of dispersion of the individual first-year ratios—the standard deviation—is about 37 percent of the average ratio for all industries. As each year passes, however, the individual completion ratios draw closer together, so that by the fifth year, the standard deviation is only 14 percent of the average ratio. Thus the inter-industry variation in response rates is much wider when short-term adjustments are considered than it is in the long run.

Long-Run Capital-Output Relationships

Putting aside for the moment further consideration of the effects of variations in response rates among industries and over time, this section will concentrate instead on the long-run implications of the equations. Each equation implies a specific value of the long-term elasticity of capital stock with respect to output. This is an interesting figure in itself, but for many purposes it is more important to know the value of the long-term marginal net capital-output ratio, or the absolute amount of net investment that would be induced for each dollar of increase in real output. This ratio is easily calculated as follows:

The long-term elasticity of capital stock with respect to output, E_y, may be written as

$$E_y = \frac{\frac{\Delta K}{K}}{\frac{\Delta Y}{Y}} = \frac{\Delta K}{\Delta Y} \cdot \frac{Y}{K}, \tag{4.1}$$

where ΔK and ΔY are respectively the absolute changes in capital stock and in output. Thus it is necessary only to multiply the long-term elasticity by the average capital-output ratio, K/Y, in order to derive the long-term marginal net capital-output ratio, $\Delta K/\Delta Y$.

$$E_y \cdot \frac{K}{Y} = \left(\frac{\Delta K}{\Delta Y} \cdot \frac{Y}{K}\right) \frac{K}{Y} = \frac{\Delta K}{\Delta Y} \,. \tag{4.2}$$

Long-term marginal net capital-output ratios computed according to equation (4.2) are presented in Table 12. Several features of these ratios should be described before the implications of the table are summarized.

First, it will be recalled that a value of unity was imposed on the long-term elasticity of capital stock with respect to output in most industries. This means that the long-term marginal capital-output ratio is constrained a priori to equal the average capital-output ratio, except in railroads and public utilities.

Second, both the long-term elasticity and the corresponding marginal capital-output ratio are net of the influence of variations in production techniques as reflected in the trend variable, and of changes in relative prices as well, wherever the latter are included in the investment equation. Hence their magnitudes may change over time as techniques and prices vary. The estimates in Table 12 are for 1960.

Finally, it is the desired or equilibrium average capital-output ratio that is relevant to the calculation of the long-term marginal net capital-output ratio. Seldom if ever does the ratio of actual stock to actual output in a given year equal the desired ratio, for seldom if ever is the industry in full long-term equilibrium. Fortunately it is easy to calculate the desired capital-output ratio in 1960 or any other year from the basic investment regression. Each investment regression implies an expression for desired stock in terms of expected or normal output, time, and (occasionally) relative prices, in the general form of equation (2.2a) in Chapter 2. Normal output itself is a weighted average of the output terms from the investment regression, and the ratio of desired stock to normal output gives the desired average long-term capital-output ratio.[1]

With the main characteristics of the estimates described, the principal findings concerning the long-run average and marginal capital-output ratios will now be summarized.

[1] The desired average capital-output ratio for the aggregate of all industries was 7 percent higher than the actual ratio for 1960. The corresponding percentages for the major sectors were: manufacturing, 4; railroads, minus 3; nonrail transportation, 0; public utilities, 14; communications, 8; commercial and other, 8; and farming, 4.

TABLE 12. *Long-Term Average and Marginal Net Capital-Output Ratios and Their Determinants*

(Based on 1960 values)

Industry or Sector	Long-Term Elasticities (E_y)	Capital-Output Ratios: Average (K/Y)	Capital-Output Ratios: Marginal $\Delta K/\Delta Y$	Addendum: Percentage Distribution of Output
	(1)	(2)	(3)	(4)
Aggregates				
All industries	1	1.12	1.12	*100.0*
Total manufacturing	1	.74	.74	*40.0*
Component Industries				
Manufacturing industries:				
Primary metals	1	1.46	1.46	*2.7*
Machinery	1	.40	.40	*6.3*
Motor vehicles	1	.56	.56	*3.2*
Nonautomotive transportation equipment	1	.44	.44	*2.1*
Stone, clay, and glass	1	.85	.85	*1.3*
Other durables	1	.42	.42	*5.7*
Food and beverages	1	.45	.45	*4.0*
Textiles	1	.88	.88	*1.4*
Paper	1	.96	.96	*1.4*
Chemicals	1	.84	.84	*3.3*
Petroleum and coal	1	2.43	2.43	*3.3*
Rubber	1	.60	.60	*.6*
Other nondurables	1	.24	.24	*4.6*
Railroads	.32	4.58	1.47	*2.5*
Nonrail transportation	1	.80	.80	*3.7*
Public utilities	.69	4.31	2.97	*4.0*
Communications	1	1.88	1.88	*2.8*
Commercial and other	1	.70	.70	*40.9*
Farming	1	2.64	2.64	*6.2*
Arithmetic mean of component industries				
Unweighted	.95	1.34	1.10	
Weighted	.97	1.10	.98	

Note: The method by which these estimates were derived is explained in the text.

One is immediately struck by the wide range of average capital-output ratios shown for the various industries in column 2. The ratios for eleven of the thirteen individual manufacturing industries are less than one, whereas the ratios in four of the six nonmanufacturing sectors exceed unity by large margins. The highest ratio is 4.6 for railroads, but it is nearly equaled by public utilities. In contrast, the large commercial and other sector has a ratio of only 0.7.

The simple average of the capital-output ratios for all industries is 1.34. This average, however, does not take account of the relative importance of the various industries in total production. A new average was therefore calculated in which each capital-output ratio was weighted by the proportion of total output produced by the industry, as shown in the last column of the table.[2] The weighted average of the capital-output ratios is 1.10, a value nearly equal to that computed directly from the aggregative equation for all industries.

In the final set of regressions, the marginal capital-output ratios differ from the average ratios in only two sectors of industry—railroads and public utilities—since unitary elasticities of capital stock to output were assumed in the remaining sectors. Nevertheless, the inclusion of only two sectors with output-elasticities other than unity considerably reduces the mean value of the marginal ratios as compared with the average ratios. This is because the marginal ratios for railroads and public utilities are markedly less than the average ratios. In these sectors the average ratios give a seriously misleading impression of the amount of net investment that would accompany a given output increase in the long run.

The weighted average of the marginal ratios for all industries is 0.98. The direct estimate of the marginal ratio derived from the aggregate investment regression is 1.12. The principal reason for this discrepancy is the choice of the unitary-elasticity form of the aggregative equation for analysis. The alternative aggregative regression implies a long-term elasticity of 0.92, which in turn implies a marginal capital-output ratio of 1.03 instead of 1.12 in 1960. Another factor contributing to the discrepancy is the influence of shifts in the composition of output on the aggregate investment-output relationship during the postwar years to which the aggregate regression was fitted. Such shifts are implicitly allowed for in the aggregative regres-

[2] The aggregate capital-output ratio is

$$\frac{K}{Y} = \frac{\sum_{i=1}^{n} K_i}{\sum_{i=1}^{n} Y_i} = \frac{\sum_{i=1}^{n} \frac{K_i}{Y_i} \cdot Y_i}{\sum_{i=1}^{n} Y_i},$$

where the symbols without subscripts refer to aggregates and those with subscripts to individual industries. It follows directly that the individual capital-output ratios should be weighted by individual outputs.

TABLE 13. *Long-Term Marginal Capital-Output Ratios, Selected Years*

Industry or Sector	1950	1955	1960
Aggregates			
All industries	1.34	1.23	1.12
Total manufacturing	.85	.82	.74
Component industries			
Manufacturing industries			
Primary metals	1.08	1.25	1.46
Machinery	.42	.41	.40
Motor vehicles	.61	.81	.56
Nonautomotive transportation equipment	.95	.64	.44
Stone, clay, and glass	.93	.99	.85
Other durables	.51	.47	.42
Food and beverages	.69	.55	.45
Textiles	1.21	1.05	.88
Paper	.97	.96	.96
Chemicals	1.42	1.12	.84
Petroleum and coal	2.43	2.43	2.43
Rubber	.72	.66	.60
Other nondurables	.32	.28	.24
Railroads	1.70	1.54	1.47
Nonrail transportation	1.17	.99	.80
Public utilities	4.73	3.71	2.97
Communications	1.75	1.84	1.88
Commercial and other	.81	.74	.70
Farming	3.20	2.74	2.64
Arithmetic mean of component industries			
Unweighted	1.35	1.22	1.10
Weighted	1.15	1.05	.98

Note: The method by which these estimates were derived is explained in the text.

sion. But the procedure of weighting the sectoral marginal ratios for 1960 by the corresponding output proportions provides a measure of what the over-all marginal ratio would be if the composition of output remained unchanged while aggregate output increased from the 1960 level.

As was noted earlier, the long-term equilibrium values of the average and marginal capital-output ratios will change over time owing to changes in techniques and relative prices. In addition the ratios will vary with the level of output in those sectors in which the elasticity of capital stock with respect to output differs from unity.[3] During the 1950's these factors resulted

[3] Let the equation for desired stock be:

$$\log K^*_t = \log a_1 + a_2 \log Y^*_t + a_3 \log P^*_t + a_4 T,$$

where Y^*_t and P^*_t are normal output and price and the a coefficients are long-term in a general decline in the equilibrium values of the average and marginal net capital-output ratios (Table 13). These declines are discussed more fully in Chapter 7.

Short-Term Investment Responses and Marginal Capital-Output Ratios

Both the time shape of the investment response to an output-induced change in capital requirements and the equilibrium, or long-term, capital-output relationship have now been discussed. The next task is to pool this information in order to derive short-term marginal capital-output ratios for the various industries. To measure the marginal relationship for response periods of up to five years it is necessary only to multiply the long-term marginal ratios from Table 12 by the completion percentages from Table 11. The results are presented in Table 14.

According to the table, the amount of net investment per dollar of output increase will average 16 cents during the first year of the increase. If output remains at the new level in subsequent years, additional investment will be forthcoming. By the end of the second year, the total net investment for the two years together will be 39 cents per dollar of output increase. After five years of adjustment to a once-for-all output increase, the total amount of net investment induced during the five years will be 75 cents per dollar of output increase. These estimates are based on weighted averages of the individual marginal ratios and are in close accord with the corresponding ratios from the aggregative equation, as can be seen by comparing the top and bottom lines of Table 14.

It was noted earlier that the average capital-output ratios were a seriously misleading guide to the marginal long-term investment responses per dollar of output increase in the case of railroads and public utilities. It is now clear that in virtually all industries the current ratio of capital stock to output will be a poor indicator of the amount of net investment to be expected per dollar of permanent output increase for two, three, or more

elasticities. The logarithm of the desired capital-output ratio is given by:

$$\log K^*_t - \log Y^*_t = \log a_1 + (a_2 - 1) \log Y^*_t + a_3 \log P^*_t + a_4 T.$$

If a_2 equals one, the capital-output ratio is invariant with respect to output, but otherwise it is not.

TABLE 14. *Short-Term and Long-Term Marginal Net Capital-Output Ratios* (Based on 1960 values)

Industry or Sector	Short-Term Ratios for Period Ending in Year:					Long-Term Ratio
	1	2	3	4	5	
Aggregates						
All industries	.14	.37	.55	.69	.79	1.12
Total manufacturing	.11	.34	.49	.59	.64	.74
Component industries						
Manufacturing industries						
Primary metals	.19	.64	1.03	1.24	1.34	1.46
Machinery	.06	.14	.21	.26	.29	.40
Motor vehicles	.06	.21	.31	.39	.44	.56
Nonautomotive transportation equipment	.12	.18	.34	.40	.42	.44
Stone, clay, and glass	.16	.33	.46	.56	.63	.85
Other durables	.11	.23	.30	.35	.38	.42
Food and beverages	.01	.15	.25	.32	.36	.45
Textiles	.14	.39	.57	.69	.76	.88
Paper	.16	.48	.67	.79	.86	.96
Chemicals	.11	.44	.71	.80	.83	.84
Petroleum and coal	.36	1.22	1.72	2.01	2.18	2.43
Rubber	.12	.34	.45	.52	.56	.60
Other nondurables	.02	.09	.14	.17	.19	.24
Railroads	.18	.50	.74	.92	1.06	1.47
Nonrail transportation	.16	.29	.39	.47	.54	.80
Public utilities	.33	.95	1.97	2.47	2.72	2.97
Communications	.21	1.50	1.79	1.86	1.88	1.88
Commercial and other	.14	.26	.35	.42	.48	.70
Farming	.42	.78	1.08	1.33	1.54	2.64
Arithmetic mean of component industries						
Unweighted	.16	.48	.71	.84	.92	1.10
Weighted	.16	.39	.56	.67	.75	.98

Note: The method by which these estimates were derived is explained in the text.

years after the increase occurs. This is a direct consequence of the sizable investment lags typical of the present-day economy and is not the result of any failure to correct current capital-output ratios for unutilized capacity. Even the corrected long-term equilibrium ratios used here must be further adjusted to allow for response lags before valid short-term marginal capital coefficients are obtained.

Replacement Investment

Both the short- and long-term marginal capital-output ratios discussed thus far were confined to the relationship between net investment and output change. Replacement investment also rises as a result of an increase in output, however, and it may be interesting to calculate by how much. This is easily done under the assumption of a constant depreciation rate, since the annual depreciation stream in our model is derived by simply multiplying the net capital stock by the depreciation rate.

In the long run the annual depreciation stream will rise in direct proportion to the capital stock. With a unitary elasticity of capital stock to output, a 1 percent output increase would call forth a 1 percent increase in capital stock and annual depreciation, and the ratio of depreciation to output would remain unchanged. The depreciation-output ratio would fall, however, in those industries where the capital-output ratio decreased because of scale economies accompanying the expansion of output.

A marginal depreciation-output ratio makes little sense in the long run. Since the capital stock will have to be maintained indefinitely, the cumulated replacement investment induced by a given once-for-all output increase will approach infinity as the time horizon comprising "the long run" is lengthened.[4]

A short-term marginal depreciation-output ratio is a more meaningful concept. Just as in the case of net investment, one can ask how much replacement expenditure will be forthcoming within a given number of years in response to an increase of one dollar of output. Table 15 shows the short-term, marginal gross capital-output ratios for intervals of up to five years. These ratios include both net and replacement investment and were calculated as follows:

In order to simplify the calculations, it was assumed that depreciation and replacement on new capital goods do not begin until the end of the year in which they are acquired. Thus during the first year of adjustment to an output increase, the only new investment is net investment, and the marginal gross ratio (column 1 of Table 15) equals the marginal net ratio (column 1 of Table 14). During the second year, however, additional new

[4] A marginal depreciation-output ratio could be defined in terms of the change in the size of the annual depreciation stream between two equilibrium positions, but it would not be comparable to the marginal net capital-output ratio, which deals with the total amount of net investment ever induced by a permanent increase of one unit of output.

TABLE 15. *Short-Term Marginal Gross Capital-Output Ratios*

(Based on 1960 values)

Industry or Sector	Short-Term Ratios for Period Ending in Year:					Depreciation Rate
	1	2	3	4	5	
Aggregates						
All industries	.14	.38	.59	.76	.92	.07
Total manufacturing	.11	.36	.54	.69	.81	.11
Component industries						
Manufacturing industries						
Primary metals	.19	.65	1.10	1.38	1.59	.08
Machinery industries	.06	.15	.24	.32	.39	.14
Motor vehicles	.06	.22	.35	.46	.55	.12
Nonautomotive transportation equipment	.12	.19	.37	.47	.54	.11
Stone, clay, and glass	.16	.35	.51	.66	.80	.11
Other durables	.11	.24	.35	.44	.51	.13
Food and beverages	.01	.15	.27	.36	.45	.12
Textiles	.14	.40	.62	.79	.93	.09
Paper	.16	.50	.74	.92	1.06	.10
Chemicals	.11	.46	.78	.95	1.08	.12
Petroleum and coal	.36	1.25	1.86	2.31	2.66	.09
Rubber	.13	.35	.51	.63	.73	.12
Other nondurables	.02	.09	.15	.20	.24	.12
Railroads	.18	.51	.79	.96	1.13	.03
Nonrail transportation	.16	.31	.46	.60	.73	.15
Public utilities	.33	.97	2.03	2.63	3.01	.05
Communications	.21	1.51	1.95	2.19	2.38	.09
Commercial and other	.14	.27	.37	.46	.55	.05
Farming	.42	.80	1.14	1.44	1.72	.05
Arithmetic mean of component industries						
Unweighted	.16	.49	.77	.96	1.11	.10
Weighted	.16	.40	.61	.76	.89	.07

Note: The method by which these estimates were derived is explained in the text.

replacement investment occurs equal to the product of the depreciation rate and the net investment of the first year. When this replacement investment is added to the net investment for the two-year period, the result is the marginal gross ratio shown in column 2 of Table 15.

In the third year of adjustment there is again additional depreciation. This time it is equal to the product of the depreciation rate and the net

TABLE 16. *Long-Term Price Elasticities of Net Investment and Completion Percentages for One to Five Years*

Industries	Long-Term Elasticities	Completion Percentage by Year:				
		1	2	3	4	5
Stone, clay, and glass	−1.76	*4.0*	*20.3*	*40.3*	*55.3*	*66.5*
Textiles	.72	*6.2*	*27.1*	*54.0*	*71.0*	*81.7*
Other nondurables	.73	*28.0*	*51.8*	*67.7*	*78.4*	*85.5*
Nonrail transportation	.78	*20.0*	*35.9*	*48.7*	*59.0*	*67.1*
Communications	.08	*0*	*77.1*	*94.7*	*98.8*	*99.6*
Commercial and other	.46	*20.5*	*36.8*	*49.8*	*60.0*	*68.2*
Farming	− .53	*16.0*	*29.5*	*40.8*	*50.3*	*58.3*
Arithmetic mean	—	*13.5*	*39.8*	*56.6*	*67.5*	*75.3*
Standard deviation	—	*8.0*	*17.7*	*17.8*	*15.5*	*13.2*
Ratio of standard deviation to mean	—	0.592	0.446	0.314	0.229	0.175

Note: The long-term price elasticities are negative if the relative price variable is the real price of capital and positive if it is the ratio of the money wage and the money price of capital. The elasticities and completion percentages are computed in the same way as are responses to output changes.

investment of the first two years, since the latter figure is the amount by which capital stock at the beginning of the third year exceeds the original level. The total replacement expenditure for the entire three-year period is therefore equal to the depreciation rate times the sum of the net investment of the first year and the net investment of the first two years taken together. This figure is added to the marginal net three-year ratio to obtain the corresponding gross ratio. The gross ratios for the four- and five-year intervals were calculated in the same way.

The differences between the gross and net ratios are small at first, but they get progressively larger as replacement expenditures cumulate over more years. The disparity between the gross and net ratios also varies with the depreciation rate, which ranges from 3 percent a year for railroads to 15 percent for nonrail transportation. The five-year gross ratios for those sectors are respectively 7 and 35 percent larger than the net ratios. The corresponding percentages for all industries and for total manufacturing are 16 and 26.

Short- and Long-Term Price Elasticities

Table 16 refers to the price elasticities of net investment calculated for the seven industries for which price terms are included in the final regressions. The long-term elasticities carry a minus sign if the variable is the real price of capital and a positive sign if it is the ratio of the money wage and the money price of capital.

Six of the seven long-term price elasticities are smaller than unity. In contrast, the elasticity for stone, clay, and glass is well above unity. This happens to be the industry with the least reliable price terms (Table 4), and it would be well to view the implied elasticity as subject to a very large margin of error. The estimates for the other industries are more reliable statistically.

The completion percentages for periods of up to five years are shown in the remaining columns of Table 16. These percentages were calculated from the coefficients of the price terms exactly as it was done earlier for the output terms. Once again it is found that only a small fraction of the total response is completed within one year and that even after five years a sizable portion of the adjustment remains to be made. It is again true, moreover, that the individual completion percentages draw progressively closer together as the adjustment period lengthens.

Stabilizing Effects of Investment Lags

Two types of lag are implied in the investment regressions. First, there is an expectational lag in most sectors, so normal output is a weighted average of current and recent outputs, and similarly for normal prices where relevant. Second, there is an adjustment lag, indicating that businessmen do not attempt to fill the entire gap between desired and actual stock within one year. In this section, measures of the short-term stabilizing effects of these lags are presented separately and in combination.

It was shown earlier that the basic regressions could be written in the following form, using only two lag terms for simplicity:

$$(4.3)\quad \log K_t - \log K_{t-1} = b[(\log a_1 + a_{21} \log Y_t + a_{22} \log Y_{t-1} + a_{31} \log P_t + a_{32} \log P_{t-1} + a_4T) - \log K_{t-1}].$$

The expression in parentheses represents desired stock as a function of expected output Y^*_t and prices P^*_t, so the equation may also be written:

$$(4.4)\quad \log K_t - \log K_{t-1} = b[(\log a_1 + a_2 \log Y^*_t + a_3 \log P^*_t + a_4T) - \log K_{t-1}],$$

where a_2 equals $a_{21} + a_{22}$ and a_3 equals $a_{31}+a_{32}$.

Suppose there were no expectational lags, so normal output always equaled current output. Then the gap between desired and actual stock, as represented by the expression in brackets, would fluctuate more widely from year to year than it actually does, leading to correspondingly wider fluctuations of net investment. Suppose additionally that b equals one, so the entire discrepancy between desired and actual stock is eliminated each year. These two assumptions would result in a maximum amplitude of year-to-year fluctuation of net investment in response to changes in output and relative prices, and amplitude measures based on them may therefore serve as a benchmark for estimating the stabilizing influence of lags.

It is a simple procedure to calculate from equation (4.4) the annual capital expansion ratio K_t/K_{t-1} if b equaled one and Y^*_t equaled Y_t. If the calculated K_t/K_{t-1} had a value of 1.10 for a particular year, for example, this would mean that under the postulated conditions net investment during the year would have amounted to 10 percent of the initial capital stock. To measure the amplitude of the change in investment between two successive years, the larger of the two capital expansion ratios is divided by the smaller. The resulting annual amplitude ratios are then averaged to provide a summary measure for the entire period 1949–60, which is put in percentage form by subtracting one from the average amplitude ratio and multiplying by 100.[5]

[5] Assume, for example, that estimated net investment for the given conditions is zero in the first year, 10 percent of capital stock in the second year, and minus 10 percent in the third. The successive ratios K_t/K_{t-1} would then be 1.00, 1.10, and 0.90. The amplitude ratio for the first pair of years would be 1.10, and for the second pair it would be 1.22. The average amplitudes presented in Table 17 are derived from the geometric means of the annual amplitude ratios. Allowance was made in the calculations for the fact that net disinvestment during any year cannot exceed depreciation for the year, since gross investment cannot fall below zero. Thus the minimum net capital expansion ratio was constrained to be no smaller than $1-d$ in any year, where d is the depreciation rate.

TABLE 17. *Estimated Average Amplitude of Investment Fluctuations Under Alternative Assumptions As to Lags*

(In percent)

Industry or Sector	No Lags	Expectational Lag Only	Expectational and Adjustment Lag	Actual Investment	
				Net	Gross
	(1)	(2)	(3)	(4)	(5)
Aggregates					
All industries	3.8	2.2	0.5	0.6	0.5
Total manufacturing	6.8	3.9	1.4	1.5	1.3
Component industries					
Manufacturing industries					
Primary metals	14.7	6.5	3.1	4.2	3.9
Machinery	11.8	8.1	1.9	2.4	2.2
Motor vehicles	18.9	12.1	3.9	4.5	4.1
Nonautomotive transportation equipment	22.0	13.2	8.1	7.3	6.7
Stone, clay, glass	11.8	10.9	2.6	2.7	2.5
Other durables	6.7	4.3	1.6	1.9	1.7
Food and beverages	2.3	2.3	0.8	1.0	0.9
Textiles	4.9	3.6	1.5	1.5	1.3
Paper	6.4	4.2	1.7	2.0	1.9
Chemicals	7.4	3.5	2.3	2.4	2.2
Petroleum and coal	4.3	3.8	1.6	1.4	1.2
Rubber	8.9	5.2	2.3	2.6	2.3
Other nondurables	2.7	2.3	0.7	0.7	0.4
Railroads	2.1	1.7	0.5	0.6	0.6
Nonrail transportation	6.5	6.5	1.3	1.3	1.0
Public utilities	2.1	1.6	0.8	1.0	1.0
Communications	3.5	2.8	2.2	1.9	1.7
Commercial and other	2.8	2.8	0.6	0.6	0.6
Farming	4.1	4.1	0.6	0.6	0.6
Arithmetic mean of component industries	7.6	5.2	2.0	2.1	1.9
Standard deviation	5.7	3.4	1.7	1.6	1.5
RATIO: standard deviation to mean	.75	.65	.84	.76	.78

Note: The method by which these estimates were derived is explained in the text.

Measures of average amplitude derived in this way are presented in Table 17. The various columns show the average annual amplitude of investment in each industry under different assumptions as to lags. The first column contains the hypothetical maximum average amplitudes for the case just discussed, in which no lags occur. Next is shown the hypothetical average amplitude if there were an expectational lag alone, derived from equation (4.3) by assuming that b equals one. Column 3 gives the average amplitude of the investment ratios as originally computed from equation (4.3) with b not equal to one. This measure reflects the combined influence of both types of lag. Finally, the average amplitudes calculated directly from the raw investment data are listed in column 4. A comparison of columns 3 and 4 should convince the reader that the average amplitude of fluctuation predicted by the equation is a reliable index of the actual average amplitude in virtually all industries.

The hypothetical maximum average annual amplitudes with no lags range from 2.1 percent for public utilities and railroads to 22.0 percent for nonautomotive transportation equipment. Differences among industries in these hypothetical maximum average amplitudes are proportional to the year-to-year variability of output or prices, or both, as weighted by the corresponding long-term investment elasticities. The more variable is output or relative prices, and the larger is the corresponding elasticity, the greater is the hypothetical amplitude of investment fluctuation.

The stabilizing power of the investment lags stands out vividly when columns 2 and 3 are compared with column 1. The expectational lags alone account for a substantial reduction in the amplitude of investment fluctuations in most industries, whereas the additional reduction due to adjustment lags is always significant and often larger. When allowance is made for both lags, the average amplitudes range from 0.5 percent for railroads to 8.1 percent for nonautomotive transportation equipment, as compared with the 2.1–22.0 range without lags.

The arithmetic mean of the individual amplitude indexes is 2.0 percent when account is taken of lags and 7.6 percent when it is not. These unweighted averages are valid measures of central tendency, but they overstate the instability of aggregate investment under either set of conditions. The aggregative equation is implicitly weighted for differences among industries in price and output fluctuations and in the size and timing of investment responses and hence provides a superior measure of the average amplitude of aggregate investment for any given set of conditions. According to that equation, the various lags reduced the average annual amplitude of total investment from a potential rate of 3.8 percent to 0.5 percent during the period 1949–60. This is an even greater relative reduction than was suggested by the unweighted averages of individual amplitudes.

The importance of investment lags for over-all economic stability can scarcely be over-emphasized. The difference between the mean investment amplitudes with and without lags, or between the corresponding measure based on the aggregative equations for total manufacturing and for all industries, is strikingly large, but it still understates the stabilizing effects of the lags. This is because the calculations of hypothetical maximum amplitudes take output movements as given, whereas aggregate output would itself fluctuate more widely if investment did. The resulting feedback effects would further amplify the investment fluctuations.

The foregoing discussion was confined to fluctuations of net investment. Similar amplitude measures for gross investment are presented in column 5 of Table 17. The first step in calculating these measures was to add the annual depreciation rate to the annual capital expansion ratio as computed from the actual stock data. Thus if net investment were 10 percent of capital stock and depreciation were 5 percent of capital stock in a given year, K_t/K_{t-1} would be 1.10, and the new ratio including replacement expenditure would be 1.15, indicating that gross investment was 15 percent of capital stock in that year. Given the new series of annual gross investment ratios, their average annual amplitude was computed by the same method as was used for net investment.

A comparison of columns 4 and 5 indicates that the amplitude of fluctuation of gross investment was only slightly smaller in most sectors than that of net investment alone. The steadier flow of replacement expenditure does reduce the year-to-year amplitude of gross, as compared to net, investment, but not a great deal.

Compositional Shifts and Aggregate Investment

The previous investigations have disclosed substantial differences among industries in the speed and magnitude of response of investment expenditure to changes in desired capital stock. These differences imply that aggregate investment can be significantly affected by shifts in the industrial composition of investment demand. Shifts in the composition of national output, for example, may raise or lower aggregate investment demand depending on whether the short-term marginal capital-output ratios of the gaining industries are higher or lower than those of the losing industries.

The direction and magnitude of the net effect of output shifts on aggregate investment expenditure during the postwar years may be estimated as follows: The investment regression for each industry yields an annual prediction of the volume of net investment associated with the output movements actually experienced. To compute the hypothetical investment of each industry in the absence of output shifts, it is necessary only to substitute for actual industry output that output which would have been produced had all industries shared equally in the actual movement of aggregate output. If the hypothetical investments are subtracted from those originally predicted and the differences are summed for all industries, the result is a summary measure for each year of the estimated net effect of output shifts on total investment. The cumulative results over a span of years would not differ much if hypothetical investment were compared with actual instead of predicted investment. However, by comparing hypothetical and predicted investment, one makes sure that the difference between the two in any one year is due only to the differing assumptions about output behavior and is unaffected by the residual error term.

The details of the procedure are as follows: The annual series of aggregate output in the covered sectors was first expressed in index form with 1947 equal to 100. The hypothetical annual output of each industry under the assumption of a fixed (as in 1947) composition of total output was then calculated by multiplying the index of aggregate output by the 1947 value of real gross product (expressed in 1954 dollars) originating in the industry. Thus both actual and hypothetical industry output are expressed in 1954 dollars for use in the regressions.

The next step was to compute the annual estimates of hypothetical net investment by iteration from the investment regression for each industry. The 1949 estimate was computed by inserting the necessary hypothetical output values and the actual price values and 1948 capital stock. The net investment thereby computed was added to the 1948 capital stock to derive hypothetical capital stock at the end of 1949. Given the latter figure and the hypothetical output for 1950, the hypothetical 1950 net investment could then be computed, and so on. Repeated applications of this procedure produced the final series on hypothetical capital stock as it would have developed in the industry since 1949 had aggregate output behaved as it actually did but with a fixed composition as in 1947.

So much for hypothetical net investment and capital stock. Hypothetical replacement investment was estimated by applying the actual annual depreciation rates for each industry to the annual estimates of hypothetical capital stock. A similar calculation was made to derive the replacement stream implied by the net capital stock predicted by the original regression

TABLE 18. *Estimated Gain or Loss of Net Investment Resulting from Output Shifts, by Industry, 1949–62*

(In billions of 1954 dollars)

Industry or Sector	1949	1950	1951	1952	1953	1954	1955	1956	1957	1958	1959	1960	1961	1962
All industries	1.33	.77	.83	1.42	1.15	1.26	1.02	1.67	1.71	1.31	.02	−.46	−.08	.02
Total Manufacturing	−.10	−.12	.95	1.10	1.07	.52	.20	.44	.30	−1.09	−1.01	−1.07	−.98	−.52
Primary metals	−.17	−.22	.10	.06	−.33	−.53	−.37	.02	.23	−.44	−.91	−.89	−.80	−.57
Machinery industries	−.12	−.11	.04	.15	.20	.08	.02	.10	.06	−.18	−.10	.02	.02	.07
Motor vehicles	.07	.14	.19	−.02	−.07	.05	.10	.24	−.13	−.19	−.23	.10	.09	.01
Nonautomotive transportation equipment	−.02	−.09	.22	.27	.70	.87	.33	.09	.08	.01	.07	−.17	−.24	−.19
Stone, clay, and glass	.06	.07	.10	.04	.01	0	.02	.05	.02	−.02	.03	.03	0	−.01
Other durables	−.05	.01	.03	0	.11	.04	0	−.06	−.08	−.14	−.01	.02	0	.04
Food and beverages	−.15	−.01	−.19	−.20	−.12	−.20	−.03	−.15	−.10	−.03	.13	−.03	−.03	.05
Textiles	−.02	−.05	−.08	−.17	−.15	−.16	−.16	−.14	−.14	−.09	−.01	−.01	−.06	−.03
Paper	−.02	−.02	.05	.01	−.01	.06	.10	.12	.04	.01	.05	.04	.07	.10
Chemicals	.11	.19	.39	.47	.38	.12	.12	.29	.36	.23	.21	.28	.25	.23
Petroleum and coal	.26	0	.17	.57	.41	.27	.11	−.06	.01	−.21	−.28	−.50	−.32	−.25
Rubber	−.05	−.04	0	−.01	0	−.02	.01	0	−.02	−.03	.01	.01	.01	.02
Other durables	0	.01	−.07	−.07	−.06	−.06	−.05	−.06	−.03	−.01	.03	.03	.03	.01
Total Nonmanufacturing	1.43	.89	−.12	.32	.08	.74	.82	1.23	1.41	2.40	1.03	.61	.90	.54
Railroads	−.61	−.71	−.38	−.37	−.56	−.67	−.55	−.32	−.32	−.44	−.48	−.49	−.45	−.46
Nonrail transportation	.11	.16	.30	.09	−.02	−.06	−.03	−.02	.02	−.04	.07	.05	.05	.16
Public utilities	.60	1.17	1.45	1.40	1.61	1.38	1.53	2.03	2.03	2.11	1.96	1.86	1.64	1.55
Communications	.46	.30	−.21	.20	.37	.19	.79	.65	.79	.74	.75	.32	.76	1.04
Commercial and other	.38	−.03	−.39	−.32	−.57	.04	−.43	−.21	−.22	.34	−.15	−.26	−.24	−.47
Farming	.49	0	−.89	−.68	−.75	−.14	−.49	−.90	−.89	−.31	−1.12	−.87	−.86	−1.28

Note: The method by which these estimates were prepared is explained in the text.

TABLE 19. *Estimated Gain or Loss of Gross Investment Resulting from Output Shifts, by Industry, 1949–62*

(In billions of 1954 dollars)

Industry or Sector	1949	1950	1951	1952	1953	1954	1955	1956	1957	1958	1959	1960	1961	1962
All industries	1.48	.93	1.05	1.78	1.67	1.93	2.19	2.57	2.82	2.48	1.23	.76	1.10	1.16
Total Manufacturing	−.13	−.10	.97	1.24	1.35	.91	.64	.95	.85	−.59	−.62	−.74	−.71	−.38
Primary metals	−.18	−.23	.07	.03	−.37	−.60	−.48	−.10	.12	−.55	−1.09	−1.15	−1.12	−.96
Machinery industries	−.13	−.13	.01	.14	.22	.11	.06	.15	.12	−.14	−.08	.04	.06	.10
Motor vehicles	.07	.15	.22	.03	−.02	.10	.15	.32	−.04	−.13	−.20	.12	.13	.03
Nonautomotive transportation equipment	−.02	−.10	.22	.29	.78	1.04	.58	.35	.37	.30	.36	.13	.04	.06
Stone, clay, and glass	.06	.07	.12	.07	.04	.03	.05	.08	.06	.02	.08	.08	.05	.03
Other durables	−.06	.01	.04	0	.12	.05	.03	−.04	−.08	−.15	−.03	0	−.02	.03
Food and beverages	−.15	−.02	−.22	−.26	−.20	−.29	−.14	−.27	−.24	−.17	−.01	−.16	−.17	−.09
Textiles	−.02	−.05	−.10	−.20	−.19	−.20	−.23	−.22	−.23	−.20	−.13	−.13	−.18	−.16
Paper	−.03	−.02	.05	.01	−.01	.06	.11	.14	.08	.04	.10	.08	.11	.15
Chemicals	.11	.22	.45	.59	.54	.32	.33	.53	.64	.56	.55	.67	.67	.69
Petroleum and coal	.27	.03	.20	.64	.53	.41	.27	.12	.17	−.06	−.14	−.41	−.26	−.23
Rubber	−.05	−.04	−.01	−.02	−.01	−.03	0	−.01	−.03	−.04	−.01	0	−.01	0
Other nondurables	0	.01	−.08	−.08	−.08	−.09	−.09	−.10	−.09	−.07	−.02	−.01	−.01	−.03
Total Nonmanufacturing	1.61	1.03	.08	.54	.32	1.02	1.55	1.62	1.97	3.07	1.85	1.50	1.81	1.54
Railroads	−.62	−.74	−.43	−.43	−.62	−.75	−.65	−.43	−.44	−.59	−.63	−.67	−.65	−.68
Nonrail transportation	.11	.18	.35	.15	.07	.03	.16	.05	.11	.05	.17	.14	.16	.28
Public utilities	.74	1.23	1.58	1.63	1.89	1.73	1.94	2.54	2.65	2.83	2.77	2.77	2.65	2.64
Communications	.48	.34	−.15	.24	.45	.29	1.24	.85	1.09	1.12	1.20	.84	1.33	1.71
Commercial and other	.39	−.01	−.38	−.32	−.62	−.03	−.51	−.30	−.32	.24	−.24	−.36	−.36	−.60
Farming	.51	.03	−.89	−.73	−.85	−.25	−.63	−1.09	−1.12	−.58	−1.42	−1.22	−1.32	−1.81

Note: The method by which these estimates were prepared is explained in the text.

with actual output. This makes it possible to compare the predicted and hypothetical values of both the gross and the net investment streams under the assumed conditions.

The results of the calculations for net investment are presented in Table 18. For 1949–62 as a whole it is estimated that output shifts added $12.0 billion of real net investment to the amount that would have occurred had national output followed its actual path but with unchanging composition. This gain raised aggregate real net investment by an estimated 13.7 percent, since the calculated amount of net investment without output shifts was $89.5 billion for the same period.

The time pattern of the investment gains will be considered in detail in Chapter 7. It is worth noting at this point, however, that the aggregate gains were large and positive until 1958 and either small or negative thereafter. For the 1949–58 period, output shifts added $12.5 billion, or 18.5 percent, to the net investment that would otherwise have occurred under *ceteris paribus* conditions. The corresponding calculations for 1959–62 show a loss of about $0.5 billion, or 2.3 percent.

The industry detail shows the precise distribution of gains and losses. It will be noted that the contribution of the nonmanufacturing industries as a group was both positive and substantial except during the Korean War, when it was negative or small. The total contribution of the manufacturing industries was positive during 1951–57 but negative before and after those years.

Table 19 contains the same calculations for gross investment as were presented for net investment in Table 18. The general effect of including replacement investment is to augment the positive or negative deviations in each industry. This is because replacement demand is a function of the size of the net stock, and a positive deviation of net investment in a given industry means that its net stock increased faster than it would have if the industry's output had increased at the average rate, so its replacement investment also increased faster than it would have otherwise.

The absolute magnitude of the total gross investment gain was larger in every year than that for net investment. The gain was smaller when measured as a percentage of the gross investment that would have occurred with an unchanged composition, however. Thus for 1949–62, the absolute and relative gross investment gains were respectively $23.2 billion and 5.5 percent. The corresponding figures for 1949–58 are $18.9 billion and 6.4 percent, whereas those for 1959–62 are $4.2 billion and 3.4 percent. The time pattern and industrial distribution of the gains and losses are similar to those for net investment.

5 / *Capacity and Capacity Utilization*[1]

THE CONCEPTS OF capacity and capacity utilization have figured prominently in discussions of business investment demand in recent years. Thus far I have worked directly with capital stock and its relation to output, instead of defining the capacity corresponding to a given stock and relating *it* to output. Not unexpectedly, however, my formulation of the investment function implies a precise relationship between capital stock and capacity. This relationship permits new measures of capacity and capacity utilization to be computed which will provide additional perspective on recent and prospective trends in investment demand.

The new estimates are necessarily provisional in character, since they are derived from investment regressions fitted to a particular time period (1949–60). However, if refitting the equations with additional observations should alter the parameter estimates, the capacity estimates for all years would be affected. Similarly, the capacity estimates would change if further investigation should lead to improvements in the specification or estimation of the investment regressions. These are inherent characteristics of the method.

The purpose of this chapter is to explain the new method and to discuss the principal properties of the resulting estimates. The new estimates of capacity and capacity utilization for manufacturing industries are also compared with those of other investigators. Analysis of the causes and implications of recent trends in capacity utilization is deferred until later chapters.

[1] Much of the material in this chapter is taken from my paper "On A New Method of Capacity Estimation," *Journal of the American Statistical Association* (June 1964).

Capital Stock and Capacity

From an economist's viewpoint, capacity is a cost concept. It is usually defined as that output which may be produced at minimum average total cost, given the existing physical plant and organization of production and the prevailing factor prices. Unit costs of production are higher than the minimum if actual output either exceeds or falls short of capacity output. This is due to decreases in efficiency because the input of labor and materials is either too large or too small to make optimum use of the physical facilities. That is, the average total cost function is U-shaped, though not necessarily symmetrically so, and capacity utilization may exceed or fall short of 100 percent as output varies to either side of the point of minimum average cost.

At any given time, then, capacity—an output concept—depends on the size of the capital stock, the level of production technique, and the prices of productive resources. But these same four variables are represented in equation (2.2a) for desired capital stock as specified in Chapter 2. In its logarithmic form, that equation is:

$$\log K^*_t = \log a_1 + a_2 \log Y^*_t + a_3 \log P^*_t + a_4 T. \qquad (5.1)$$

The underlying rationale of this equation is that K^*_t is the optimum capital stock to use in combination with the labor input implied by Y^*_t, given the production techniques and expected relative prices of time t. By the same token, the equation also specifies the optimum or capacity output Y^c_t that would be produced with the actual capital stock K_{t-1} if labor input were adjusted to yield the least-cost combination with existing capital under existing conditions as to techniques and factor prices. That is, if actual stock is substituted for desired stock in equation (5.1) and the equation is solved for output, now regarded as the unknown, the result is:

$$\log Y^c_t = \frac{\log K_{t-1} - \log a_1 - a_3 \log P^*_t - a_4 T}{a_2}. \qquad (5.2)$$

Thus all that is necessary to estimate capacity at time t in a given industry is to derive equation (5.2) from the original investment regression and calculate the optimum output corresponding to the actual capital stock.

According to equation (5.2), the capacity output corresponding to a given level of capital stock depends on relative prices and time. Since a_4 usually has a negative value in equation (5.1), signifying that the effect of technical progress is generally to reduce the capital stock necessary to produce a given output, the capacity of a given capital stock as computed from equation (5.2) usually increases over time. Similarly the economic capacity of a given capital stock will vary if relative prices change and thereby alter the optimum combination of capital and labor inputs.[2]

Notice also that the effects of scale economies are allowed for in equation (5.2). If there are constant returns to scale, a_2 will have a value of one, so that a doubling of capital stock (and labor input) would double capacity. If a_2 is less than unity, capacity will more than double with a doubling of capital stock and other inputs—the case of increasing returns to scale. As was pointed out in Chapter 3, however, it was necessary to impose an a priori value of unit on a_2 in the regressions for most sectors, including the aggregate of all covered industries.

Certain features of this method of estimating capacity call for comment. First, it is consistent with the basic theory of optimum economic production.

Second, although it is consistent with production theory, the measurement technique does not require the estimation of either a production or a cost function including all inputs. Instead, the relationship between capacity and capital stock is inferred from the hypothesis that net investment will occur in proportion to the excess of normal output over the optimum output that can be produced with the existing capital stock under existing techniques and prices. That is, the hypothesis of the original model that net investment is proportional to the excess of desired stock over actual stock has been transformed into the equivalent hypothesis that net investment is proportional to the excess of normal output over capacity.[3] Since

[2] Meaningful price variables were obtained for only 7 of 19 industries, however. And they do not appear in the aggregative regressions for total manufacturing and for all covered industries.

[3] That these are two different ways of looking at the same thing is easily seen. The original model combined the adjustment hypothesis

$$\log K_t - \log K_{t-1} = b(\log K^*_t - \log K_{t-1})$$

with the desired stock relationship

$$\log K^*_t = \log a_1 + a_2 \log Y^*_t + a_3 \log P^*_t + a_4 T$$

to give

$$\log K_t - \log K_{t-1} = b(\log a_1 + a_2 \log Y^*_t + a_3 \log P^*_t + a_4 T - \log K_{t-1}).$$

the two hypotheses are equivalent, an empirical estimate of the relationship between desired capital stock and normal output derived from the original model can readily be translated into a corresponding relationship between capacity output and actual capital stock.[4]

Third, the derived capacity estimates depend in a critical way on the accuracy with which expected long-term, or normal, output is specified and estimated in the basic investment regression. Since capacity is inferred from the inverted functional relationship between desired stock and normal output, any bias in the original estimates of normal output will produce a corresponding bias in the capacity estimates. For reasons to be discussed presently, it is possible that the capacity estimates made in this study by applying the method are biased downward because of a tendency to underestimate expected output. To give a simple example, suppose that net investment is zero in a particular year. According to the model this means that normal output is equal to capacity in that year. But if the true normal output is underestimated in the original investment regression, so also will the true capacity be underestimated. The causes and consequences of such bias will be discussed in detail below.

Fourth, the utilization ratio relating actual output to capacity may easily exceed one. In most other published measures "capacity" means the maximum output attainable under normal conditions of production, and actual operations are therefore almost always at less than 100 percent of capacity.

This equation must hold when the gap between $\log K^*_t$ and $\log K_{t-1}$ is zero (that is, when desired and actual stock are equal), in which case the expression in parentheses may be rearranged to yield

$$\log K_t - \log K_{t-1} = b\left[\log Y^*_t - \left(\frac{\log K_{t-1} - \log a_1 - a_3 \log P^*_t - a_4 T}{a_2}\right)\right],$$

which is seen to be equal to

$$\log K_t - \log K_{t-1} = b(\log Y^*_t - \log Y^c_t)$$

from the specification of the capacity relationship in equation (5.2) above. For gaps different from zero, it is easy to verify that

$$\log K_t - \log K_{t-1} = b(\log K^*_t - \log K_{t-1}) = b[a_2(\log Y^*_t - \log Y^c_t)].$$

[4] Murray Brown has pointed out, however, that inverting (5.1) to derive (5.2) may involve some error because (5.1) is derived from a regression, and unlike exact linear relations, regressions are in general irreversible (see "Discussion," *Proceedings of the Business and Economic Statistics Section*, American Statistical Association [1963], p. 228). Although this is a valid point, it should be stressed that the error will be small when the investment regression has a high correlation coefficient. Moreover, the derived capacity measures can be tested directly for consistency with independent capacity estimates, as is done below for manufacturing.

This holds alike for capacity estimates based on engineering information, questionnaires, or capital-output ratios or production levels at cyclical peaks. In economic terms, such estimates imply a concept more like peak capacity—the output at which the marginal cost of producing an additional unit of output becomes prohibitively high, given the existing facilities—than like optimum capacity as it is defined here.[5]

Fifth, allowance has been made in the underlying regressions for most of the major determinants of investment demand. Since the resulting capacity estimates reflect the influence of relative prices (where significant) and technical progress on production costs, changes in those variables will alter the relationship between capacity and output. Thus a utilization rate based on these capacity estimates is a kind of summary index of the entire set of underlying investment determinants.

Finally, once the underlying investment regression has been fitted for a particular period, the derived capacity relationship may be used to make forward projections of the capacity growth implied in alternative rates of capital formation. Such projections would be subject to the usual risks and qualifications concerning the extrapolation of economic relationships beyond the original period of observation. The 1961–62 figures on capacity and utilization shown in some of the later tables were estimated by extrapolating the capacity relationships obtained from the investment regressions for the period 1949–60.

The Capacity Estimates

The complete set of annual estimates of capacity is shown for the years 1949–62 in Table 20. The estimates are given in index form to facilitate comparison of trends in the various sectors. It is worth taking a moment to highlight the principal findings concerning postwar capacity growth before turning to an appraisal of the quality of the estimates.

According to the estimates, the growth of aggregate capacity averaged 4.1 percent a year between 1949 and 1962. Manufacturing capacity grew

[5] See my earlier paper on "Capacity, Capacity Utilization, and the Acceleration Principle," in *Problems of Capital Formation*, Studies in Income and Wealth, Vol. 19 (Princeton Univ. Press, 1957) for a more extensive discussion of the relations between economic and engineering concepts of capacity.

at about the same average rate, but other major industrial sectors diverged considerably from the over-all average. Railroads showed the slowest growth rate at 1.9 percent, whereas the fastest rate was achieved by public utilities—10.5 percent.

There was a general deceleration of capacity growth during 1953–62 as compared with 1949–53. Only communications grew as rapidly after 1953 as before.

Although the growth deceleration began during the period 1953–57, it became more pronounced after 1957. Indeed, manufacturing capacity increased as rapidly in 1953–57 as it had in 1949–53, but its growth rate was halved in 1957–62. The other major sectors also decelerated after 1957, most of them markedly.

The principal reason for the deceleration of capacity growth during recent years is the diminished rate of business fixed capital formation. Equation (5.2) shows that capacity is a function of capital stock, relative prices, and technical change as reflected in the time trend. Thus the slower the growth of capital, the slower that of capacity. Since the capacity equation for most industries contains a constant logarithmic trend, no general deceleration of capacity growth is attributable to that source.[6] Finally, whereas it is true that the rate of change of relative prices affects the estimated capacity change in the three manufacturing and four nonmanufacturing industries for which significant price relationships were uncovered, this does not appear to have been a generally significant influence over postwar capacity growth.

These broad findings concerning capacity trends are certainly consistent with general expectations. A close inspection of the industry detail reveals some features that may be surprising, however. For example, the estimates for railroads, farming, and primary metals show substantial decreases in capacity during the last few years of the period. This may be an unexpected result, especially in the case of primary metals, which is not usually thought of as a lagging or declining industry.

One reason for the apparent decline of primary metals capacity is the presence in the original investment regression of a substantial estimated

[6] The manufacturing capacity equation has a curvilinear trend, implying a small degree of acceleration over time, but this would tend to augment rather than retard capacity growth. The aggregative capacity equation has a linear logarithmic trend, implying neither acceleration nor deceleration of capacity growth relative to capital growth.

uptrend in the desired capital-output ratio, or what amounts to the same thing, an implied downtrend in capacity per dollar of capital stock. Quite possibly this result is a valid reflection of a heavily capital-using form of technical change. But even so, the time rate of decline of capacity per unit of capital may be overestimated. The only other industry with a positive trend in the desired capital-output ratio is communications, where the estimated increase is at a much slower rate. Moreover, the original investment regression for primary metals was one of the poorest of the group, with an $\bar{R}^2$ of only .534, which necessarily casts doubt on the accuracy of the derived capacity relationship. All the same, a reduction in capacity cannot be ruled out as implausible a priori, despite its possible overstatement in the present estimates.

Motor vehicles is another troublesome sector. Although the original investment regression had an $\bar{R}^2$ of .868, it will be recalled that the equation contained a curvilinear net trend, which implied an increase in the desired capital-output ratio until 1954–55 and a fall thereafter. Hence the derived capacity estimates show a decline during the Korean War and do not recover to the 1949 level until 1955, after which they rise rapidly. This curvilinear pattern may have resulted from a radical change in the nature of technical progress or perhaps more plausibly from an intra-industry shift toward defense production during the Korean War and away from it thereafter. Other rationalizations could doubtless be advanced, but no matter what the true explanation, it seems plausible that the observed curvilinear trend is an approximation of what was actually a reversal from a linear uptrend to a linear downtrend, since there is little evidence of persistent acceleration or deceleration of unit capital requirements in other industries. This last speculation in turn suggests that capacity growth for motor vehicles may be seriously overestimated for the last few years shown in Table 20, since the curvilinear trend implies a rapidly accelerating rate of decrease of unit capital requirements toward the end of the period.

Attention should also be called to the curvilinear trends in the capacity equations for total manufacturing and the commercial and other sector. The degree of curvature in the former equation is so slight as to pose little difficulty. With regard to the commercial sector, however, the trend reverses direction after 1960, implying a gradually accelerating rise of unit capital requirements in subsequent years. This is troublesome particularly because the capacity estimates after 1960 are extrapolations beyond the original period of fit. However, the bias, if any, is probably not large in

TABLE 20. *Indexes of Capacity, 1949–62*[a]

(1949 = 100)

Industry or Sector	1949	1950	1951	1952	1953	1954	1955	1956	1957	1958	1959	1960	1961	1962
Major Sectors														
All industries	100	105	110	116	121	127	131	137	143	148	151	156	161	166
Manufacturing	100	102	107	113	120	126	132	138	145	150	152	156	162	168
Railroads	100	106	111	118	123	126	127	129	132	133	132	131	130	128
Nonrail transportation	100	99	108	111	112	114	117	125	132	134	135	138	139	138
Public utilities	100	116	133	150	169	188	204	222	245	270	294	318	343	366
Communications	100	105	110	116	123	131	140	152	168	182	190	199	208	218
Commercial and other[b]	100	102	110	113	116	116	120	125	131	131	135	136	136	136
Farming	100	107	106	116	127	135	144	146	148	144	154	156	154	153
Manufacturing Industries														
Primary metals	100	100	103	113	121	121	118	118	123	125	123	121	118	114
Machinery	100	101	105	111	118	124	128	134	144	148	148	150	155	159
Motor vehicles	100	89	86	87	89	95	103	114	127	133	140	155	176	206
Nonautomotive transportation equipment	100	105	117	144	188	268	351	389	420	447	468	492	518	550
Stone, clay, and glass	100	103	102	111	118	113	106	109	126	139	137	140	143	141
Other durables	100	103	109	116	121	126	130	136	141	143	144	148	152	157
Food and beverages	100	107	113	118	123	127	130	134	137	140	143	147	153	160
Textiles	100	105	110	114	118	118	118	119	122	124	124	124	125	125
Paper	100	104	110	115	119	123	129	139	151	158	161	165	170	174
Chemicals	100	104	112	125	138	149	157	167	182	195	205	218	235	253
Petroleum and coal[c]	100	106	111	119	127	134	140	146	153	157	157	158	159	160
Rubber	100	101	105	111	117	120	122	127	133	135	136	141	147	152
Other nondurables	100	103	108	111	113	112	116	121	128	127	131	133	135	138

[a] Sources and methods are described in the text.
[b] Includes trade, services, finance, and contract construction.
[c] Includes petroleum mining.

1961 and 1962, since the curvature is gentle and it was shown in Chapter 3 that the investment regression for the commercial sector was a fairly accurate predictor during 1961–62.

The final industry to be singled out for special comment is nonautomotive transportation equipment. According to the estimates, capacity in this industry expanded more than five-fold during 1949–62. This rapid growth reflects the enormous expansion of aircraft production during the period, and there can be no doubt that the industry's capacity did increase strikingly. However, much of the capital formation in this industry during, and for some years after, the Korean War was on government account and may not be fully reflected in the capital stock estimates here despite the crude adjustment for government capital formation described in Appendix B. Thus the actual rise of net capital stock may be greater than is indicated in the series in this study, implying that more of the capacity increase than is presently estimated should be attributed to capital stock growth and less to a downtrend in unit capital requirements. The precise effect that more accurate capital stock estimates would have on the time pattern of capacity growth in the industry is difficult to gauge, since both the capital series and the trend factor would differ.

Table 21 shows the annual rates of capacity utilization implied by the new capacity estimates. Utilization is measured by the ratio of actual output to estimated capacity and is expressed as a percentage of capacity.The postwar trend of capacity utilization will be analyzed in later chapters. For the present, attention will be focussed on other properties of the estimates.

One important question concerns the internal consistency of the capacity and utilization estimates. The estimates for all covered industries and for total manufacturing shown in Tables 20 and 21 were derived from the corresponding aggregative investment regressions. How do they compare with aggregative estimates built up from the component industries? The answer depends partly on the method of aggregation.

The simplest aggregation technique is to sum the individual industry capacities and outputs and then to divide the latter sum by the former in order to estimate the aggregative utilization rate. This is equivalent to calculating a weighted average of the individual utilization ratios in each year, with the weight for each industry determined by its capacity in the particular year.

As deLeeuw has pointed out, however, this sort of weighting system is not the most valid one for analyzing the relation of aggregate investment

TABLE 21. *Actual Rates of Capacity Utilization, 1949–62*[a]

(In percent of capacity)

Industry or Sector	1949	1950	1951	1952	1953	1954	1955	1956	1957	1958	1959	1960	1961	1962
Major Sectors														
All industries	110	117	117	114	114	107	114	113	108	101	108	107	105	108
Manufacturing	102	114	118	114	117	104	113	111	105	94	105	105	102	106
Railroads	102	113	118	105	98	88	100	103	94	86	90	90	90	91
Nonrail transportation	87	101	106	98	98	93	102	97	94	89	100	100	101	113
Public utilities	137	136	136	129	124	121	126	128	124	117	120	118	116	116
Communications	108	107	112	113	110	112	118	117	113	106	109	111	111	113
Commercial and other[b]	102	109	104	104	105	105	110	109	105	104	108	109	110	115
Farming	135	134	126	120	113	111	110	106	103	107	100	104	105	106
Manufacturing Industries														
Primary metals	96	122	129	107	115	93	123	122	113	86	101	103	103	112
Machinery	95	110	125	131	132	110	116	123	112	92	111	113	109	118
Motor vehicles	97	140	132	113	140	118	154	112	107	78	97	101	80	82
Nonautomotive transportation equipment	99	87	154	223	212	137	107	111	116	99	100	90	87	89
Stone, clay, and glass	93	109	121	106	102	103	125	127	109	93	109	107	104	110
Other durables	100	110	109	107	113	101	108	104	99	93	105	104	101	106
Food and beverages	111	107	103	102	99	97	99	100	97	97	99	99	98	96
Textiles	102	110	103	98	99	90	100	100	92	89	103	99	100	109
Paper	103	118	119	108	115	112	121	118	107	103	112	110	113	116
Chemicals	100	118	122	114	111	102	112	114	109	101	110	110	107	110
Petroleum and coal[c]	110	115	123	118	116	108	111	111	106	99	104	104	105	107
Rubber	93	110	111	105	108	99	113	104	99	93	111	108	104	115
Other nondurables	102	105	100	100	101	101	104	103	98	98	106	108	107	108

[a] Sources and methods are described in the text.

[b] Includes trade, services, finance, and contract construction.

[c] Includes petroleum mining.

TABLE 22. *Alternative Estimates of Capacity Utilization, 1949–60*
(In percent of capacity)

Industry	1949	1950	1951	1952	1953	1954	1955	1956	1957	1958	1959	1960
All industries												
Direct (I)	110	117	117	114	114	107	114	113	108	101	108	107
Indirect (II)	104	113	111	109	110	105	111	110	105	99	106	106
Indirect (III)	111	117	117	113	111	106	112	111	106	101	105	106
Manufacturing												
Direct (I)	102	114	118	114	117	104	113	111	105	94	105	105
Indirect (II)	101	113	116	113	116	104	113	111	105	94	105	105
Indirect (III)	102	114	120	115	117	104	114	112	105	94	105	104

Note: Estimate I is derived from a regression fitted directly to aggregative data. Estimates II and III are weighted averages of the utilization rates of the component industries, based respectively on the capacity and investment weights shown in Table 23.

demand to capacity utilization.[7] If the marginal capital-output ratio of industry *A* exceeds that of industry *B*, *A* will invest more per dollar of capacity than does *B* at the same rate of utilization, and hence *A* should be given more weight per dollar of capacity in the aggregative utilization measure. Specifically, the utilization rate for each industry should be weighted by the product of its marginal capital-output ratio and its capacity in order to provide the appropriate investment weight.[8]

As it turns out, the results for manufacturing are much alike under the alternative weighting schemes. The direct estimates (I) of manufacturing capacity utilization shown in Table 22 are derived from the single aggregative equation for that sector. The two indirect estimates are weighted averages of the utilization rates in the thirteen individual manufacturing industries, based respectively on capacity (II) and investment (III) weights.[9] It will be seen that variants II and III differ by one point or less in most

[7] Frank deLeeuw, "The Concept of Capacity," *Proceedings of the Business and Economics Statistics Section*, American Statistical Association (1961), pp. 320–29.

[8] This weighting scheme is a refinement of the one that I used in the paper cited in note 1 to this chapter. The weights for variant III in that paper were based on marginal capital-output ratios instead of the products of those ratios and the corresponding capacities. The present weights are preferable because they allow for differences in both capacity and capital intensity. It is clear that these weights, instead of the ones I used earlier, are what deLeeuw had in mind in his paper.

[9] The weights for variant III are the products of the desired long-term marginal capital-output ratios shown in Table 13 and the corresponding industry capacities. Allowance for changes in these desired ratios and capacities over time was made by averaging the weights based on the 1950 and 1960 distributions. The single set of constant weights derived by this simple procedure yields virtually the same results as those obtained by allowing for continuous annual variation in the weights.

years, although the gap is larger during the Korean War years of 1951–52. Moreover, either weighting scheme produces an average utilization measure for total manufacturing that conforms well with the one based directly on the aggregative manufacturing equation.

In contrast to the results for manufacturing, a comparison of the two versions of economy-wide capacity utilization based on weighted averages of individual utilization rates reveals substantial differences in level and trend. The investment-weighted estimates (III) lie above those based on capacity weights (II) and also trend sharply downward after 1951, whereas the capacity-weighted estimate for 1955 is nearly as high as that for 1951. The investment-weighted series conforms much more closely to that based directly on the aggregative equation than does its capacity-weighted counterpart.

The discrepancies between variants II and III are greater for the economy-wide measures than for manufacturing alone because the capacity and investment weights vary more radically among the nonmanufacturing industries (Table 23). These weighting differences would still be comparatively unimportant, of course, were it not for the considerable diversity in the trends and fluctuations of capacity utilization in the several industries as shown in Table 21. Because the Korean War depressed utilization rates in some sectors while abnormally stimulating others, the discrepancy between variants II and III is especially large during the early 1950's.

That the conformity of the investment-weighted series is superior to that of the series based directly on the aggregative equation is in accord with a priori expectations. For reasons already discussed, an aggregative utilization index which takes account of inter-industry differences in capital intensity as well as capacity should correlate better with aggregate investment than does a capacity-weighted index. Since the direct estimate of aggregate utilization is inferred from a relationship between aggregate investment and aggregate output, it allows implicitly for differences in the capital intensities of the various industries and should therefore be similar to the investment-weighted index.

"Normal" Versus Actual Utilization Rates

It was noted above that a utilization rate based on the present capacity estimates is a kind of summary index of the entire set of determinants specified in the original investment regression. This is strictly true only if the utilization rate is based on the relation of expected or normal output to capacity. The ratio of actual output in year *t* to capacity measures the pressure of current operations on capacity, but current investment will not be proportional to the actual utilization rate unless businessmen expect the current level of production to persist indefinitely. In most industries, however, the best investment regressions were obtained by assuming that normal output was not equal to current output but instead was a weighted average of current and recent outputs. It follows that investment in year *t* will not be closely related to capacity utilization in year *t* alone unless the utilization rate is based on normal output. If actual utilization rates were to be used to explain current investment, for example, by regression analysis, it would be necessary for best results to include lagged as well as current rates in order to allow for the lag of normal output relative to current output.

This point is illustrated in Chart IV. The chart shows both the actual and the normal utilization rates for the aggregate of all covered industries. It is noticeable at a glance that the normal utilization rates fluctuate in a considerably different pattern from the actual rates. Their amplitude is much narrower, and their peaks and troughs do not always coincide with those of the actual rates.

More to the point, the normal utilization rates are correlated much more closely with current investment expenditures than are the actual utilization rates. This may be seen by comparing the utilization estimates with the capital expansion ratios also shown in the chart. The capital expansion rates are shown on both a net and a gross basis. On the net basis a rate of 100 percent means that there was zero net investment and hence no capital expansion during the year, whereas a rate of 105 percent indicates that net investment during the year amounted to 5 percent of the initial capital stock. Similarly a gross expansion rate of 110 percent would indicate that gross investment expenditure during the year equaled 10 percent of the capital stock at the beginning of the year.

The superior correlation of the normal utilization rates with current investment expenditures is borne out by formal analysis. With regard to net investment (net capital expansion rate), it is found from a linear least-squares regression that the coefficient of determination for the normal utilization rates is .967, as compared with .643 for the actual rates. The corresponding coefficients of determination for the gross investment relationship are .932 and .619. A similar improvement would be observed for any individual industry if normal utilization rates were substituted for actual rates.

CHART IV. *Actual and Normal Utilization Rates and Gross and Net Capital Expansion Rates*

All Covered Sectors, 1949–60

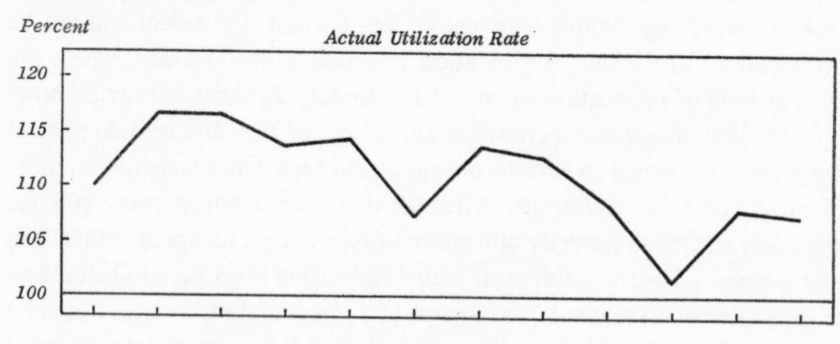

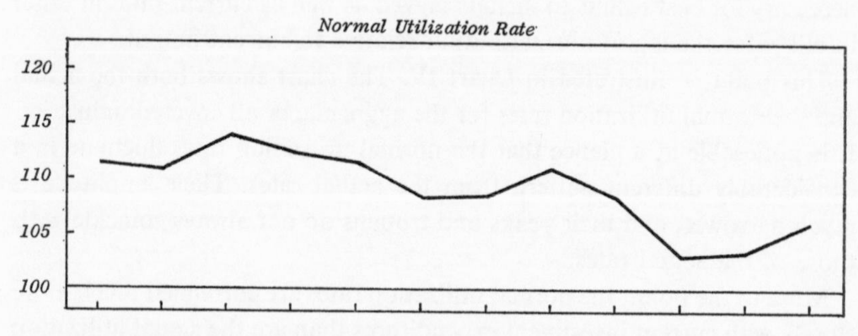

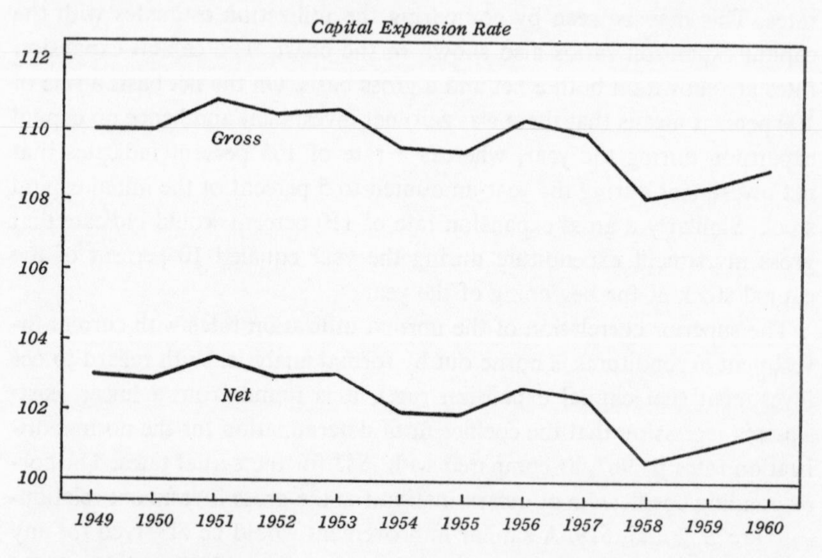

See text for explanatory remarks.

TABLE 23. *Distribution of Capacity and Investment Weights, Average for 1950 and 1960*
(In percent)

Industry	Capacity Weights	Investment Weights
Primary metals	3.12	3.76
Machinery	5.82	2.28
Motor vehicles	3.11	1.73
Nonautomotive transportation equipment	1.60	.86
Stone, clay, and glass	1.33	1.13
Other durables	5.88	2.63
Food and beverages	4.38	2.37
Textiles	1.66	1.66
Paper	1.32	1.22
Chemicals	2.74	2.82
Petroleum and coal	3.38	7.90
Rubber	0.59	.38
Other nondurables	4.78	1.26
Railroads	3.16	4.78
Nonrail transportation	3.98	3.72
Public utilities	2.71	9.37
Communications	2.37	4.19
Commercial and other	41.67	30.16
Farming	6.40	17.78
Total	100.00	100.00

Note: See text for description of the derivation of the capacity and investment weights.

It is inevitable, of course, that higher correlations would be obtained from the regressions involving the normal utilization rates. This is simply another way of stating that better fits were obtained in the original investment regressions by assuming that normal output depends on lagged as well as on current output. Expressing that important conclusion through the concept of the normal utilization rate, however, serves to make the point that investigators using other estimates of capacity utilization for current investment analysis should experiment with utilization rates based on some concept of normal or permanent output.

The normal utilization rates for all industries are given in Table 24.

TABLE 24. *Normal Rates of Capacity Utilization, 1949–62*[a]

(In percent of capacity)

Industry or Sector	1949	1950	1951	1952	1953	1954	1955	1956	1957	1958	1959	1960	1961	1962
Major Sectors														
All industries	111	111	114	112	111	108	109	111	108	103	103	106	105	105
Manufacturing	105	105	113	112	112	109	105	109	105	99	98	104	102	102
Railroads	114	104	113	108	99	92	94	101	97	89	88	90	90	91
Nonrail transportation	87	101	106	98	98	93	102	97	94	89	100	100	100	113
Public utilities	124	118	114	115	113	110	110	112	112	110	108	107	108	108
Communications	107	104	104	106	107	105	107	110	107	104	103	105	107	107
Commercial and other[b]	102	109	104	104	105	105	110	109	105	104	108	109	110	115
Farming	135	134	126	120	113	111	110	106	103	107	100	104	105	106
Manufacturing Industries														
Primary metals	108	106	114	113	106	104	107	116	116	104	97	100	104	108
Machinery	100	103	117	125	128	116	113	118	113	98	103	112	109	113
Motor vehicles	95	120	140	124	121	126	124	128	103	92	82	92	85	73
Nonautomotive transportation equipment	101	94	109	114	140	128	110	102	101	99	102	90	89	84
Stone, clay, and glass	94	104	118	107	101	104	121	125	109	95	105	107	104	109
Other durables	101	106	107	106	109	103	104	104	100	94	101	104	102	104
Food and beverages	110	104	101	99	98	95	94	96	97	95	95	96	95	94
Textiles	107	103	104	98	96	94	95	98	95	90	95	100	99	104
Paper	105	106	115	112	109	111	112	114	108	103	106	109	109	113
Chemicals	100	100	106	108	104	100	100	103	103	100	99	101	101	100
Petroleum and coal[c]	114	108	114	116	112	100	106	108	106	102	100	104	104	105
Rubber	98	100	108	105	103	102	104	106	99	96	101	107	104	106
Other nondurables	102	101	100	98	99	101	99	101	98	98	98	105	106	106

[a] Sources and methods are described in the text.
[b] Includes trade, services, finance, and contract construction.
[c] Includes petroleum mining.

On the Level of Capacity Utilization

The reader will have noticed that the utilization rates computed by the new method are generally over 100 percent during 1949–62. Capacity utilization in manufacturing did fall to 94 percent during the 1958 recession, but the rate for all covered industries remained above 100 percent even in that year. Similarly the normal utilization rate for manufacturing dipped slightly below 100 percent during 1958–59, but again the aggregate rate did not. These figures may look suspiciously high in view of the widespread talk about the development of "excess capacity" in recent years. Are the suspicions justified?

The answer is in two parts. On the one hand, there is nothing inherently suspicious about utilization rates consistently in excess of 100 percent, given the definition of capacity used here. On the other hand, there is reason to suspect an indeterminate amount of upward bias in the actual utilization estimates.

With regard to the first point, it must be remembered that capacity is defined here as that output which minimizes average cost per unit, rather than the maximum output attainable under normal operating conditions. If optimum capacity is estimated accurately, a utilization rate in excess of 100 percent means that current output lies in the range between optimum and peak capacity. Unless marginal cost rises quite steeply beyond the point of minimum cost, the range between optimum and peak capacity may be wide. According to the estimates in Table 21, the maximum average over-all utilization rates attained during the period 1949–62 were about 117–18 percent. Rates in about half of the individual industries ranged higher, of course. But even so, 12 of the 19 industries had maximum rates of less than 125 percent, and only 3 industries exceeded 132. These figures do not appear to imply an inherently implausible range between optimum and peak capacity.

There is reason, nonetheless, to suspect some bias in the estimates. It was stressed earlier that the capacity estimates rest on the hypothesis that net investment will be positive only if normal output exceeds capacity. But there is an element of bias in this assumption for an industry in which "building ahead of demand" instead of "catching up with demand" is the typical practice. For such an industry, capital expansion may occur even when normal output as it is defined here is less than optimum capacity. This is because the concept of normal output used is an average of recent and current outputs and makes no provision for the possibility that expected long-term output may be larger than actual current output during periods of rising demand.[10]

The assumption that firms typically base their capital expansion plans on an estimate of expected long-term output that is lower than actual current output is not implausible even for a growing economy. The risks and penalties of premature expansion must be weighed against the costs when capacity is inadequate to meet peak cyclical demands. Provided there is a sufficient range between optimum and peak capacity to permit expected peak demands to be met without prohibitive marginal costs, it may be entirely rational to err on the side of too little rather than too much optimum capacity—especially since underutilization of optimum capacity may raise short-run unit costs just as much as would over-utilization.

Let us suppose, nevertheless, that normal output is indeed an underestimate of expected output in some industries and investigate the consequences for the capacity estimates. In particular, assume that the true expected output is a multiple $k > 1$ of normal output as presently estimated —surely as reasonable as any other simple assumption about the relationship. In that case the output terms in the basic investment regression should be multiplied by k, and since the regression is fitted in logarithmic form, this amounts to adding $\log k$ to each output term. Since $\log k$ is added to each output observation, the moments of the deviations of the observations from their means are unaffected, and hence the slope coefficients of all variables are unaffected. The standard error of estimate and the coefficient of multiple determination are also unaltered. The only change is to force the constant term $\log a_1$ to be smaller than before in the amount $a_2 \log k$ to offset the additional contribution of the new output variables to the regression. Since the true $\log a_1$ is smaller than the original estimate by $a_2 \log k$, it follows that true capacity is k times that estimated from equation (5.2).

It is important to realize what such a constant bias does and does not imply about the estimates. In the first place, it affects only the level, and not the changes over time, of the capacity estimates. The year-to-year percentage changes in capacity are the same in either case.

Second, it also affects the level of the estimates of actual capacity utiliza-

[10] Normal output usually exceeds actual output during brief contractions even under this definition, of course.

tion. Since capacity is underestimated, utilization is overestimated—by how much it is impossible to say. Again, however, it is only the level of the utilization series that is biased, and not its trend or cyclical variations.

Third, the normal utilization rates as presently estimated do not differ *even in level* from those that would be derived if kY^* were substituted for Y^*. Whereas it is true that estimated capacity would then be larger in the multiple k, so also would be the new value of normal (expected) output, and hence their ratio would be unchanged. Thus the utilization rates that are critical for investment analysis—the normal rates—are not biased even for industries that build in advance of demand, at least under the assumption that the normal output variable itself has a constant proportional bias to the unknown value of expected output.

Fourth, the fact that the normal utilization rates would be unaffected by a biased estimate of normal output is another way of stating that (1) the speed of adjustment and (2) the level of desired stock and its relationship to actual capital stock are also invariant to such bias (see note 3 to this chapter). What is at issue is merely the interpretation to be placed on certain characteristics of the investment equation and not the predictive ability of the equation as originally formulated and estimated. This means that none of the conclusions about recent and prospective investment trends reached in later chapters is affected by the possible bias in the measurement of normal output.

To sum up: the possible bias in the present estimates of normal output implies that capacity may be correspondingly underestimated. The mere fact that the estimated utilization rates tend consistently to exceed 100 percent does not prove that such bias exists, however. It would not be irrational in an uncertain world for most business firms to plan consistently to operate in the range between optimal and peak capacity rather than to attempt an exact accommodation of optimal capacity and expected output some years hence. While the possibility of bias must be conceded, there is no obvious way to determine its magnitude and no persuasive reason to believe that it is large. Most important of all, it is only the level of the capacity estimates and current utilization rates that would be affected by the bias. Neither their movements over time, nor the level of the normal utilization rate, nor the investment predictions of the basic regressions would be affected in any way.

A final implication of the "catching up with demand" hypothesis of investment behavior should be mentioned. It is the fact that even in the "long run" and under conditions of steady growth of aggregate demand a perfect adjustment of capacity to output would not be achieved if by that is meant operating consistently at 100 percent of optimum capacity. What would be achieved under those conditions would be an equality between the growth rates of capacity and output that would preserve the same rate of "over-utilization" of capacity indefinitely. Evidently it would be useful to know what this "equilibrium" rate of "over-utilization" would be, but discussion of its determinants is best postponed until Chapter 8.

Some Comparisons with Other Measures of Capacity and Utilization in Manufacturing

The direct estimates of manufacturing capacity (variant I) prepared for this study are compared with indexes of manufacturing capacity developed by three other investigators in Table 25. It will be seen that the trends of

TABLE 25. *Indexes of Manufacturing Capacity as Shown in the Present Study and Three Other Sources*
(1953=100)

Year	Present Study (Variant I)	Federal Reserve Board[a]	National Industrial Conference Board[b]	McGraw-Hill[c]
1948	79	81		
1949	83	84		
1950	85	87		
1951	89	91		86
1952	94	95		92
1953	100	100	100	100
1954	105	104		107
1955	110	108	110	114
1956	115	114	115	121
1957	121	119	118	128
1958	125	123		135
1959	127	126	124	140
1960	130	131		146
1961	135	135	132	151

[a] Newly revised estimates obtained from Frank deLeeuw of Federal Reserve Board.

[b] Daniel Creamer, *Recent Changes in Manufacturing Capacity,* Studies in Business Economics, No. 79 (National Industrial Conference Board, 1962), Table 4.

[c] Releases of McGraw-Hill Department of Economics, except end-of-year estimates, were averaged to center them in mid-year for comparability with other series.

the Federal Reserve and National Industrial Conference Board indexes are similar to the present series, whereas the McGraw-Hill index rises at a substantially more rapid rate. The latter index is known to be subject to an upward bias, which accounts for part, though not necessarily all, of its more rapid rise.[11]

Since the FRB and NICB indexes are both tied to capital stock series, it is not particularly surprising that they agree fairly closely with the new estimates. The similarity of method is especially marked in the case of the NICB series, since its construction involves a correction of capital stock for increases in output-capital ratios above preceding peaks. This device closely resembles the procedure used in this study of allowing for a continuous trend in the ratio of normal output to desired stock. Capital stock is also an important ingredient of the FRB capacity index for manufacturing, although its construction involves use of the McGraw-Hill indexes of capacity and utilization as well.[12]

Granted the foregoing similarities, it is nonetheless of considerable interest that the three estimates agree as closely as they do, since they were derived by different statistical techniques and are based on independent data sources, including independent estimates of capital stock in all three cases.

When capacity utilization in manufacturing is considered, comparisons of independent estimates can be broadened to include two additional indexes—from the Wharton School and *Fortune* magazine.[13] The utilization rates as reported by the several sources are shown in the top half of Table 26.

It will be seen that the rates calculated for the present study exceed 100 percent in all years except 1958, whereas those from the other sources seldom if ever do. As was explained above, the concept of capacity used here refers to the level of output at which average cost is a minimum and not to the maximum attainable output. Hence utilization may readily exceed 100 percent of capacity. In contrast, the utilization estimates of the NICB and the Wharton School are constructed in such a way that utilization cannot exceed 100 percent by assumption. The *Fortune* utilization index was derived by dividing an output index by a capacity index, each of which was on the base 1956=100. Hence the utilization index is arbi-

[11] Statement by Douglas Greenwald in *Measures of Productive Capacity*, Hearings before the Subcommittee on Economic Statistics of the Joint Economic Committee, 87 Cong. 2 sess. (May 1962), pp. 19–20. Cited hereinafter as JEC Hearings.

[12] JEC Hearings, testimony of Frank deLeeuw, pp. 129–30.

[13] *Ibid.*, testimony of Lawrence R. Klein (pp. 43–66) and Morris Cohen (pp. 67–81).

TABLE 26. *Measures of the Rate of Capacity Utilization for Total Manufacturing As Shown in the Present Study and Five Other Sources*

Year	Present Study (Variant I)	Federal Reserve Board[a]	Wharton School[b]	National Industrial Conference Board[a]	*Fortune* Magazine[b]	McGraw-Hill[a]
		A. As Reported (in percent of capacity)				
1948	113	87	93		96	
1949	102	79	83		88	
1950	114	88	90		99	
1951	118	92	92		102	
1952	114	91	91		101	
1953	117	93	94	100	104	
1954	104	83	86		94	84
1955	113	90	94	97	102	92
1956	111	89	95	91	100	86
1957	105	85	93	88	96	78
1958	94	76	84	87	87	80
1959	105	84	92	94	97	85
1960	105	83	92	93	96	77
1961	102	81	90	92	95	83
		B. Index (1955=100)				
1948	100	97	99		94	
1949	90	88	88		86	
1950	101	98	96		97	
1951	104	102	98		100	
1952	101	101	97		99	
1953	104	103	100	103	102	
1954	92	92	91		92	91
1955	100	100	100	100	100	100
1956	98	99	101	94	98	93
1957	93	94	99	91	94	85
1958	83	84	89	90	85	87
1959	93	93	98	97	95	92
1960	93	92	98	96	94	84
1961	90	90	96	95	93	90

[a] For source, See Table 25.

[b] *Measures of Productive Capacity*, Report of the Subcommittee on Economic Statistics to the U.S. Congress, Joint Economic Committee, 87 Cong. 2 sess. (July 24, 1962), p. 16.

trarily set at 100 in 1956 and does not purport to show actual levels of utilization. The definition of capacity is left to respondents in the McGraw-Hill surveys, but "in general, companies follow a commonsense definition of capacity, such as maximum output under normal work schedules," and the reported utilization rates clearly are based on a conceptual peak of 100 percent, which is almost never reached in any industry.[14] Finally, owing to its method of construction, the general level of the FRB utilization index is determined essentially by that of the McGraw-Hill utilization series.

In order to abstract from differences in level and to concentrate on the trends in utilization rates, all six utilization series were put on the basis 1955 = 100 (the earliest year for which all indexes are available) in the lower half of Table 26. The new index and that of the Federal Reserve Board move closely together during the 1950's, since the trends of the two capacity series are quite similar and the output indexes used to compute the utilization ratios are highly correlated. According to both indexes, the rate of capacity utilization in manufacturing was 10 percent lower in 1961 than in 1955.

The McGraw-Hill series also shows a 10 percent decrease in utilization between 1955 and 1961, but the observations for many of the intervening years differ substantially from the first two series. The McGraw-Hill data refer to operating rates at the end of the year, however, whereas the first two indexes apply to the average utilization rate for the entire year. If the McGraw-Hill estimates are adjusted to an annual basis by multiplying the utilization rates for each year by the ratio of total production for the year to December production (Federal Reserve index of manufacturing production), the result is the following series of utilization rates (1955 = 100):

1954	91	1958	84
1955	100	1959	93
1956	94	1960	92
1957	94	1961	89

It appears reasonable to infer that were the McGraw-Hill utilization estimates based on average utilization rates for the whole year, they would agree closely with the series in this study and that of the Federal Reserve Board, except during 1956. Evidently the systematic upward bias suspected in the McGraw-Hill capacity index does not extend to the series of reported operating rates.

The *Fortune* utilization index remained consistently higher than those

[14] *Ibid.*, testimony of Douglas Greenwald, p. 4.

already discussed from 1958 on and showed a net decline of 7 instead of 10 percent between 1955 and 1961. The Wharton and NICB indexes declined even less, registering decreases of 4 and 5 percent respectively between 1955 and 1961. The NICB index refers to the peak quarterly rate of utilization during the year, but correction to an annual rate would reduce the 1961 rate on a 1955 base by only one point. Of the remaining four-point difference between the 1961 value of the NICB index and my own, half is due to a higher output estimate and half to a lower capacity estimate in the NICB index. With regard to the Wharton utilization index, only two points of the six-point spread in 1961 between it and my own index can be traced to faster output growth in the numerator of the Wharton index. The slow growth of the Wharton capacity index between 1955 and 1961 is explained partly by the downward bias inherent in its method of construction (trend line through successive output peaks) when one or more weak cyclical peaks follow a strong one.[15]

Individual Manufacturing Industries

Utilization rates have also been published for a number of individual manufacturing industries by NICB and McGraw-Hill. It is possible to compare these estimates with my own for the eleven industries shown in Chart V, after making several adjustments to put the various series on a comparable basis.

Both McGraw-Hill and NICB present separate utilization estimates for electrical and nonelectrical machinery, so these were combined to form a single machinery index by using the same weighting procedures as did the compilers. Similarly the McGraw-Hill estimates for iron and steel and nonferrous metals were combined into a primary metals index comparable in coverage to my own.

Next, all series were converted to the base 1955 = 100 in order to abstract from differences in the level of the utilization estimates. Except for this conversion to a common base year, the utilization rates graphed in the left-hand column of Chart V are just as reported in the three sources.

A final adjustment was made to increase the comparability of the

[15] *Measures of Productive Capacity*, Report of the Subcommittee on Economic Statistics to the U. S. Congress, Joint Economic Committee, 87 Cong. 2 sess. (July 24, 1962), pp. 18–19.

indexes. The McGraw-Hill data refer to operating rates at the end of the year, and they were converted to annual rates by the same method as is described above in connection with the comparisons for total manufacturing. The NICB estimates were similarly adjusted from peak quarterly to annual rates. The adjusted McGraw-Hill and NICB series are plotted, along with my own estimates, in the right-hand portion of the chart, and it is apparent that the three series do draw closer together in most industries than before the conversion to annual operating rates. The following discussion is based on the adjusted rates.

It is apparent from a glance at the chart that the utilization estimates for the individual industries diverge considerably more than those for total manufacturing. The disparities are largest in the durable goods industries and are especially marked for motor vehicles and other transportation equipment. Generalization about the relationships among the series is difficult because they frequently cross one another, but there is a clearly discernible tendency for the NICB estimates to exceed the others after 1957. The estimates in this study are rarely either the highest or the lowest of the three, tending instead to occupy an intermediate position or to fluctuate around the others. The two clear exceptions are primary metals after 1958 and motor vehicles after 1956, which tends to confirm my earlier speculations about possible biases in the capacity estimates for those industries. It is a fair generalization, however, that the estimates made here differ less from either the McGraw-Hill or NICB series than those two do from each other.

In conclusion, neither the comparisons for individual industries nor those for total manufacturing have uncovered any egregious flaw or systematic bias in the new estimates of capacity and operating rates insofar as trends are concerned. There may be some bias in the level of the new estimates—downward for capacity and upward for utilization—but if so, it is unimportant for analysis of changes over time.

The principal import of these conclusions lies in the fact that they confirm the validity of the new estimating technique. Other estimates of manufacturing capacity are available and differ little from the new series. But the new method makes it possible to present estimates on a virtually economy-wide basis, embracing most nonmanufacturing industries as well. To my knowledge these are the first such estimates of aggregate plant capacity. In the past, investigators have often depended on the civilian unemployment rate or on closely related estimates of the ratio of actual to potential

CHART V. *Comparison of Capacity Utilization Estimates of Present Study (——), McGraw-Hill (——), and N.I.C.B. (- - - -), Selected Manufacturing Industries, 1955–61*
(1955=100)

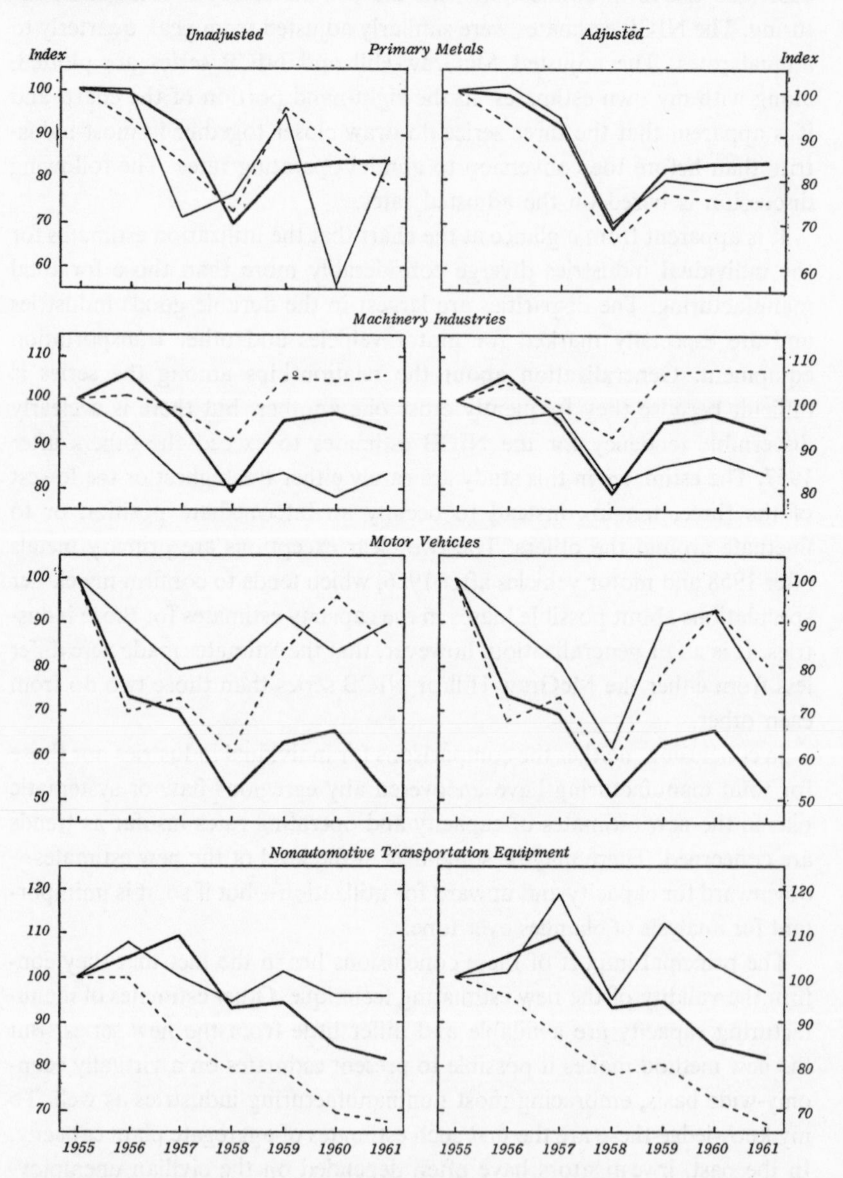

Note: No estimate for 1956 is available in the McGraw-Hill series for motor vehicles. The estimates for 1955 and 1957 are connected by a straight line in the chart.
See text for explanatory remarks.

CHART V. (continued)

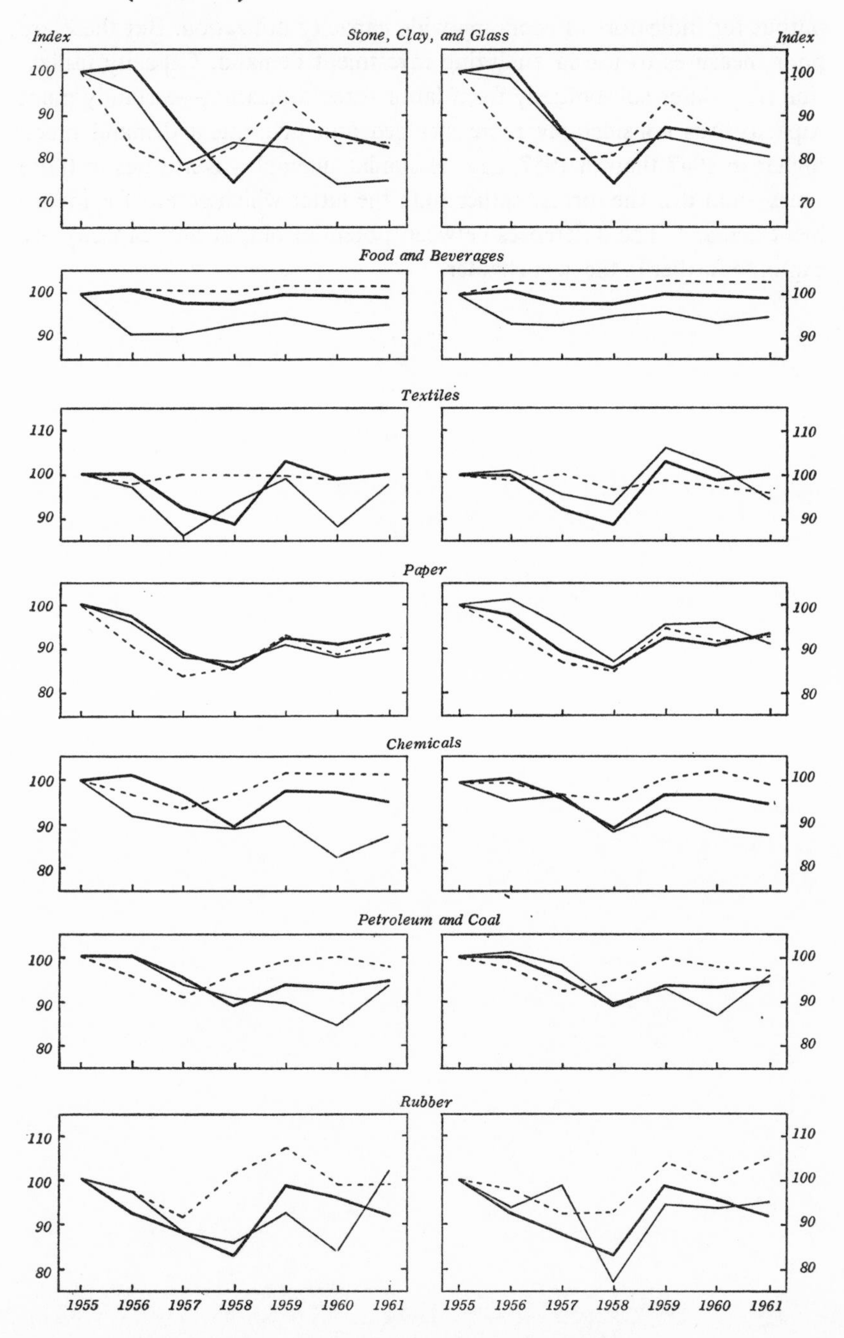

output for indicators of economy-wide capacity utilization. But these are poor measures to use in analyzing investment demand. Capacity utilization may differ substantially from labor force utilization—certainly plant capacity was considerably more strained and investment demand much higher in 1947 than in 1957, despite similar unemployment rates in those years—and it is the former rather than the latter which counts for investment demand. The differences between potential output and capacity are explored further in the next chapter.

PART III

6 / *Growth Deceleration and Aggregate Demand*

THE SLOWDOWN IN the growth of real GNP and the associated rise of unemployment in recent years were due proximately to a deficient rate of increase of aggregate demand. One of the primary purposes of this study is to analyze the role of business fixed investment in the demand lag, but this is impossible without giving some attention to other components of aggregate demand. The growth pattern of actual and potential GNP and the behavior of the major components of gross national expenditure during the postwar years are examined in this chapter as a prelude to the subsequent analysis of recent and prospective trends in investment demand.

Aggregate Demand and Potential Output in the Postwar Economy

Real GNP in 1954 dollars increased at an average annual rate of 3.5 percent between 1947 and 1963, but there was a marked difference in the growth rate before and after the Korean War (Chart VI). Between 1947 and 1953 real output increased 4.6 percent a year, whereas the rise averaged only 2.9 percent annually from 1953 to 1963.

Some retardation in the rate of increase of national output was only to be expected after the Korean War ended in 1953. Under the war stimulus, aggregate demand had been unusually high during 1951–53, and the unemployment rate averaged only 3.1 percent during those years, as compared with an average of 3.9 percent in 1947–48. Thus part of the output

CHART VI. *Real Gross National Product and Civilian Unemployment, 1947–63*

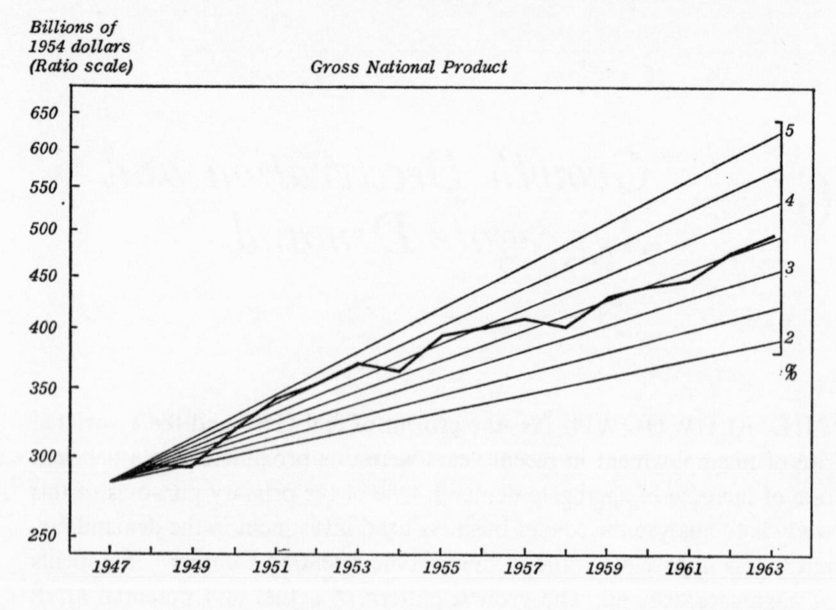

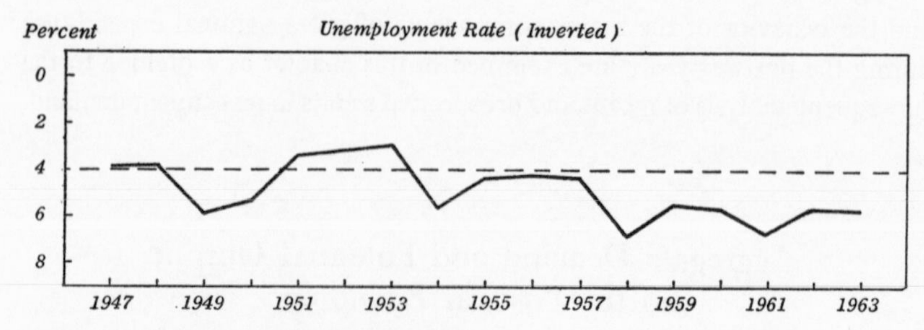

Source: U. S. Departments of Commerce and Labor.

increase between 1947 and 1953 was accomplished by reducing unemployment to a level that was abnormally low by peacetime standards.

It is primarily for this reason that the deceleration of output growth during the first post-Korean business cycle aroused comparatively little concern. The average annual rate of increase of real GNP dropped to 2.6 percent between 1953 and 1957. The accompanying growth of unemployment was not alarming, however, since it began from such a low level in 1953. Unemployment averaged about 4.3 percent of the civilian labor force during 1955–57, or only a little above the commonly accepted goal of 4.0 percent.

The sluggishness continued after 1957, however, and as a result output did not increase enough to keep unemployment from rising to a definitely unsatisfactory level. Between 1957 and the next cyclical peak in 1960, output increased at a 2.5 percent annual rate, and unemployment rose to 5.6 percent of the labor force. The pace of output increase quickened to 3.9 percent a year between 1960 and 1963, and this proved sufficient to keep the unemployment rate approximately constant—5.7 in 1963, as compared with 5.6 in 1960—but not to improve it.

If the observed deceleration after 1953 had occurred without an accompanying rise of unemployment, it could be attributed to a slowdown in the growth of resources or productivity. Indeed, there is good reason to believe that potential GNP (or the output that can be produced under conditions of full employment, given the existing stock of capital, state of technology, and supply of natural resources) did increase more rapidly in the period 1947–53 than in 1953–63. Thus some growth deceleration would have occurred after 1953 even at full employment. It is equally apparent, however, that the slowdown was due partly to a deficient growth rate of aggregate demand, for otherwise unemployment would not have increased as it did.[1]

There have been several attempts to quantify the concept of potential output for the postwar years.[2] Perhaps the best known is that of the President's Council of Economic Advisers. Chart VII, which is reproduced from the *Economic Report of the President* of January 1964, gives the Council's estimate of potential output for the years 1953–63. According to the Council, "the path of potential is represented by a $3\frac{1}{2}$ percent trend line through actual output in mid-1955, which is taken as a period of approximately full use of resources."

Although the trend line is intended only as a smooth approximation of what is conceptually a rather irregular path, the reader will observe that

[1] It is possible that a small fraction of the rise in aggregate unemployment after 1957 was due to structural transformations in the occupational and industrial distribution of the labor force, but there is abundant evidence that the overwhelmingly important factor was insufficient aggregate demand. See *Higher Unemployment Rates, 1957–60: Structural Transformation or Inadequate Demand*, U. S. Congress, Joint Economic Committee, 87 Cong. 1 sess. (1961) and *Economic Report of the President* (January 1964), Appendix A.

[2] For a review of the estimates developed by Edward Denison, James Knowles, and Arthur Okun, see Michael E. Levy, *Fiscal Policy, Cycles and Growth*, Studies in Business Economics, No. 81 (National Industrial Conference Board, 1963), Chap. 5. Okun prepared the estimates used by the Council of Economic Advisers.

CHART VII. *Gross National Product, Actual and Potential, and Unemployment Rate*

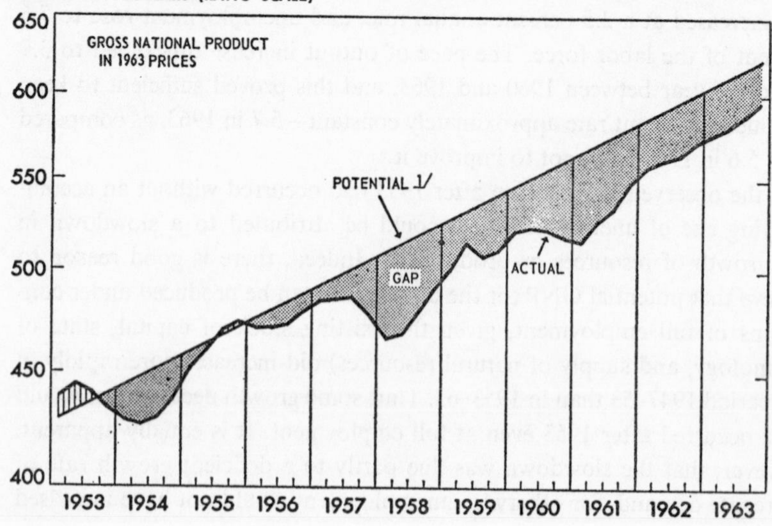

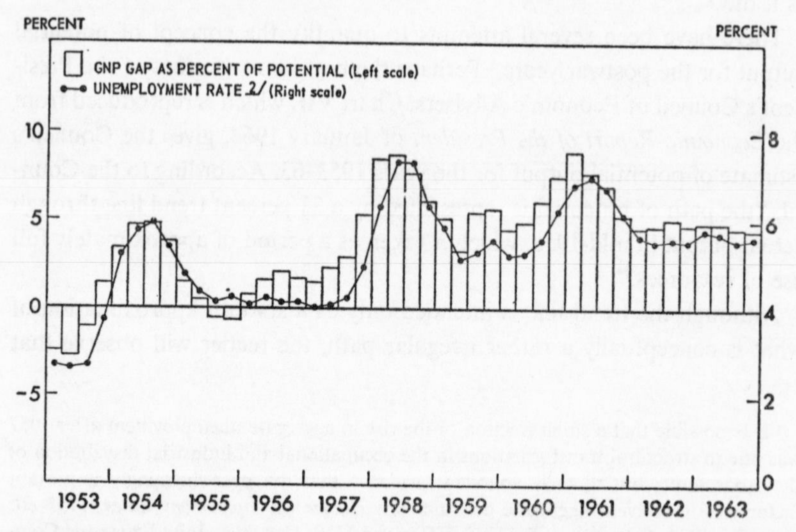

Sources: U. S. Department of Commerce, Department of Labor, and Council of Economic Advisers.

* Seasonally adjusted annual rates.

[1] 3½% trend line through middle of 1955.

[2] Unemployment as percent of civilian labor force; seasonally adjusted.

the deviations of actual from estimated potential output correspond fairly closely to the fluctuations in the rate of unemployment during business cycles and as between business cycle peaks. The gap between actual and potential output is an estimate of the size of the excess or deficiency of aggregate demand relative to the output that would be produced at "full employment," that is, at an unemployment rate of 4 percent. It is avowedly only an approximation to the true gap, and other reasonable estimates of potential output yield somewhat different results.[3] All estimates agree, nevertheless, that aggregate demand has lagged far behind potential output ever since the business cycle peak of 1957.

Notice, however, that the amount of the demand lag was about the same in 1962–63 as at the preceding cyclical peak in 1960 (Chart VII). That is, the gap between actual and potential GNP that had developed between 1957 and 1960 owing to the slow growth of aggregate demand in that period, neither widened nor narrowed appreciably following the 1961 recovery. Because actual output growth quickened in 1960–63 as compared with 1957–60, some observers have concluded that the economy was not really sluggish in the latter period, although conceding that it may have been in the former. But this argument misses the point. Once output has fallen below potential, aggregate demand must increase faster than potential for a time if chronic underemployment of human and capital resources is to be avoided.

With regard to the early postwar years, the Council has stated that the rate of increase of actual GNP is a reasonable approximation to that of potential GNP.[4] Real GNP increased at an annual rate of 4.3 percent between the first quarter of 1947 and the last quarter of 1953. The corresponding rate based on annual data is 4.6 percent. The Council places the rate of growth of potential at about 4.5 percent during 1947–53. However, since unemployment stood at 3 percent in 1953 instead of the 4 percent which is used to define potential output and which actually prevailed in 1947, the rate of growth of actual GNP during 1947–53 must have exceeded the rate of growth of potential GNP. According to the Council's estimates,

[3] *Ibid.* For a vigorous critique of the Council's estimates, see Arthur F. Burns, "Examining the New Stagnation Theory," *The Morgan Guaranty Survey* (May 1961). The Council's estimate of potential output, which was originally derived for 1953–60, continued to yield fairly close agreement between the quarterly GNP gaps and the unemployment rate when it was extrapolated through 1963.

[4] *Economic Report of the President and the Economic Situation and Outlook* (January 1961). Hearings Before U. S. Congress, Joint Economic Committee, 87 Cong. 1 sess. (Feb. 9, 10, March 6, 7, 27, and April 10, 1961), pp. 335–36.

a reduction of one percentage point in the unemployment rate at a given time would be associated with an increase in real GNP of slightly more than 3 percent. This implies that actual GNP was about 3 percent above potential in 1953, which in turn leads to an estimated growth rate of potential of 4 percent during 1947–53.[5]

It appears, then, that potential or full-employment GNP increased at about 4 percent during 1947–53 and 3.5 percent thereafter. The corresponding rates of actual increase are 4.6 and 2.9 percent. Thus most of the post-Korean deceleration was due to a slowed rate of increase of aggregate demand, and not to the slowdown in the growth of potential output. The deceleration of aggregate demand during 1953–57 returned the economy to, or slightly below, the path of potential output which it had exceeded during the Korean War, but the continued sluggishness of demand after 1957 left the economy far short of full employment even during business expansions.

Additional evidence on recent trends in the over-all rate of resource usage is provided by the estimates of capacity and capacity utilization developed in Chapter 5. Whereas the concept of potential output relates to full utilization of the labor force, the concept of capacity as defined in this study relates to optimal utilization of the fixed capital stock. Given the existing stock of productive facilities, potential output is defined as that output which would be produced if 96 percent of the labor force were employed, whereas capacity is defined as that output which would be produced if no more labor were used than was necessary to operate all plants at minimum average cost. Thus capital stock growth affects both potential output and capacity. But potential output and capacity may increase at

[5] The one-to-three relationship between a reduction of unemployment and an increase of GNP was proposed by Okun and is summarized in "Okun's Law":

$$P = A[1 + .032(u - 4)],$$

where P is potential GNP, A is actual GNP, and u is the unemployment percentage. The formula may be used to make quarterly estimates of potential output from data on actual output and unemployment. Levy computed the average growth rate of potential output implied by such estimates by fitting a semilogarithmic trend to the quarterly figures. The growth rate of potential output implied by Okun's formula for post-1953 agreed exactly with the figure of 3.5 percent adopted by the Council. The implied rate for 1947–53 was 3.7 percent, however, rather than the rate of 4.3 or 4.5 percent suggested by the Council. (Levy, *op. cit.*, p. 69 and Table 5). See Arthur M. Okun, "Potential GNP: Its Measurement and Significance," *Proceedings of the Business and Economic Statistics Section*, American Statistical Association (1962) for a general discussion of the concept of potential GNP and a comparison of the estimates obtained by three different approaches to its measurement.

different rates unless they initially coincide or unless there is no attempt to eliminate or at least to reduce the implied long-run disequilibrium between capital and labor inputs if they do not initially coincide.[6]

As a result of fifteen years of depression and war, the capital stock of 1947–48 was inadequate to meet postwar demands. The estimated rate of aggregate capacity utilization in 1948 was 120 percent—a figure far in excess of the 100 percent rate associated with the optimum combination of capital and labor. The heavy investment programs of the next five years resulted in a 17.8 percent increase of net capital stock and a 28.5 percent growth of capacity. The difference between these two gains reflects, of course, the increased efficiency of the capital stock. Aggregate demand also increased rapidly during the Korean period, but some catching-up of capacity was accomplished nonetheless, and the aggregate utilization rate had dropped to 114 percent by 1953 (Chart VIII).

Thus the capital stock growth of the early postwar years augmented both potential output and capacity, but the annual rate of increase was smaller for the former than for the latter—about 4 percent as compared with 5 percent. The rate of capacity utilization dropped from 120 to 114 percent between 1948 and 1953 despite the rise of labor force utilization from 96 to 97 percent. In other words, even in the "over-full" employment situation of 1953, the degree of over-utilization of plant and equipment was smaller than in the immediate postwar years, because the capital stock had grown fast enough in the interim to improve the relationship of capital and labor inputs.

The postwar downtrend in capacity utilization continued after 1953, despite the deceleration of capacity growth from an annual rate of 5.2 percent in 1948–53 to 3.5 percent in 1953–62. Aggregate output increased even more slowly than capacity during 1953–62—at an annual rate of 2.8 percent as compared with 3.5 percent—so that the utilization rate dropped from 114 percent in 1953 to 108 percent in 1962. It must not be thought, however, that the continued downtrend of capacity utilization was due primarily to a deficiency in the rate of growth of demand. The utilization rate would have fallen about as much by 1962 had actual output moved along the potential path after 1953. That is, there would have been a downtrend of capacity utilization between 1953 and 1962 even if output had in-

[6] As was noted in Chapter 5, it would not be irrational in an uncertain world for businesses to plan consistently to operate in the range between optimum and peak capacity, implying some "overutilization" of optimum capacity even in the long-run. This point is discussed further in Chapter 8.

CHART VIII. *Capacity, Output, and Capacity Utilization, All Covered Industries, 1948–62*

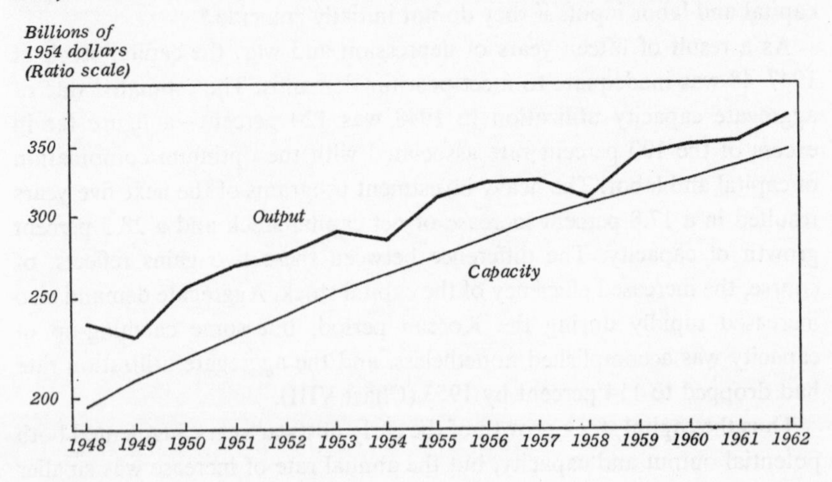

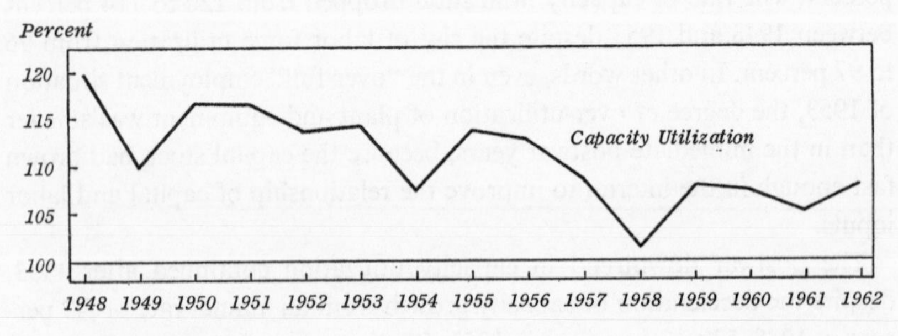

Source: Tables 20 and 21.

creased fast enough to keep the unemployment rate at 4 percent during all the intervening years, since businessmen would have continued to improve the long-term relationship of capital and labor inputs by gradually narrowing the gap between the actual and desired stock of capital.

The aggregate demand lag did have important consequences for the level of capacity in 1962 if not for its rate of utilization, however. The aggregative equation is used in Chapters 7 and 8 to calculate the course that capital stock would have taken had output followed the potential path during 1955–62. Since actual output was well below potential during most of those years, the utilization rate, and hence net investment, fell considerably below the levels that would have been realized at potential output. By 1962 the cumulative investment lag had reduced net capital stock, and hence capacity, 5 percent below what it otherwise would have been. Since actual output was also 5 percent below potential in 1962, however, the actual utilization rate of 108 percent was about the same as would have been realized in 1962 had output followed its potential throughout 1955–62.[7] Of course, had output taken its actual course until 1961 and then recovered to potential in 1962, the utilization rate would have been about 113 percent instead of 108 percent in the latter year, since capacity would then have been the same as actually realized but output would have been 5 percent higher.

One final point is in order before turning to an analysis of the deceleration of aggregate demand. Because capacity utilization and investment demand were lower in 1957–62 than in 1953–57, the growth rates of capital stock and capacity were correspondingly lower in the years since 1957. Thus the net capital stock increased at 2.4 percent a year during 1953–57 and 1.2 percent a year during 1957–62, and the corresponding growth rates of capacity were respectively 4.2 and 3.0 percent.

Since capital stock growth affects the growth of potential output as well as capacity, these facts suggest that potential output increased more slowly in 1957–62 than in 1953–57, despite the contrary estimates of the Council of Economic Advisers. It would be easy to overstress this point, however, since potential output is far less sensitive than is capacity to changes in the level of capital stock.

For example, suppose that fixed capital stock were 1 percent higher in a given year than is actually the case. This means that optimum capacity would be 1 percent higher as well, given the (reasonable) assumption of constant returns to scale of plant. Potential output would also be higher in this situation—but by only a minor fraction of 1 percent. This is because potential output is defined for a given labor input (that necessary to employ 96 percent of the labor force), and the increase of capital would therefore increase potential output only in proportion to the marginal productivity of capital. The elasticity of national output with respect to business fixed capital when other inputs are held constant is in the neighborhood of 0.18.[8] Thus a difference of 1 percent in the level of capital stock implies a difference of only about 0.18 percent in the level of potential output.

[7] According to the calculations in Chapter 8, the utilization rate under the latter conditions would have been 109 percent in 1962, but that estimate is based on capital stock at mid-year. The rate would be 108 percent if based on capital stock at the end of 1962.

[8] Edward F. Denison estimates the income share from business fixed capital, and hence

The Deceleration in the Growth of Aggregate Demand

Any analysis of the deceleration in the rate of growth of aggregate demand since 1953 must begin with the cutback of defense spending after the Korean War. Largely under the spur of rising defense expenditures, total purchases of goods and services by federal, state, and local governments rose at an annual rate of 14.6 percent in constant dollars between 1947 and 1953. In marked contrast, the annual rate of increase of real government expenditure between 1953 and 1963 averaged a miniscular 1.1 percent. Indeed, the initial impact of the defense cutback had caused a reduction of 13.2 percent in real government purchases between 1953 and 1955. The absolute decline of federal spending for defense and other purposes was reversed in 1956–57, but it was not until 1961 that the renewed expansion of federal purchases and the continuing uptrend of state and local expenditures carried the government total back to the 1953 level (Chart IX).

Clearly the cutback in federal spending after Korea was a powerful autonomous force acting directly to slow the rate of growth of national output from the side of demand. The cutback posed difficult problems of readjustment, but nonetheless it provided the opportunity to re-employ resources elsewhere and even to stimulate the growth of potential GNP by permitting an increase in the investment share. Thus the significant analytical question is why the defense reduction was followed by an insufficient adjustment of private demand to maintain a full-employment growth rate.

At first the adjustment went well. The main brunt of the absolute reduction of defense spending was felt between the second quarters of 1953 and 1954, when real federal expenditures fell 20 percent and GNP declined 3.7 percent. Not only was the shock of this and other deflationary influences soon overcome, but the ensuing upswing quickly carried the economy back to a satisfactory level of employment. The unemployment rate fell to 4.2 percent by mid-1955 and stayed at about that level for the next two years.[9]

---

the elasticity of national income with respect to such capital under constant returns to scale, at 0.13 (*The Sources of Economic Growth in the United States* [Committee for Economic Development, 1962], pp. 30–31). The share would be 0.18 on a GNP basis, with depreciation added to net income from capital.

[9] For a detailed analysis of the cyclical factors at work during 1953–57, see Chaps. 6 and 7 of my *Growth and Stability of the Postwar Economy* (Brookings Institution, 1960).

CHART IX. *Real Gross National Product and Major Components, 1947–63*

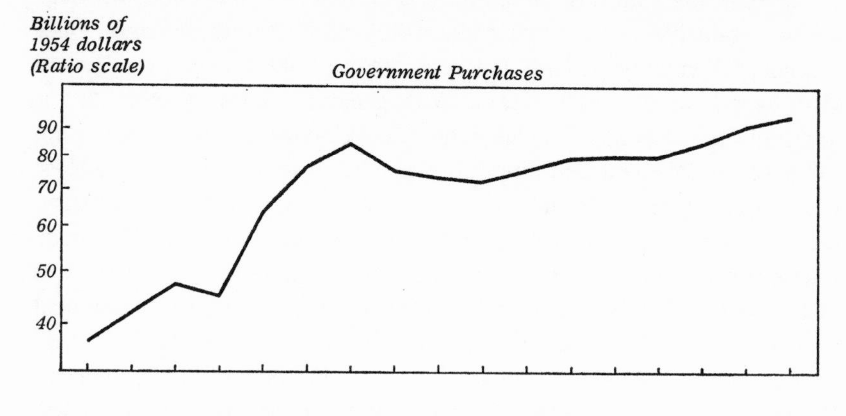

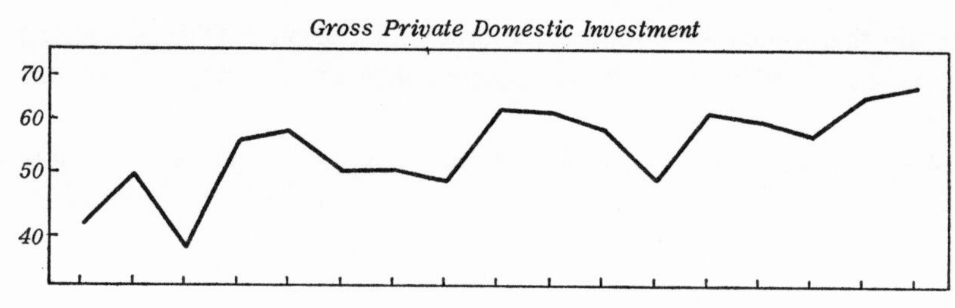

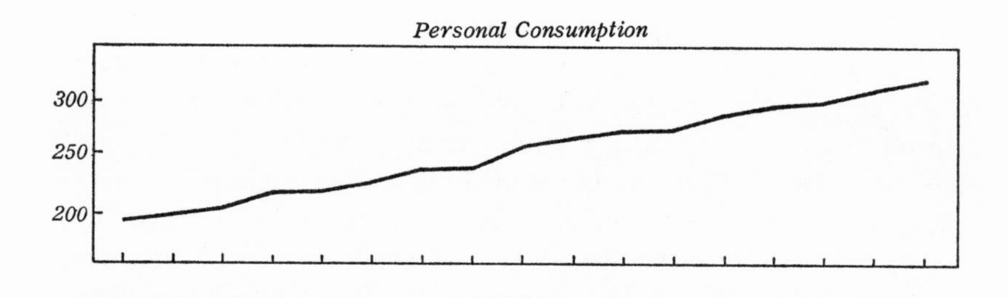

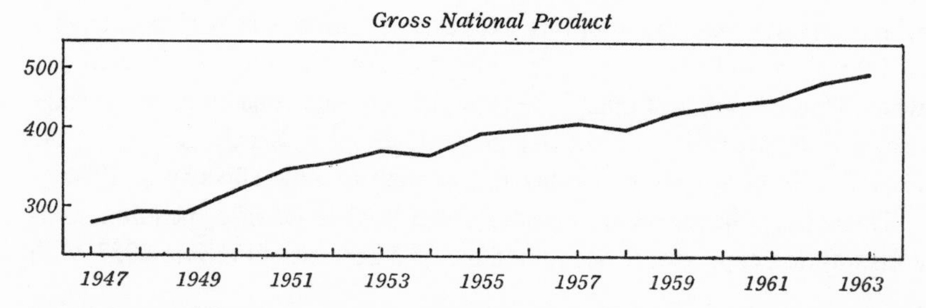

Source: U. S. Department of Commerce.

The difficulty with this initial adjustment, however, was that it involved an unsustainable shift in the composition of aggregate demand. Once reached, full employment will not be maintained unless aggregate demand rises as fast as potential output. With given tax rates, whether this is accomplished depends primarily on the behavior of nonconsumption expenditure. Personal consumption expenditure is not likely to increase more rapidly than GNP under conditions of steady growth at full employment, since gross private saving tends to be a stable fraction of GNP in all but severely depressed years,[10] and since tax receipts will rise at least as fast as potential GNP at fixed tax rates. Hence the sum of government expenditure, gross private domestic investment, and net exports would have to rise as fast as potential GNP in order to sustain full employment. If one of these components of nonconsumption demand increased less rapidly than potential output, some other component would have to rise correspondingly more rapidly than potential to prevent the growth of unemployment.

A convenient way to examine the relative growth rates of the various components of aggregate demand is to observe changes in the composition of GNP over time since the share of a given component will increase or decrease according to whether it grows more or less rapidly than GNP. Table 27 shows the percentage distribution of the major GNP components at the four postwar business cycle peaks and in 1963, the latest year for which data are available at the time of writing. These years were chosen for the comparison because our concern is with the failure of aggregate demand to grow fast enough in recent years to achieve full employment even during the most prosperous phase of the business cycle.

The table shows that federal purchases of goods and services declined from 15.9 percent of GNP in 1953 to 11.2 percent in 1957, or 4.7 percentage points. The largest offsetting increase occurred in the state and local share, which rose 1.5 percentage points. Net exports came next with an increase of 1.2 points, to be followed closely by gross private domestic investment, which rose 1.1 points. Finally, the share of personal consumption expenditure was augmented by 0.7 of one percentage point, largely because of the reduction in personal income tax rates which became effective in 1954.

Thus after adjustment to a post-Korean level of defense spending, nonconsumption expenditure accounted for 35.5 percent of GNP in 1957, with

[10] For documentary evidence, see Edward F. Denison, "A Note on Private Saving," *Review of Economics and Statistics* (August 1958), pp. 261–67, and his *The Sources of Economic Growth in the United States* (Committee for Economic Development, 1962), pp. 121–24.

gross private domestic investment and net exports absorbing 16 percent and total government expenditure 19.5 percent. The private nonconsumption share had been even higher under full employment conditions in 1948, when gross private domestic investment and net exports together totaled 18 percent of GNP. Both export demand and domestic investment demand had been swollen by abnormal postwar backlogs in 1948, however, and these had long since been eliminated. As it turned out, even a 16 percent share for gross private domestic investment and net exports proved to be unsustainable at a full-employment growth rate after 1957.

The 1957 spurt in net exports was augmented by the Suez crisis. The actual share of net exports in GNP decreased substantially after 1957, and the decrease would doubtless have been greater had GNP increased at the potential rate since exports are determined largely by external factors and imports would have risen more if GNP had done so.

TABLE 27. *Percentage Distribution of Components of GNP at Business Cycle Peaks, Current Dollars, 1948–63*

Component	1948	1953	1957	1960	1963[a]
Government purchases	13.3	22.7	19.5	19.8	21.4
Gross private domestic investment	16.6	13.8	14.9	14.3	14.1
Personal consumption	68.7	63.7	64.4	65.3	63.8
Net exports	1.3	−0.1	1.1	0.6	0.7
Total	100.0	100.0	100.0	100.0	100.0
Government purchases:					
Federal	7.4	15.9	11.2	10.6	11.4
State and local	5.8	6.8	8.3	9.2	10.0
Total	13.3	22.7	19.5	19.8	21.4
Gross private domestic investment:					
Business fixed investment[b]	10.9	9.9	10.7	9.4	9.0
Residential construction	3.9	3.8	3.8	4.2	4.3
Inventory investment	1.8	0.1	0.4	0.7	0.8
Total	16.6	13.8	14.9	14.3	14.1
Personal consumption:					
Durable goods	8.8	9.0	9.1	8.9	8.8
Nondurable goods	38.0	32.3	31.1	30.2	28.6
Services	21.9	22.4	24.2	26.2	26.4
Total	68.7	63.7	64.4	65.3	63.8

[a] Latest year available, not business cycle peak.
[b] Producer's durable equipment plus nonresidential construction.
Note: Details may not add to totals because of rounding.

The gross private domestic investment share also decreased, from 14.9 percent in 1957 to 14.3 in 1960 and 14.1 in 1963. The weakness was confined to business fixed investment, however, since the shares of residential construction and inventory investment increased. In contrast, business fixed investment fell from 10.7 percent of GNP in 1957 to 9.4 percent in 1960 and 9.0 percent in 1963. These are percentages of actual GNP, but it will be shown in the next chapter that the business fixed investment share would have decreased substantially even under full employment conditions.

Given the deceleration in the rate of increase of gross private domestic investment and net exports, full employment could not be maintained without an offsetting acceleration in the growth rate of government purchases of goods and services or personal consumption expenditures. Government purchases did increase somewhat relative to actual GNP, especially between 1960 and 1963. The level of government spending on goods and services is largely independent of the level of GNP at any particular time, however, so that the actual share overstates the implicit full employment share whenever GNP falls short of potential output. If the level of actual government purchases is expressed as a percentage of potential GNP, the 1960 and 1963 figures are respectively 18.7 and 20.4.[11] The former figure is below the 19.5 percent share that actually prevailed in 1957, whereas the latter is not far above it.

It is noteworthy, moreover, that the great bulk of the rise in the government share was due to state and local spending. It is probable that a large part of the rise in such spending was financed by increases in tax rates, thereby inducing offsetting reductions of private demand at any given level of GNP.[12]

Finally, although there was a spurt of consumption expenditure relative to GNP in 1960, this was followed by a fall in the consumption share in 1963 to a level below that of 1957. While there is considerable variability in the short-term income-consumption relationship, owing both to the built-in income stabilizers and to independent fluctuations in the personal

[11] The estimates of potential GNP in current dollars were made by extrapolating the 1955 level of real GNP at 3.5 percent a year and multiplying the resulting real estimates by the GNP implicit price index for 1960 and 1963. If actual GNP had equaled potential GNP in those years, prices might have been higher. But if they had been, they would have been higher for government purchases as well as for other goods and services, so the implicit government share at full employment would have been about the same as calculated.

[12] The income elasticity of state and local taxes is not far from one, to judge from an average of the elasticities for individual taxes presented in Otto Eckstein, *Trends in Public Expenditures in the Next Decade* (Committee for Economic Development, 1959), p. 44. Using 1958 tax receipts as weights, the implied over-all elasticity of state and local revenues at 1958 rates was found to be 1.1.

saving rate, a permanent increase in the share of consumption in GNP is highly unlikely without a reduction in personal tax rates.[13]

It is apparent from this brief survey of the major components of GNP that the retardation in the growth rate of business fixed investment demand was at the heart of the aggregate demand lag after 1957, given the fiscal policies of the period. It is equally evident that the deceleration in the growth of investment demand could have been offset by a faster growth of government expenditure or by a tax reduction to stimulate consumption demand. It is worth considering this last point somewhat further before turning to a detailed analysis of investment demand.

If there were no government spending or taxes, full employment would be achieved whenever private investment was large enough to absorb the private saving that would be forthcoming with the economy operating at its potential. This would still be true if the tax revenue generated at full employment were just equal to government expenditure. Suppose, however, that tax rates were set to yield a surplus of government revenue at a full-employment level of GNP. Then full employment would require that private investment be large enough to offset both the private *and* the government saving at potential GNP.

This reasoning underlies the recently developed concept of the implicit federal surplus or deficit at full employment, representing the amount of positive or negative saving on federal account that would occur at potential GNP.[14] As in the case of potential GNP itself, quantitative estimates of the full-employment surplus are subject to a considerable margin of error. Again it is true, however, that all estimates indicate that the federal surplus would have been substantial at a full-employment level of GNP during recent years. The estimates of the Council of Economic Advisers, shown in Table 28, are the most conservative of the available alternatives since other estimates range up to one percentage point higher in relation to potential GNP.[15]

The table shows that the estimated full-employment budget surplus has ranged between 1 and 2 percent of potential GNP since 1956. The near approach to full employment in 1956 and the first half of 1957 meant a comparatively small divergence between the actual and implicit surpluses

[13] See Hickman, *Growth and Stability of the Postwar Economy*, Chaps. 9 and 10, for a discussion of income-consumption relationships in the postwar economy.

[14] The Council of Economic Advisers discussed the new concept in considerable detail in its 1962 Annual Report, printed in the *Economic Report of the President* (January 1962), pp. 78–84. For a review and critique of the various methods by which the implicit surplus may be estimated, see Levy, *op. cit.*, Chap. 6.

[15] Levy, *op. cit.*, Table A-3.

TABLE 28. *Actual and Estimated Full-Employment Federal Budget Deficits or Surpluses, 1956–62*[a]

Year	Actual[b]		Estimated Full-Employment[c]	
	Billions of dollars	Percent of actual GNP	Billions of dollars	Percent of potential GNP
1956	5.7	*1.4*	7.5	*1.7*
1957	2.0	*0.5*	6.1	*1.3*
1958	−9.4	*−2.1*	4.5	*0.9*
1959	−1.1	*−0.2*	6.0	*1.1*
1960	3.5	*0.7*	12.1	*2.3*
1961	−4.5	*−0.9*	9.0	*1.6*
1962	−4.3	*−0.8*	7.1	*1.2*

[a] On national-income-accounts basis.
[b] Data from *Survey of Current Business* (July 1962 and 1963).
[c] Averages of semi-annual estimates as given in Levy, *op. cit.*, Table A-3.

for those years. Beginning in 1958, however, actual deficits were run in every year save one, and the actual surplus of 1960 was still far short of the implicit surplus for that year. These budgetary shortfalls are due, of course, to the loss of tax receipts incurred when actual GNP is lower than potential GNP. But whether or not full employment is attained in the first instance is importantly affected by the size of the implicit budgetary surplus, since the larger the surplus at potential GNP, the larger must be private investment in order to provide a demand offset to the government saving.

Denison has shown that the gross private saving rate is remarkably stable during reasonably prosperous peacetime years (including the moderate postwar recessions), fluctuating narrowly around 15 percent of GNP.[16] This means that unless private investment demand (including net foreign investment) is sufficient to account for more than 15 percent of potential GNP, an implicit budgetary surplus of 1 percent or more is almost certain to result in substantial unemployment. Indeed, if private investment demand were to fall much below 15 percent of potential GNP, tax rates or government expenditure would have to be adjusted to yield a deficit at potential GNP in order to attain full employment—unless investment demand could be raised sufficiently by other policy instruments to make a deficit unnecessary. Clearly the question whether private investment opportunities are sufficient to assure a full-employment growth rate for a given period cannot be answered without considering the concomitant fiscal and monetary conditions, as was stressed in Chapter 1.

[16] *Sources of Economic Growth*, p. 121.

7 / *Recent Trends in Business Fixed Investment Demand*

IT IS CONVENIENT to begin the analysis of recent trends in business expenditures for plant and equipment by exploring the implications of the equation for aggregate net fixed investment developed in Chapter 3. Chart X traces the main elements of that equation during the period 1949–62. The actual and computed capital expansion ratios K_t/K_{t-1} for each year are shown in the top section. The computed expansion ratio is proportional to the gap between desired and actual stock in any year, as is shown in the middle section. Desired stock itself depends on normal output and time, and the relative contributions of these two variables are shown in the lower portion of the chart.

The chart reveals a clear decline in the average level of the aggregate capital expansion ratio between the Korean War period and 1954–57 and again between the latter interval and 1958–62. According to the equation, this occurred because the gap between desired and actual stock narrowed in each successive period, owing to a progressive deceleration of the growth of aggregate normal output. May one not conclude from this observation that the deceleration of capital stock growth was caused by the deceleration of output growth?

Such a simple cause-and-effect interpretation of the equation would be seriously misleading mainly for two reasons. In the first place, it implies that all net investment is induced investment in the sense that it results solely from the growth of aggregate output. It will be shown presently, however, that a substantial fraction of aggregate investment demand is related to income-autonomous shifts in the composition of national output. For any given level of national output, the aggregate desired stock will vary according to the direction and magnitude of the output shifts. Since the effects of the compositional shifts on desired stock are implicit in the parameters of the aggregative equation, it is incorrect to think of the latter

CHART X. *Major Elements in the Aggregative Investment Equation and Actual and Computed Changes in Capital Stock, 1949–62*

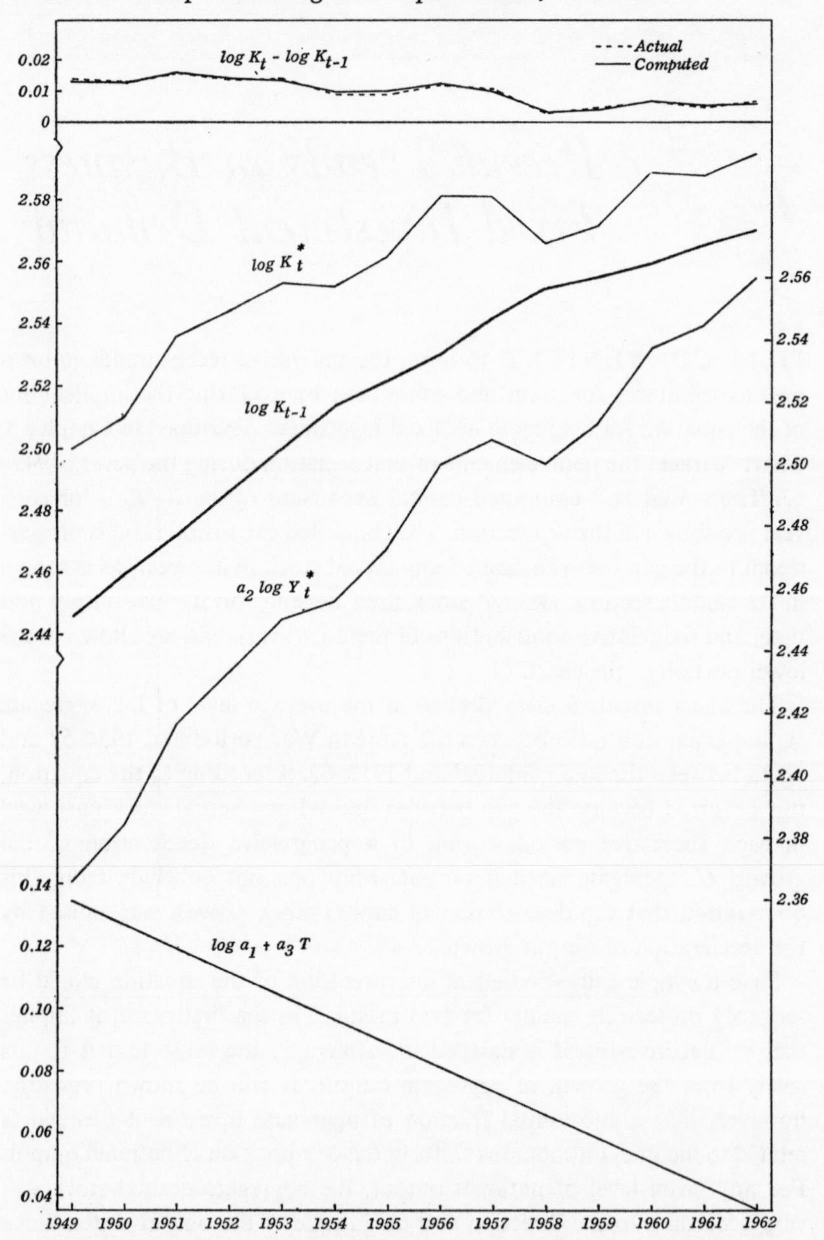

Note: The computed change in capital stock shown in the upper panel is a constant proportion (b = 0.24) of the estimated gap between desired and actual stock in the lower panel.

as referring only to the investment induced by the expansion of real national income.

Second, it must be remembered that aggregate investment affects the level of aggregate output as well as being affected by it. Since investment and output are determined simultaneously, it is invalid to take the latter as given in order to explain the behavior of the former. Indeed one of the principal purposes of this study is to analyze the causal role of investment demand in the deceleration of the growth of aggregate demand. In order to do so, however, it is necessary to go beyond the investment equation itself.

The essential point was made in the preceding chapter, where it was emphasized that full employment will not be attained unless investment demand is sufficient to offset both private and government saving at potential GNP. From the side of investment demand, therefore, the important question is: how much investment would be forthcoming at potential output? If the volume of full-employment investment demand consistently falls short of full-employment saving, the failure of actual output to follow the potential path—with given federal fiscal policies and private saving propensities—is clearly traceable to a deficiency of private investment opportunities.

Thus the real significance of the aggregative equation is that it can be used to estimate business fixed investment demand under alternative assumptions about the level and trend of aggregate output. In particular it can be used to calculate the implicit volume of business fixed investment demand at potential GNP, for comparison with the implicit saving rate. This use of the equation as an investment demand function may be questioned on the grounds of single-equation bias, but it is unlikely that the parameters would differ significantly if they were estimated in the context of a complete model.[1]

Investment Demand at Full Employment

The procedure for estimating business demand for plant and equipment along a full-employment growth path is straightforward, given the aggregative equation. Starting from some base year in which actual and potential

[1] See the discussion in Chapter 3.

output are equal, the first step is to compute the potential growth path of net stock by inserting the successive annual estimates of potential output into the regression. The net stock series is then first-differenced to yield the annual estimates of net investment demand. Finally, potential replacement is estimated from the net stock series by applying the annual depreciation rates shown in Appendix Table B-8, and added to net investment to yield the desired values of potential gross investment.[2]

The estimates of potential real gross investment for 1956–63 presented in column 2 of Table 29 were made by this procedure, except that they required an additional adjustment for coverage. The estimates of business purchases of plant and equipment used in this study omit some categories of investment expenditure and some industrial sectors that are included in the more global figures on construction and producers' durable equipment in

TABLE 29. *Gross Business Fixed Investment at Actual and Potential GNP, 1956–63*

(In billions of constant [1954] dollars)

Year	Business Fixed Investment		Gross National Product		Investment-GNP Ratios (in percent)	
	Actual (1)	Potential (2)	Actual (3)	Potential (4)	Actual (5)	Potential (6)
1956	41.1	41.6	400.9	406.4	*10.2*	*10.2*
1957	41.1	42.1	408.6	420.6	*10.0*	*10.0*
1958	34.2	42.4	401.3	435.3	*8.5*	*9.7*
1959	36.3	42.6	428.6	450.5	*8.5*	*9.5*
1960	38.9	43.3	439.9	466.3	*8.8*	*9.3*
1961	37.6	43.9	447.7	482.6	*8.4*	*9.1*
1962	40.6	44.6	474.8	499.5	*8.6*	*8.9*
1963	42.3	45.4	493.0	517.0	*8.6*	*8.8*

Sources and notes: Actual investment and GNP from *Survey of Current Business* (July 1963). Real potential GNP assumed equal to actual GNP in 1955 and to increase at 3.5 percent a year thereafter. Potential real investment demand estimated by method explained in text.

[2] More precisely, potential gross investment is estimated from the formula

$$I_t = \frac{K_t - K_{t-1} + dK_{t-1}}{1 - d/2}, \quad \text{where } d \text{ is the depreciation rate.}$$

This formula allows for one-half year of depreciation on the gross investment of period t. Since 1962 was the last year for which a direct estimate of the depreciation rate was available, it was assumed for the purposes of these calculations that the rate was the same in 1963 as in 1962.

the GNP accounts. The under-coverage amounted to about 16 percent in 1956. Moreover, there is an uptrend of about 1 percent a year in the ratio of business fixed investment on the national-accounts basis to business purchases of plant and equipment as measured here. Therefore, the underlying estimates of potential investment from the equation were adjusted upward each year by this moving ratio.

According to the estimates, potential gross business fixed investment in 1954 dollars increased from $41.6 billion in 1956 to $45.4 billion in 1963. This is based on the assumption that potential GNP was actually attained in 1955 and increased at 3.5 percent a year thereafter (column 4 of Table 29). Since the increase of potential investment averaged only 1.2 percent a year, there was a steady downtrend in the investment share of potential output, from a ratio of 10.2 percent in 1956 to 8.8 percent in 1963 (column 6).

The next task is to express the estimates of potential investment demand in current prices. An obvious procedure would be to use the actually observed implicit price indexes for business fixed investment (nonresidential construction and producers' durable equipment) and GNP to make the conversion from constant to current dollars. These price indexes are shown in columns 1 and 2 of Table 30, and their ratio is given in column 3. The estimated potential real investment shares from Table 29 are reproduced in column 5 of the new table. If these real shares are multiplied by the corresponding relative price ratios of column 3, the result is the series of current-dollar potential investment shares given in column 6. These are the same shares as would be derived, of course, from a separate conversion of the constant-dollar estimates of potential investment and potential GNP by the price indexes given in columns 1 and 2.

Since capital goods prices rose relative to other prices for several years after 1954, the relative price ratio on a 1954 base exceeds unity in all years, and the estimated current-dollar shares in column 6 range about 0.5–0.7 percentage points higher than the corresponding real shares in column 5. Notice, however, that the relative price ratio dropped steadily after 1959. But the trend of the current dollar share depends on (a) the trend in the constant-dollar share and (b) the trend of capital goods prices relative to the GNP price index. This means that if the price indexes in Table 30 are accepted at face value for present purposes, the effect of relative price trends was to reinforce the estimated decline of potential real investment demand during 1959–63. Hence the estimated current-dollar shares in column 6 decline even faster than the estimated real shares after 1959.

TABLE 30. *Estimated Shares of Gross Business Fixed Investment at Potential GNP, Current Prices, 1956–63*

Year	Price Indexes (1954=100)		Relative Price Ratio		Real Potential Investment Share (Percent)	Alternative Estimates of Current Price Potential Investment Share (Percent)	
	Capital Goods	GNP	Actual	Hypothetical		(3)×(5)	(4)×(5)
	(1)	(2)	(3)	(4)	(5)	(6)	(7)
1956	109.7	104.6	1.049	1.049	*10.2*	*10.7*	*10.7*
1957	115.7	108.4	1.067	1.067	*10.0*	*10.7*	*10.7*
1958	118.3	110.8	1.068	1.075	*9.7*	*10.4*	*10.4*
1959	120.9	112.6	1.074	1.083	*9.5*	*10.2*	*10.3*
1960	121.6	114.2	1.065	1.091	*9.3*	*9.9*	*10.1*
1961	122.4	115.7	1.058	1.099	*9.1*	*9.6*	*10.0*
1962	123.0	116.9	1.052	1.107	*8.9*	*9.4*	*9.8*
1963	124.3	118.7	1.047	1.115	*8.8*	*9.2*	*9.8*

Notes: The relative price ratios in column 3 are based on the actually observed implicit price indexes for capital goods (nonresidential construction and producers' durable equipment) and GNP, as reported in the official GNP statistics and listed in columns 1 and 2. The hypothetical price ratios in column 4 are equal to the actual ratios in 1956–57 and assume an annual increase of 0.75 percent thereafter. The real investment shares in column 5 are reproduced from Table 29. The estimated current-price investment shares in columns 6 and 7 were obtained by multiplying the real shares respectively by the actual and hypothetical price ratios.

The relative decline of capital goods prices after 1959, however, is in marked contrast to the long-term trend. The implicit price indexes for capital goods and GNP are plotted annually for the 1929–63 period in the upper panel of Chart XI, and their ratio is shown in the lower panel. Over the thirty-year span between 1929 and 1959, the relative price ratio on a 1954 base rose from .815 to 1.074, or by 0.9 percent a year. In view of this long-standing uptrend (interrupted only during the World War II period of price and investment controls), it appears reasonable to attribute the post-1959 decline to the pronounced relative deceleration of growth of demand for durable goods, which occurred for largely cyclical reasons after 1957 (see Chapter 9). In support of this interpretation it may be noted that the postwar intervals of fastest relative rise of capital goods prices came during the fixed investment booms of 1947–48 and 1955–57 and that the relative gain of capital goods prices between 1957 and 1959 was small even though positive.

What this interpretation implies, of course, is that a relative rise would have occurred in capital goods prices if the economy had stayed on the

CHART XI. *Implicit Price Indexes for Business Fixed Investment (——) and GNP (- - - -), and their Ratio, 1929–63*

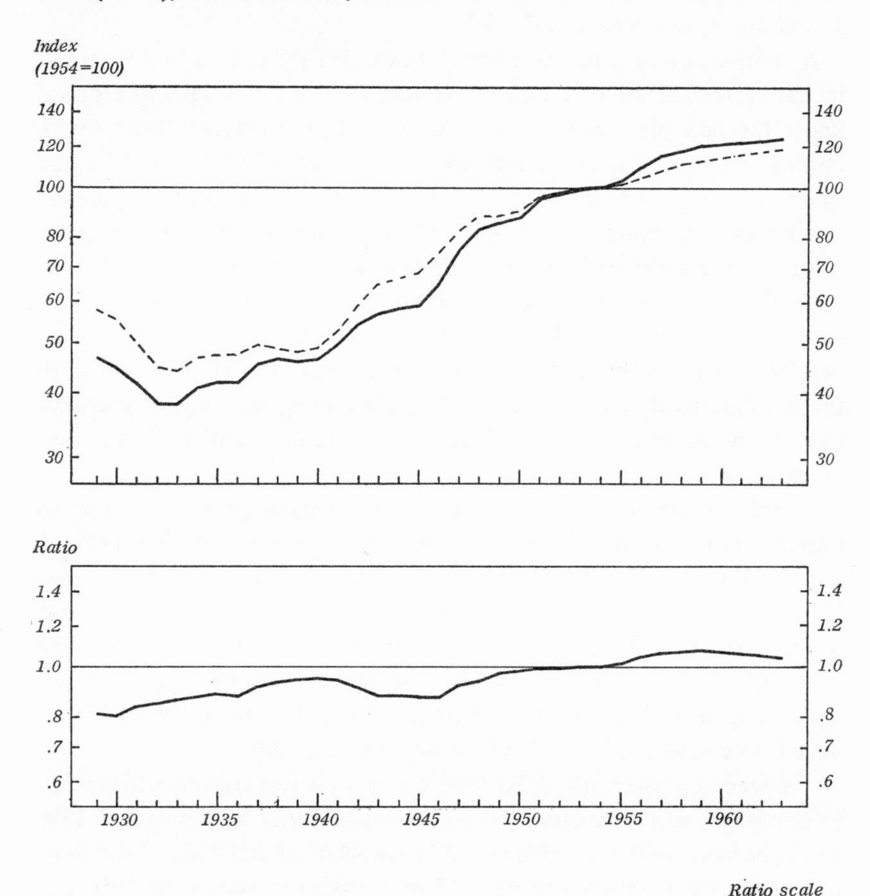

Source: U. S. Department of Commerce.

potential path instead of falling below it in recent years. The substantial downtrend in real business fixed investment demand at potential output would have reduced the relative upward pressure on capital goods prices that had been evident in the first postwar decade, however. All this is necessarily problematical, but it indicates that some upward adjustment in the estimated current-dollar potential investment shares should be made to reflect the postulated relative increase in capital goods prices under full-employment conditions. In column 4 of Table 30 I have assumed that the relative price ratio would have increased 0.75 percent each year if the economy had operated along the potential path after 1957.[3] This assumed rate of relative price increase is one-half the average annual rate actually observed during the period 1947–57.

A comparison of columns 6 and 7 shows that the estimated downtrend in the current-dollar potential investment share is substantially reduced under the new price assumptions. As a result, the current-dollar shares decline less rapidly than the real shares (compare columns 5 and 7), just as has been true over the long run.[4] Even after this allowance for a possible relative price increase for capital goods along the full-employment path, however, the estimated potential investment shares on a current-price basis diminish from 10.7 percent in 1956 to 9.8 in 1963. Thus these estimates confirm the active role of business fixed investment demand in the growth deceleration since the mid-fifties, since they indicate that it would have fallen substantially as a share of GNP, even along the path of potential output, and hence that it was a steadily diminishing potential offset to full-employment saving.

In order to establish the basic conclusion just stated, it was necessary to estimate how investment demand would have behaved during 1956–63 under conditions of continuous full-employment growth. This means asking how much investment would have been forthcoming in, say, 1960 if the economy had operated at potential output in that and every preceding year back to 1955. It is important to observe, however, that this is not the same thing as asking how much investment would occur in 1960 if output were below potential in 1959 but recovered to it in 1960.

The second answer may differ from the first for two reasons which work in opposite directions. First, the actual capital stock at the end of 1959 would be lower than that which would have accumulated under continuous full-employment growth during 1955–59, tending to widen the 1960 gap between desired and actual stock in the recovery model. Second, however, because desired stock depends partly on lagged output, it would be lower in 1960 under recovery conditions than under continuous full-employment growth, tending to narrow the gap between desired and actual stock.

[3] Notice that no assumption is made about the trend of either the GNP or the capital goods price index, but only about the trend in their ratio. It is much less restrictive to assume a trend in the relative price ratio than in the price indexes themselves, of course, and the former is all that is necessary for an estimate of the current-dollar investment *shares*, in which our interest lies. These same shares would be consistent with a falling, constant, or rising price level, provided only that the prices of capital goods changed relative to the over-all average of prices at the stipulated rate.

[4] See Appendix A for a comparison of secular trends in the capital-output and investment-output ratios in current and constant dollars.

TABLE 31. *Two Concepts of Real Potential Gross Business Fixed Investment Demand, 1956–63*

Year	Potential Investment (in billions of 1954 dollars) Under:		Investment as Percent of Potential GNP Under:	
	Steady Growth	Recovery	Steady Growth	Recovery
1956	41.6	41.6	*10.2*	*10.2*
1957	42.1	42.1	*10.0*	*10.0*
1958	42.4	40.9	*9.7*	*9.4*
1959	42.6	38.5	*9.5*	*8.6*
1960	43.3	42.8	*9.3*	*9.2*
1961	43.9	43.4	*9.1*	*9.0*
1962	44.6	43.4	*8.9*	*8.7*
1963	45.4	45.8	*8.8*	*8.9*

Note: The steady growth estimates are repeated from Table 29. The recovery estimates of net investment were made for each year by inserting potential output of the same year and actual output and capital stock from the preceding year into the investment equation. Replacement demand was estimated from actual capital stock at the beginning of the year in the recovery model.

Since these stock and output influences oppose one another insofar as net investment demand is concerned, the final outcome is uncertain. The depressing output effect is apt to predominate when comparison periods are short, however, since it takes several years of below-potential operations for the cumulative stock lag to become substantial. Moreover, although a lower actual stock will raise net investment demand for any given desired stock level, it will also depress replacement investment. For comparisons spanning no more than a few years, therefore, gross investment demand at potential output is apt to be smaller under recovery conditions than under continuous full employment.

Thus it is necessary to distinguish between two concepts of potential investment demand. Both concern investment demand at potential output in a given year, but one is a longer-run concept relating to steady growth conditions, whereas the other focusses on the short-term consequences of recovery to potential during the year. The former is the more appropriate measure for present purposes, but the reader may be interested in a comparison of the estimated potential real investment shares under the two concepts (Table 31).

Potential investment demand is estimated to be smaller under the recovery concept in every year between 1957 and 1962. The margin by which it falls short of long-run potential demand varies from year to year, however. The shortfall tends to be greater the larger is the output increase necessary to restore full employment in a given year. This explains why the shortfall is so large in 1959, following the 1958 recession. The extent of the shortfall in a given year also depends on the gap between actual stock and the stock which would have accumulated along the potential growth path, however, and this influence grows in relative importance the longer is the span over which comparisons are made. This is the reason why potential investment demand under the recovery assumption finally surpassed the steady-growth estimate in 1963.

It would be possible to introduce a further refinement into the estimates of potential investment demand under recovery conditions. The recovery estimates take cognizance of the fact that past departures from potential output affect the amount of investment demand to be undertaken upon a return to full employment, but they do not allow for the influence of past departures on present potential itself. A shortfall of actual output below potential will reduce capital stock growth below its long-term potential rate, however, and capital stock growth itself affects the growth of potential. Thus a third measure of potential investment demand could be developed in which potential output under recovery conditions is corrected for the debilitating effects of past shortfalls on present potential.

This correction has not been made, however, since it would be of minor significance for the investment estimates. This is because, as was discussed in Chapter 6, the level of potential output is rather insensitive to differences in the level of capital stock at a given time. The output increase to be obtained from a 1.0 percent increase of capital with labor input held constant is much smaller than that which would be forthcoming if all inputs were increased proportionally, being on the order of 0.18 percent. Since actual capital stock at the outset of 1963 was 5 percent below the level it would have reached under steady growth along the potential path during 1955–62, the correction factor for the 1963 potential would be less than 1 percent. Even if it were as much as 1 percent, the corrected potential investment share for 1963 under the recovery assumption would be 8.85 instead of 8.88 percent in 1954 prices, and the correction would be progressively smaller for earlier years.

The Downtrend in Unit Capital Requirements

The proximate cause of the downtrend in both the actual and potential ratio of business fixed investment to GNP is the downtrend in the amount

TABLE 32. *Estimated Investment Shares at Alternative Assumed Annual Growth Rates of GNP, 1956–63*
(In percent of real GNP)

Year	At 3.0% Growth Rate	At 3.5% Growth Rate	At 4.0% Growth Rate
1956	10.2	10.2	10.2
1957	9.9	10.0	10.0
1958	9.6	9.7	9.8
1959	9.3	9.5	9.6
1960	9.1	9.3	9.5
1961	8.9	9.1	9.3
1962	8.7	8.9	9.2
1963	8.5	8.8	9.0

Note: Calculated by same method as was used in Table 29.

of capital stock desired per unit of output (Chart X). The parameters of the aggregative regression imply a long-term elasticity of capital stock with respect to output of unity. This means that in the absence of a downtrend in the stock of desired capital at a given output, the rate of increase of the net capital stock would equal that of output under steady growth conditions.[5] Net investment would therefore be a constant fraction of GNP. Abstracting from changes in the depreciation rate, replacement investment would also be a constant fraction of GNP, since it would be proportional to capital stock and the capital-output ratio would be constant. Thus the gross investment share would follow a horizontal trend apart from short-term variations associated with fluctuations in the growth rate.

Because of the downtrend in the desired capital-output ratio, however, the long-term growth rate of the capital stock is smaller than that of output. Although this implies a secularly falling proportion of net and gross investment to GNP, the rate of decline of the investment share is not invariant to the growth rate of output. This fact is quantified in Table 32, which shows the estimated investment shares corresponding to output growth rates of 3.0, 3.5, and 4.0 percent after 1955. Notice that the faster the growth rate, the slower is the decline of the investment share. Can any general statement be made about what determines the rate of decline of the investment share?

The first point to notice is that the *level* of the *desired* investment share—the share that would be achieved if there were no lags in the adjustment of

[5] More precisely, the rate of increase of net capital stock would approach that of output asymptotically from an initial disequilibrium position.

capital to output—will vary positively with the rate of output growth. Thus if $\alpha = \Delta K/\Delta Y$ is the desired long-term marginal capital-output ratio, the corresponding net investment share is $\Delta K/Y = \alpha g$, where $g = \Delta Y/Y$ is the growth rate of output. Similarly, if the depreciation rate is d, the desired replacement demand is $D = dK$, and the corresponding replacement share is $D/Y = dK/Y = \alpha d$, since the average and marginal capital-output ratios are equal under the assumption of constant returns to scale. Hence the gross investment share is $I/Y = \alpha(g+d)$, and the higher the rate of output increase g, the larger the investment share for given α and d. This is the basic reason why the investment shares for, say, 1963 in Table 32 increase progressively with the assumed growth rate. The α and d values for 1963 are the same for all three growth rates, of course.

Thus the *level* of the gross investment share varies positively with g, but it does not follow that the rate of output growth should affect the *trend* in the investment share. As a matter of fact, the rate of decline of the *desired* investment share does *not* depend on g. This is because the down-trend in the desired marginal capital-output ratio α is independent of g, given the assumption of constant returns to scale (see Chapter 4, note 3). Thus for *any* given value of g, the desired gross investment share $\alpha(g+d)$ will decline from one year to the next in the same proportion as the decline in α.

Why, then, do the investment shares for different growth rates in Table 32 show different rates of decline between 1955 and 1963? The answer is that the same initial conditions—the same values of output and actual capital stock in 1955—were accepted for each growth rate assumption, and the initial position was one of long-term disequilibrium in each case. Because of lags in the adjustment process, the actual paths can never catch up with the desired ones, although they would eventually parallel the latter. Since the desired path which is being "chased" is higher the faster is the rate of growth, however, the decline from the same initial position will be smaller, the higher the growth rate.

To probe more deeply into the fall in the investment share requires an investigation of the factors underlying the decline in the aggregate capital-output ratio. The first step is to examine the determinants of the postwar trends in sectoral capital coefficients.

Trends in Sectoral Capital-Output Ratios

The postwar downtrend in capital requirements per unit of output has occurred across the broad range of industries included in the analysis (Table 33). Eleven of the thirteen manufacturing groups showed declines in the actual capital-output ratio between 1948 and 1962, as was true also of three of the six nonmanufacturing sectors. The actual capital-output ratios understate the downtrend in the amount of capital desired per unit of output under long-term equilibrium conditions, however, because productive facilities were so heavily utilized in the early postwar years that actual output was far above optimum or capacity output. The desired capital-output ratio provides a superior measure for studying the secular trend in capital requirements, since it is free of the distortions introduced by temporary variations in the rate of utilization of capacity. When measured in this way, only the primary metals and communications industries show an increase in desired unit capital requirements between 1948 and 1962.

In terms of the investment model the desired capital-output ratio can be affected by scale economies, price-induced factor substitution, or technical change. With regard to scale economies, the regressions for railroads and public utilities imply increasing returns to scale of plant, thus reinforcing the downtrend in unit capital requirements due to technical change.

The final regressions for seven of the industries included in Table 33 contain price terms. Over the postwar period as a whole, relative price trends have tended to reduce desired capital-output ratios in stone, clay, and glass, textiles, other nondurables, and farming. There was no pronounced trend of relative prices in either direction in nonrail transportation, communications, or the commercial and other sector. Short-term price fluctuations induced corresponding fluctuations in the desired capital-output ratios in several industries during 1948–62, but these oscillations are largely suppressed in Table 33 because it records only peak cyclical observations.

With regard to technical change as reflected in the time trends of the investment regressions, only primary metals, stone, clay, and glass, com-

TABLE 33. *Actual amd Desired Capital–Output Ratios, Business Cycle Peaks, 1948–62*[a]

Industry or Sector	Actual Ratio					Desired Ratio[b]				
	1948	1953	1957	1960	1962	1948	1953	1957	1960	1962
All covered industries	1.19	1.13	1.11	1.05	1.01	1.39	1.27	1.18	1.12	1.09
Total Manufacturing	.78	.73	.77	.71	.66	.85	.84	.80	.74	.70
Primary metals	.90	1.06	1.23	1.43	1.38	1.05[c]	1.18	1.17	1.46	1.57
Machinery	.38	.32	.38	.36	.34	.42	.41	.41	.40	.40
Motor vehicles	.56	.58	.71	.55	.48	.45	.78	.75	.56	.40
Nonautomotive transportation equipment	.99	.40	.47	.48	.42	1.03[c]	.75	.55	.44	.37
Stone, clay, and glass	.97	.85	.87	.81	.79	.95[c]	.86	.94	.85	.86
Other durables	.50	.44	.45	.41	.39	.53	.48	.45	.42	.41
Food and beverages	.64	.61	.52	.45	.42	.77	.61	.51	.45	.41
Textiles	1.10	1.10	1.04	.89	.81	1.24[c]	1.10	.97	.88	.88
Paper	.89	.86	.93	.89	.83	.98	.97	.96	.96	.96
Chemicals	1.45	1.15	.95	.78	.68	1.48[c]	1.24	1.10	.84	.74
Petroleum and coal	2.01	2.16	2.34	2.35	2.28	2.43	2.43	2.43	2.43	2.43
Rubber	.72	.64	.65	.57	.52	.74	.69	.63	.60	.58
Other nondurables	.31	.28	.26	.22	.22	.34	.28	.25	.24	.24
Railroads	4.42	4.88	4.63	4.72	4.63	4.83	4.81	4.45	4.58	4.57
Nonrail transportation	1.45	1.07	.91	.80	.70	1.24	1.05	.86	.80	.79
Public utilities	5.72	5.06	4.19	3.78	3.54	7.21	5.86	4.87	4.31	3.97
Communications	1.56	1.70	1.73	1.74	1.73	1.72	1.80	1.86	1.88	1.91
Commercial and other	.80	.71	.67	.65	.65	.85	.74	.70	.70	.73
Farming	2.21	2.67	2.63	2.55	2.57	3.66	2.99	2.71	2.64	2.71

[a] Capital stock at end of year. The year 1962 is a last observation rather than a cyclical peak.
[b] Ratio of desired stock and normal output.
[c] Ratios for 1949.

munications, and farming show a continuous increase in the desired capital-output ratio from this source, and the increase is insignificant for farming. The curvilinear trend for motor vehicles indicates a rise in desired capital per unit of output until 1955 and a decline thereafter. With one exception, the remaining fourteen industries exhibit a negative time trend throughout the postwar period, in most cases at a constant percentage rate. The exception is the commercial sector, whose negative trend gradually decelerates during 1949–60 and becomes slightly positive in 1960–62.

A note of caution is in order concerning the foregoing. Although it is believed that the regression results establish the correct order of importance of the various factors theoretically capable of explaining the behavior of desired capital-output ratios, it is not claimed that the effort to measure the separate effects of relative prices, scale economies, and technical change was completely successful, for reasons discussed at length in Chapter 3.

Compositional Shifts and Aggregate Investment

It appears from the preceding survey of sectoral capital-output ratios that the basic force making for the pervasive decline of unit capital requirements since World War II is technical change, although economies in the use of capital have evidently been encouraged by relative price trends or scale economies in a few industries. Thus the postwar downtrend in the aggregate ratio is not due primarily, if at all, to a decrease in the relative importance of industries with high unit capital requirements. Shifts in the composition of investment demand must surely make some difference for the behavior of aggregate investment, however, despite the general fall in unit capital requirements. It would be surprising indeed if compositional shifts did not augment or diminish total investment demand at a given level of national output, given the wide range of capital-output ratios and adjustment lags in the various industries.

A method of measuring the relative importance of compositional factors in total investment demand was developed in Chapter 4. The method makes it possible to estimate annually the amount by which net or gross investment diverges from the level that would have obtained in each industry had the composition of output remained unchanged while aggregate output followed its actual path. The investment difference is positive for industries growing more rapidly than the average and negative for the lagging industries, but the magnitude of the difference in each industry depends also on its equilibrium unit capital requirements and the speed of its short-term responses. Whether aggregate investment is augmented or diminished on balance by the output shifts is determined by summing the industrial differences.

As a first step in the analysis of compositional factors in investment demand, it is convenient to consider their effect on capital stock growth and the trend of the aggregate capital-output ratio during 1949–62. Column 1 of Table 34 shows the value of actual net capital stock at the end of each year during 1948–62, whereas column 2 contains the corresponding estimates as computed from the aggregative equation. It will be seen that the aggregative equation predicts the time path of net capital stock with considerable fidelity, including the 1961–62 values, which lie beyond the period of original fit. The aggregative equation actually predicts the capital expansion ratio K_t/K_{t-1} rather than K_t, of course, but it is easy to chain

TABLE 34. *Comparison of Actual, Computed, and Hypothetical Capital Stock and Capital-Output Ratios, All Covered Sectors, 1948–62*

(In billions of 1954 dollars)

Year	Net Capital Stock				Output	Capital-Output Ratios			
	Actual	Computed		Hypo-thetical		Actual	Computed		Hypo-thetical
		I	II				I	II	
	(1)	(2)	(3)	(4)	(5)	(6)	(7)	(8)	(9)
1948	279.5	279.5	279.5	279.5	235.3	1.19	1.19	1.19	1.19
1949	287.9	287.7	287.8	286.5	228.7	1.26	1.26	1.26	1.25
1950	296.2	295.8	296.3	294.2	254.9	1.16	1.16	1.16	1.15
1951	306.7	306.3	306.4	303.5	267.2	1.15	1.15	1.15	1.13
1952	316.0	316.0	316.2	311.8	274.1	1.15	1.15	1.15	1.14
1953	325.9	325.4	325.1	319.6	288.7	1.13	1.13	1.13	1.11
1954	332.6	332.3	331.7	325.0	282.8	1.18	1.18	1.17	1.15
1955	339.0	339.5	339.3	331.5	311.2	1.09	1.09	1.09	1.06
1956	348.3	349.0	348.9	339.5	321.1	1.08	1.09	1.09	1.06
1957	356.6	356.4	356.4	345.3	322.5	1.11	1.10	1.11	1.07
1958	358.8	359.0	359.6	347.1	311.1	1.15	1.15	1.16	1.12
1959	362.4	362.1	362.4	350.0	340.0	1.07	1.06	1.07	1.03
1960	367.8	367.6	367.8	355.8	348.7	1.05	1.05	1.05	1.02
1961	371.7	372.0	373.5	361.6	351.9	1.06	1.06	1.06	1.03
1962	377.4	376.9	381.0	369.0	372.4	1.01	1.01	1.02	.99

Note: See text for a discussion of the assumptions and methods underlying these estimates.

the expansion ratios to the actual 1948 stock in order to derive the net stock series of column 2.

The next column shows how well the behavior of aggregate net stock was predicted by the set of industry equations. That is, the predicted net stock series was calculated for each industry separately from its own regression, and the results were summed to yield an aggregative prediction, variant II. The predicted values are again close to the actual ones although not as close in most years as the values computed directly from the aggregative equation, especially after 1960.

Finally, column 4 contains the estimates of hypothetical aggregate net stock as it would have developed had the output of each industry remained a constant fraction of national output throughout the period. It is immediately apparent that the growth of net capital stock would have been substantially slower were it not for the compositional shifts that actually occurred. The estimated increase of total capital stock with an unchanged output composition would have been $89.5 billion between 1948 and 1962. The actual increase was $97.9 billion, but the increase as computed from the individual equations with their actual outputs (variant II) is a better basis for comparison. The latter amounted to $101.5 billion. On this basis, investment due to output shifts increased aggregate net investment by $12.0 billion, or 13.4 percent, during 1948–62.

This means, of course, that output shifts caused the aggregate capital-output ratio to fall less than it otherwise would have over the postwar years (Table 34). The absolute decline of the capital-output ratio between 1948 and 1962 was about 15 percent smaller than it would have been without the output shifts. As was mentioned earlier, these compositional effects are implicitly reflected in the parameters of the aggregative regression despite the fact that it was fitted directly to aggregative data. This is clear from a comparison of the capital-output ratios as computed directly from the aggregative equation (column 7) and indirectly from the industry equations (column 8).

The conclusion from all this is that shifts in the composition of output, far from being responsible for the downtrend in the aggregate capital-output ratio, actually offset part of the decline stemming from the pervasive effects of technical change. The next task is to examine the time pattern and industrial distribution of the shift effect.

Annual estimates of the gain or loss of invesment from output shifts by industry and in the aggregate were presented for both net and gross investment in Tables 18 and 19. For present purposes it is preferable to concentrate on gross investment, which summarizes the effects of the shifts on both capital stock growth and replacement demand. As was pointed out in Chapter 4, the inclusion of replacement demand serves to augment the deviations between hypothetical and computed investment in each industry. This means that the time pattern of the aggregate shift effect is the same for both net and gross investment, so there is no loss in that respect from concentrating on the latter. The principal difference between the net and the gross measures is that the gross investment deviations are smaller in relative terms, though larger in absolute amount, than the net deviations. Thus it is estimated that output shifts raised net investment by a total of $12.0 billion, or 13.4 percent, during 1949–62, whereas the corresponding values for gross investment are $23.2 billion and 5.5 percent.

The ratio of computed to hypothetical gross investment provides a convenient index of the shift effect. For instance, it is estimated that in 1949 gross business fixed investment would have been $26.3 billion with an unchanged output composition, whereas its value as computed from the industry regressions with actual outputs was $27.8 billion. The ratio of investment with and without output shifts was therefore 1.06, or 106 in percentage terms. Thus output shifts added an estimated 6 percent to gross investment expenditure in 1949. If the ratio were to fall below 100 percent, a loss of aggregate investment demand from output shifts would be indicated.

Chart XII includes annual indexes of the shift effect for the aggregate of all covered industries and for manufacturing and nonmanufacturing industries separately. According to the aggregate index, compositional shifts added about 5 percent to gross investment on the average during the Korean War years. With the end of hostilities, the index rose gradually to a peak of 109 in 1957–58, from which it fell abruptly to an average level of 103 in 1959–62. Thus output shifts have augmented investment demand less during recent years than at any time during the postwar period, and especially as compared with 1954–58.

In evaluating the quantitative importance of the shift factor, it is useful to remember that the constant-dollar share of gross business fixed investment in GNP is on the order of 9 or 10 percent. Hence a 9 percent increase in the level of gross investment, such as occurred from the shift factor in 1957, means an increase in the investment share of GNP of about one percentage point.

The industrial pattern of the compositional shifts is quite interesting. The group indexes for the manufacturing and nonmanufacturing industries

CHART XII. *Index of Gross Investment Gains from Output Shifts, 1949–62*
(No gain = 100)

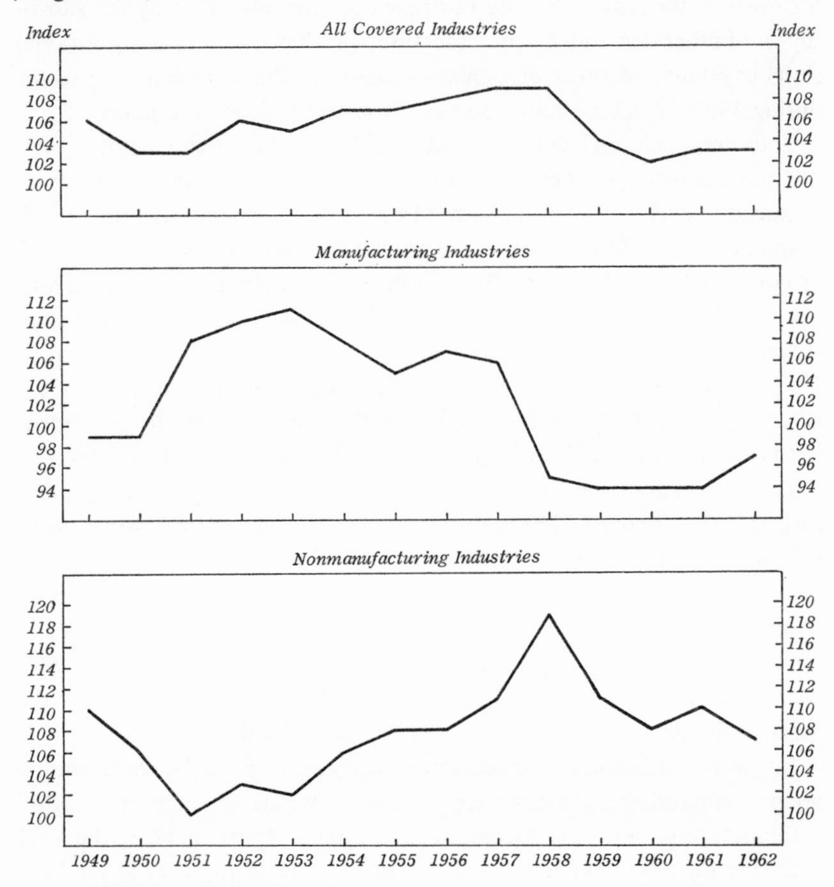

See text for explanatory remarks.

followed radically different paths. During 1949–50 the shift effect increased the gross investment of the nonmanufacturing industries by an average of 8 percent and decreased that of the manufacturing group by 1 percent. These roles were reversed by the Korean mobilization, which shifted the composition of output strongly in favor of the manufacturing industries. The investment gain for manufacturing averaged nearly 10 percent during 1951–53, as compared with only 2 percent for nonmanufacturing.

The post-Korean military cutback freed resources for other purposes, and one result was a resurgence of demand among nonmanufacturing industries during the business expansion of 1954–57. By 1956–57 the shift index for the nonmanufacturing sector was back to the pre-Korean level. Meanwhile, the loss of defense business was partially offset by the substitution of other demands for manufactured products, so that compositional shifts continued to favor investment demand in the manufacturing sector during 1954–57, although not so heavily as in the Korean expansion.

Thus compositional shifts favored investment in the manufacturing and nonmanufacturing sectors alike during the first post-Korean business cycle expansion. This is why business fixed investment demand held up so well despite the sharp deceleration in the growth of aggregate output in 1953–57 as compared with 1948–53. The investment gain from output shifts was nearly twice as great in 1957 as in 1953—9 instead of 5 percent. The actual share of gross business fixed investment in real GNP was 9.9 percent in 1953 and 10.0 percent in 1957. The 1957 share would have been only 9.6 percent ($1.05/1.09 \times 10.0$) had output shifts added no more to investment in that year than in 1953, with GNP remaining at the actual 1957 level.

This estimate of the differential shift effect is based on *ceteris paribus* assumptions, of course. The realized investment share in 1957 would probably have been even lower than 9.6 percent if the shift effect had indeed been on the order of 5 instead of 9 percent. This is because in the absence of an offsetting change in some other category of investment demand or in government saving, GNP as well as business fixed investment would have been smaller with smaller output shifts, and it was shown earlier that the investment share varies positively with the growth rate of GNP.

Investment demand continued to be augmented by output shifts among nonmanufacturing industries after 1957, but this was no longer true within manufacturing. With the exception of a cyclical spurt in 1958, the shift index for the nonmanufacturing sector has continued to hover around the 1956–57 level during recent years. In melancholy contrast, the manufacturing index fell to 95 percent in 1958 and has stayed about the same ever since. Hence more than half the investment gain in the nonmanufacturing sector was offset by a net loss in manufacturing during 1959–62, with the result that the aggregate gain averaged only 3 percent during those years. Had the aggregate gain from compositional shifts remained at the 9 percent level after 1957, the 1962 share of gross business fixed investment in real GNP would have been 9.1 percent, instead of the actual 8.6 percent, under the usual *ceteris paribus* assumptions.

In summary, output shifts have augmented aggregate business fixed investment demand throughout the post-World War II period, but to a degree which has varied over time. Investment demand was favored relatively more by compositional shifts during the first few post-Korean years than before, but this has not been true since 1959. Thus the adverse effects of output retardation on investment demand were partly offset by an enlarged shift effect during 1953–57, but compositional shifts exerted a debilitating influence on the growth of aggregate investment demand thereafter.

8 / *Looking Ahead*

THIS CHAPTER TRIES to look into the future by extrapolating the estimates of investment demand until 1970, or ten years beyond the period to which the aggregative equation was fitted. Needless to say, this is a risky business, made only somewhat less so by the fact that the equation was reasonably successful in projecting investment demand during 1961 and 1962 (see Chapter 3). Nevertheless, it is so vitally important to form a judgment on the prospects for business fixed investment demand some years ahead that the attempt should be made despite the possible pitfalls.

The estimates of future investment demand are conditional projections rather than forecasts. That is, they are estimates of what investment demand would be under specific assumptions about the path of aggregate output. If aggregate output followed a different course, so also would investment demand, and this would be true even if the aggregative regression continued to provide an accurate empirical relationship between output and investment. For this reason, investment projections will be presented for several alternative growth paths of actual and potential output. Similarly at the end of the chapter the projections of real investment demand will be converted into several different current-dollar alternatives, corresponding with different assumptions about relative price trends.

Investment Demand at Potential Output, 1956-70

Table 35 shows annual projections of potential real investment demand during the period 1956–70 under three alternative assumptions about the path of potential output. Actual output is assumed to equal potential in 1955 in all three projections, but each variant assumes a different rate of

TABLE 35. *Alternative Projections of Potential Gross Business Fixed Investment Demand, Constant Prices, 1956–70*

Year	Potential Investment (in billions of 1954 dollars)			Investment as Percent of Potential GNP:		
	Low (1)	Medium (2)	High (3)	Low (4)	Medium (5)	High (6)
1956	41.3	41.6	41.8	*10.2*	*10.2*	*10.2*
1957	41.4	42.1	42.7	*9.9*	*10.0*	*10.0*
1958	41.2	42.4	43.5	*9.6*	*9.7*	*9.8*
1959	41.0	42.6	44.3	*9.3*	*9.5*	*9.6*
1960	41.3	43.3	45.3	*9.1*	*9.3*	*9.5*
1961	41.6	43.9	46.4	*8.9*	*9.1*	*9.3*
1962	41.9	44.6	47.3	*8.7*	*8.9*	*9.2*
1963	42.4	45.4	48.6	*8.5*	*8.8*	*9.0*
1964	43.2	46.6	50.0	*8.4*	*8.7*	*8.9*
1965	43.8	47.6	51.4	*8.3*	*8.6*	*8.8*
1966	44.7	48.7	52.9	*8.2*	*8.5*	*8.7*
1967	45.4	49.8	54.4	*8.1*	*8.4*	*8.6*
1968	46.2	51.0	56.0	*8.0*	*8.3*	*8.6*
1969	47.2	52.2	57.6	*7.9*	*8.2*	*8.5*
1970	48.0	53.2	59.3	*7.8*	*8.1*	*8.4*

Note: Low projection assumes growth of potential output at 3.0 percent a year during 1956–70. The growth rates assumed in the medium and high projections are respectively 3.5 and 4.0 percent. See text for description of method of estimating potential investment demand.

growth of potential in subsequent years. The medium projection is based on an assumed potential growth rate of 3.5 percent during 1956–70, whereas a growth rate of 4.0 percent is assumed for the high projection and 3.0 percent for the low one. The medium path is the one that has been assumed by the Council of Economic Advisers for the period since 1955. I am accepting this path as the most probable one, and the higher and lower paths have been chosen merely to illustrate the effects on the estimated investment shares of varying the assumptions about potential growth rates over a wide range. For reasons given below, the investment projections based on these alternatives imply that the potential growth rates differ only because of differing growth rates of the labor force and not because of differing rates of technical progress or capital deepening. The medium projection implies a labor force growth rate of about 1.5 percent, and a variation of 0.5 percent above or below that rate would be substantial indeed. Thus the range between the high and low projections is clearly wide enough to embrace any reasonable alternative.

Each of the alternative projections assumes steady growth along the potential path during 1956–70. As was pointed out in Chapter 7, the level of potential investment demand in a given year would in general depend not only on the level of potential GNP in that year but also on the path by which it was approached. The projections shown in Table 35 for the mid- and late 1960's, therefore, are not realistic estimates of the investment demand to be expected should actual GNP now return to the potential path and move along it. Such estimates will be given later, but in the meantime the present projections will serve to draw out the implications of the aggregative equation concerning investment behavior under conditions of steady expansion and for alternative growth rates of labor force and potential output.

The estimates of potential real investment demand for the medium variant during 1956–63 are repeated from Table 29 in the preceding chapter. It will be recalled that the initial estimates were made by substituting potential for actual output in the investment equation and computing the implied path of potential capital stock, after which it was a simple procedure to calculate the corresponding values of net investment and replacement demand. It was necessary, however, to adjust the resulting gross investment estimates upward to allow for the greater coverage of the gross business fixed investment concept in the GNP accounts.

The same general procedures were followed in extending the estimates to 1970, but in order to do so, it was necessary to make specific assumptions about the depreciation rate and the coverage adjustment factor. Potential replacement demand had been estimated for 1956–62 by applying the actual annual depreciation rates from Table B-8 to the projected net stock figures. The assumption used in extending the estimates through 1970 was to hold the depreciation rate constant at the 1962 level. As for the coverage adjustment factor, it was assumed to increase at the same rate during 1963–70 as it had during 1956–62.

The high and low projections of potential investment demand during 1956–70 parallel those just described in every respect except for the assumption about the growth path of potential output. In particular they make use of the same depreciation rates and coverage adjustment factors as in the medium projection.

All three variants indicate a continuous downtrend in the implicit long-term or steady-growth share of real business fixed investment at potential GNP during 1956–70. According to the medium, or 3.5 percent, growth rate projection, the real investment share at full employment would drop from an estimated 10.2 percent in 1956 to 8.1 percent in 1970. The drop would be greater for a potential growth rate of 3.0 percent and smaller for one of 4.0 percent, for the reasons noted in Chapter 7. Hence the lower the growth rate assumed for potential output after 1955, and hence the lower the level of potential output in any later year, the smaller the estimated investment share. The low projection is therefore the most pessimistic of the three from the standpoint of the implied contribution of business fixed investment demand to the attainment of a full-employment level of aggregate demand.

Another, more optimistic, property of the alternative projections also merits comment. This is the implication that the investment share required to provide the expansion of capital facilities needed for a 4.0 percent growth rate of potential output is not greatly in excess of that needed for a 3.0 percent growth rate, *assuming that labor force growth is not a constraint in that range and that techniques improve at the same rate in the two cases.* The largest spread between the projected annual investment shares is 0.6 of a point, and it is not reached until 13 years after the comparison is begun. Thus if capital expansion rather than labor force growth were the limiting factor, it would not require an implausible diversion of resources into additional investment to sustain a markedly higher growth rate—plausibility being judged by comparison with the fixed investment shares of past years.

To avoid misunderstanding, it must be stressed that the foregoing calculations do *not* refer to the investment quotas necessary to support alternative growth rates of potential output for a given growth rate of labor input. This is because projection of the trend term in the aggregative equation implies a continuation of the same rate and character (factor-bias) of technical change as in the period of fit and because the absence of a relative price term precludes examining the effects on the growth rate of potential GNP of price-induced changes in the capital-labor ratio. It is assumed instead that each potential growth rate corresponds to a different growth rate of the labor force, so the question becomes: how much investment is necessary to supply the same average complement of plant and equipment per worker each year along each alternative path? If, as appears realistic, the growth of labor input implies a 3.5 percent growth rate of potential GNP for the given rate and character of technical progress, faster growth could still be achieved through capital formation. But this could be done only by raising the ratio of capital to labor. To obtain a given acceleration of potential output by a capital-deepening process, however, would require a much larger investment increase than that needed when the growth of labor input can also be accelerated, since diminishing returns to capital are encountered in the former case but avoided in the latter. This is the same point, of course, that was discussed above in connection with the distinction between capacity and potential output, where it was emphasized that the investment-elasticity of potential output was much smaller than that of optimum capacity (Chapter 6).[1]

Granted the general nature of the projections in Table 35, they are still only as accurate as the assumptions underlying them. To cite a few possibilities, there could be inaccuracies (1) because of faulty specification or estimation of the original equation, or (2) because some investment determinant, not explicitly represented in the regression, changed in direction or relative importance following the period of fit, or (3) because the rate or character of technical progress changed after the equation was fitted. To repeat, the equation did predict actual investment reasonably well during 1961–62, but this is no guarantee that it will do as well in subsequent years.

Experience will provide the only conclusive test of the projections, but it is possible to indicate the margins of tolerance associated with some of the underlying assumptions. This has already been done with respect to the growth path assumed for potential output, of course, by presenting alternative projections for several growth rates.

The projections may also be sensitive to variations in the definition and measurement of capital stock. This question is investigated systematically in Appendix A, where investment regressions are presented for six alternative measures of capital stock prepared by the Office of Business Economics of the United States Department of Commerce and based on varying

[1] Robert M. Solow has presented estimates of the amounts of fixed investment necessary to support alternative growth rates of potential output for specified rates of technical progress and labor force growth in "Technical Progress, Capital Formation, and Economic Growth," *American Economic Review* (May 1962), pp. 76–86. His estimates of the investment quota required for a growth rate of 3.5 percent range from 8.4 to 9.7 percent of GNP (1960–61 level), depending on the particular assumptions about technical progress and labor force growth. My own average estimate for the same period and growth rate is 9.2 percent (an average of the 1960 and 1961 shares), near the middle of the range. However, Solow's estimates indicate that for any given combination of technical progress and labor force growth, the investment quota would have to be increased by at least one percentage point to raise the growth of potential from 3.5 to 4.0 percent a year. As would be expected, this quota increase is five times as large as would be required under my assumptions, which allow for an acceleration in the growth of labor input as well as of capital input in going from the 3.5 to the 4.0 percent growth rate.

assumptions about useful lives, depreciation methods, and gross *versus* net stock concepts. It suffices at this point to report that the major discrepancies between the present capital stock series and the various OBE net stock variants are traceable to the use of different underlying gross investment data rather than to differences in the depreciation assumptions. The stock estimates used here were built up from the investment data contained in a joint survey of business expenditures for new plant and equipment by the Office of Business Economics and the Securities and Exchange Commission, whereas the OBE stock variants were derived from the data on nonresidential construction and purchases of producers' durable equipment as measured in the GNP accounts.

Because the latter investment estimates exceed the former in both level and rate of increase over time, the OBE net stock series all rise more rapidly over the postwar years than does my series. Consequently investment regressions based on the OBE net stock variants show a smaller downtrend in the desired capital-output ratio, and hence imply a slower decline in the estimated gross investment share at potential output, than does the original regression. Some allowance for the difference between the two gross investment series has already been made, of course, in the estimates of potential investment demand shown in Table 35, since the original predictions were multiplied by a moving coverage adjustment factor in order to put them on a parity with business fixed investment as measured in the GNP accounts. However, the results presented in Appendix A show that projections of investment demand made from regressions based directly on the OBE net stock variants would decline more slowly than those in Table 35 despite the coverage adjustment. There is virtually no discrepancy in 1960, but by 1970 the potential investment share as estimated from any of the OBE net stock variants would be about 0.5 percentage points higher than that shown for the medium projection in Table 35; that is, it would be about 8.6 instead of 8.1 percent.[2] It is believed, however, that the original projections of gross business fixed investment are more firmly based than the new ones despite the need for a coverage adjustment in the former, since the OBE-SEC investment data are conceptually better than those from the GNP accounts for empirical implementation of my investment model (see Appendix A).

[2] The direct comparison in Appendix A is for investment shares excluding construction of farm residences. On that basis the OBE net stock variants imply an investment share of 8.4 percent in 1970, as compared with 7.9 percent for my investment concept (see Table A-3).

Capacity Utilization at Potential Output

Each of the projections of potential GNP implies a specific path of capital stock growth and hence a specific development of capacity and capacity utilization. The implicit utilization rates are shown for each of the potential output projections for each year in Table 36.

It will be noted that each projection implies a downtrend of capacity utilization during 1956–70. Moreover each projection involves a gradual approach to an apparently stable utilization rate during the closing years of the period. The stable terminal rate is not the same for each projection, however, but rather varies positively with the growth rate assumed for potential GNP. These observations suggest that (1) capacity utilization is approaching a long-term equilibrium along each growth path, (2) the equilibrium utilization rate is a function of the growth rate of output, (3) the

TABLE 36. *Capacity Utilization Rates Under Alternative Projections of Potential Output and Investment, 1956–70*

(In percent)

Year	Potential Output Projection		
	Low	Medium	High
1956	112	113	113
1957	111	112	113
1958	110	111	112
1959	109	110	112
1960	108	110	111
1961	108	109	111
1962	107	109	111
1963	107	109	111
1964	107	109	111
1965	107	109	111
1966	106	108	111
1967	106	108	110
1968	106	108	110
1969	106	108	110
1970	106	108	110

Note: These utilization rates were calculated from the output and capital stock projections underlying Table 35, using the method described in Chapter 5.

equilibrium rate differs from 100 percent. That all these implications are correct follows from certain properties of the aggregative investment equation.

In the first place, the basic investment model implies that the capital expansion ratio is directly proportional to the expected or normal capacity utilization rate, where the factor of proportionality b depends on the speed with which businessmen act to reduce the gap between expected output and capacity.[3] In the case of the aggregative equation the numerical estimate of b is 0.24. Thus the percentage increase of capital stock during a given year will be about one-fourth of the percentage gap between normal output and capacity. For example, a normal utilization rate of 108 percent implies a capacity gap of 8 percent and would therefore elicit a 2 percent increase of capital stock during the year. Put the other way around, this means that capital stock will not increase at x percent a year unless the capacity gap is about $4x$ percent.

Suppose that output is growing at a constant rate of 3.5 percent a year. How fast must capital stock increase if capacity is to grow at the same rate as output? The trend term in the aggregative equation implies that capacity would increase at an average rate of 1.8 percent a year even if the capital stock were constant, owing primarily to improvements in the productivity of capital goods of successive vintages. Thus in order for capacity to increase at 3.5 percent a year, capital stock must increase annually by 1.7 percent (3.5–1.8). But this implies that expected or normal output must continuously exceed capacity by about 6.8 percent (4×1.7), or, in other words, that the equilibrium normal utilization rate would be about 107 percent for a growth rate of 3.5 percent. This in turn implies that the equilibrium rate of current utilization of capacity would be about 108 percent, which is the value approached for the medium, or 3.5 percent, growth-rate projection in Table 36.[4]

[3] Unless constant returns to scale are assumed, the proportionality factor will be ba_2 instead of b. See Chap. 5, note 3. Strictly speaking the proportionality holds between the logarithms of the capital expansion and capacity utilization ratios rather than between the ratios themselves.

[4] In order to go from the normal to the actual current utilization rate, two corrections are necessary. In the aggregative equation, normal output is an average of the outputs of the current and the preceding year. Assuming a 3.5 percent growth rate, this means that current output and utilization would be about 1.75 percent above normal output and utilization. However, the capacity estimates underlying the utilization rates shown in Table 36 were centered on the middle of the year by averaging capital stock at the beginning and end of the year. Since capital stock is increasing by about 1.7 percent a year in the medium projection, the middle-of-the-year capacity is about 0.85 percent higher

The same analysis can be applied to determine the equilibrium utilization rate consistent with any output growth rate. The equilibrium rate varies positively with the growth rate because the capacity trend factor is constant, and a higher growth rate of capacity therefore requires a faster growth of capital stock. It is easily calculated that the terminal rates shown for the high and low projections in Table 36 are indeed the equilibrium rates consistent with the assumed potential growth rates, just as was true of the medium projection.

Two implications of these findings should be made explicit. First, the aggregative utilization rate dropped from 120 percent in 1948 to 114 percent in 1955. According to Table 36, capacity utilization would have continued to decline after 1955 even at full employment, but at a gradually diminishing rate, as the long-term equilibrium was approached. Hence it is unrealistic to expect the postwar downtrend of utilization rates to be prolonged indefinitely unless there is a continuous deceleration of output growth. At the same time, it is important to note that a constant equilibrium utilization rate does *not* imply a constant share of gross investment in output. On the contrary, a constant utilization rate implies a falling real investment share, owing to continuous improvements in capital productivity. Hence the investment share would continue to decline even after capacity utilization had reached its equilibrium level under steady growth (compare Tables 35 and 36).

Second, although the normal or expected utilization rate must exceed 100 percent in order for positive net investment to occur in the model, this is not necessarily true of the actual utilization rate. In the empirical implementation of the model it has been assumed that expected long-term output is always less than actual current output during expansion periods. This carries the corollary that, even under steady growth, the equilibrium value of the actual utilization rate must exceed the normal rate on which investment plans are based and hence must exceed 100 percent. If it were assumed instead that expected output is greater than current output, the equilibrium value of the actual utilization rate would be less than the expected rate and might even be 100 percent, implying a perfect adjustment of capital stock and capacity to output.

---

than the beginning-of-the-year capacity, so the normal utilization rate would have to be reduced by that percentage to make it comparable to the centered current rates. The net adjustment factor to convert from the normal to the actual equilibrium rate is therefore about 1 percent when output is assumed to grow at 3.5 percent. Of course, the size of the adjustment factor varies positively with the growth rate.

It was argued in Chapter 5 that in an uncertain world businessmen may deliberately err on the side of overutilization of plant and hence that actual utilization rates consistently in excess of 100 percent are not necessarily irrational. On the other hand, there may be some upward bias in actual capacity utilization as measured in this study if businessmen typically build ahead of demand in the sense of attempting an adjustment of optimal capacity to a higher output expected some years hence even though current utilization does not exceed the optimum rate. If independent evidence were available on the determinants of expected output, the extent of such possible bias could be investigated. Barring such evidence, any adjustment in the level of the capacity estimates would be a matter of arbitrary judgment, which I have preferred not to make, since it would not affect the conclusions of this study in any significant way.

The reasons why the conclusions would not be affected were discussed in Chapter 5. The only point that need be added here is that it makes no real difference whether the actual equilibrium utilization rate under steady growth would be 110, 108, 106, or 100 percent, provided one knows which of these it would be for a particular set of assumptions. If the level of each of the projected utilization series were shifted to make the equilibrium rate 100 percent, for example, none of the implications of Table 36 would be altered. The 1956 rate would still be closer to its eventual equilibrium value, the higher the growth rate assumed for potential output. Moreover, the eventual equilibrium value would still be approached in the same time pattern and at the same rate as presently shown. The only difference is that the starting level and intermediate values for each series would be lower in the same proportion as the equilibrium level itself.

Alternative Paths to Potential GNP

The foregoing projections of potential business fixed investment demand were based on the assumption of steady growth along the path of potential GNP during 1956–70. As has already been stressed, however, departures from full employment in previous years will affect investment demand at potential GNP in a given year. This is because investment demand is affected by past events—by lagged output and lagged capital stock—as well as by current output. In view of this fact, it is interesting to explore the investment implications of four alternative paths from actual GNP in 1962 to potential GNP in 1970.

The four paths were chosen to represent a wide range of possible approaches to potential GNP as defined in the medium, or 3.5 percent, projection. All four paths begin from actual output in 1962. Path A assumes a full recovery to potential GNP in 1963 and steady growth along the potential path through 1970. In path B it is assumed that GNP rises at a constant rate from its actual 1962 level to potential GNP in 1966 and follows the potential path thereafter. The path assumed in C shows output growing steadily from its actual level in 1962 to its potential level in 1970. Path D also assumes that potential output is not reached until 1970, but the approach is different from C in that it is assumed that actual output parallels potential between 1962 and 1966 and then rises steadily to equal potential in 1970.

The real investment shares implied by each output path are shown annually for 1963–70 in Table 37. Notice that these are not estimates of investment demand at potential output except for those years in which actual and potential output are assumed to be equal. For other years they show the estimated share of the assumed actual output. It is only for path A that actual output is assumed equal to potential for all years. Indeed, actual is equal to potential in only the last year for paths C and D.

TABLE 37. *Investment Implications of Four Alternative Paths to Potential GNP in 1970*

(Gross Business Fixed Investment as Percent of Real GNP)

Year	Path A (1)	Path B (2)	Path C (3)	Path D (4)
1963	8.9	8.6	8.6	8.6
1964	9.4	8.8	8.6	8.5
1965	9.1	8.9	8.6	8.4
1966	8.9	8.9	8.6	8.4
1967	8.7	8.9	8.6	8.3
1968	8.5	8.7	8.6	8.4
1969	8.4	8.5	8.5	8.6
1970	8.2	8.3	8.4	8.6

Notes: Potential real GNP in 1970 is from medium projection assuming a 3.5 percent growth rate of potential during 1956–70. Path A assumes that realized GNP rises from its actual level in 1962 to the potential level in 1963 and grows along the potential path thereafter. Path B assumes that GNP rises at a constant rate, from its actual level in 1962 to the potential level in 1966, and then moves along the potential growth path until 1970. Path C assumes a constant rate of increase from actual GNP in 1962 to potential GNP in 1970. Path D assumes that actual GNP parallels the path of potential GNP during 1962–66 and then rises at a constant rate to potential GNP in 1970.

The estimates were made in the usual way—accepting the actual 1962 values of output and capital stock as initial conditions and extrapolating the subsequent growth path of capital corresponding to each assumed output path. The same assumptions as before were made about the depreciation rate and coverage adjustment factor.

Path A is included in Table 37 primarily for comparison with the earlier estimates of long-term potential investment demand for 1963–70, which assumed continuous full-employment growth beginning in 1955. Although path A also refers to investment demand at potential output during 1963–70, it accepts past departures from potential during 1956–62 as given and proceeds from there. A comparison of column 1 of Table 37 with column 5 of Table 35 will show that the implicit full-employment investment share is larger under the present recovery assumption than in the earlier projection in every year between 1963 and 1970. Desired stock is exactly the same in both projections from 1964 onward, since the same output is assumed for both after 1963, but the initial gap between desired and actual stock is larger in the recovery model than it would have been had growth occurred steadily along the potential path beginning in 1955. The investment shares for 1964 are substantially different under the two projections—9.4 as compared with 8.7 percent—but the gap between them narrows rapidly in later years owing to the faster approach of actual stock to the same desired level under the recovery assumption.

It is important to observe that even under the immediate-recovery assumption, the implicit real investment share at full employment never rises above 9.4 percent during 1963–70 and that it ranges down to 8.2 by the end of the period. These figures are notably lower than the 10.0 percent share actually attained in 1957, the latest year of approximately full employment.

Path B, in which output is assumed to rise at a constant rate from the 1962 actual to the 1966 potential, was chosen to illustrate a moderately rapid approach to sustained full employment in the years ahead. Path A would have required an increase of 8.9 percent from actual GNP in 1962 to potential in 1963. The average annual rate of output increase required to go from the 1962 actual to the terminal year potential would be 6.2 percent for 1962–64, 5.3 percent for 1962–65, and 4.8 percent for 1962–66. Since the actual increase of real GNP during 1962–63 was only 3.8 percent, however, any one of these approaches would require an acceleration of output growth during the remainder of the period if potential were still to be reached in the same terminal year. Thus the average annual rate of increase necessary to go from actual 1963 output to the 1966 potential would be 5.1 percent instead of the 4.8 percent assumed under path B.

Path B implies a gradual rise in the investment share of assumed actual GNP until 1965–67 and a decline thereafter as GNP moves along the potential path at 3.5 percent a year (column 2). The maximum share is 8.9 percent. By 1970 the estimated share is virtually the same for paths A and B.

The assumption underlying the two remaining paths is more pessimistic than the others: that actual output does not reach potential until 1970. In path C it is assumed that the 1970 potential is approached at a steady rate during 1963–70, whereas D parallels the path of potential during 1963–66 and only then begins to rise more rapidly than potential to meet the latter in 1970. The maximum real investment share is 8.6 percent under either assumption, but there are easily understandable differences in the time pattern of the shares in the two cases.

It is interesting to compare the terminal positions under the four growth paths in order to see how full-employment investment demand in 1970 would be affected by the alternative approaches. The differences are smaller than one might expect. The real estimated investment shares for 1970 range only from 8.2 to 8.6 percent.

Because there is a greater cumulative lag of actual behind desired stock for each successive growth path, the 1970 investment share rises progressively as one moves across the table from A to D. Indeed, desired stock is exactly the same in 1970 for A and B, and it is a lower value for either C or D, rather than the higher level that would tend to increase their investment demand relative to A and B. Thus the investment share is largest in 1970 for path D because it was assumed to be the smallest for that path in the intervening years after 1962, leaving a larger gap between actual and desired stock to be filled in 1970.

Another way to look at the cumulative investment lag implied by the alternative growth paths is to ask by how much plant capacity would increase between 1962 and 1970 under each assumption. Beginning with A the 1962–70 increases in capacity for the alternative paths would be respectively, 38.4, 37.7, 35.8, and 33.9 percent. To put the same point a little differently, the 1970 capacity attained via paths B, C, and D would be respectively, 0.5, 1.9, and 3.2 percent below that reached by path A. Although these differences are not inconsequential, they do not imply that 1970 plant capacity would be greatly affected by moderate departures from full employment in the interim period. Potential output in 1970 would be

TABLE 38. *Projected Capacity Utilization Rates for Alternative Paths to Potential GNP in 1970*

(In percent)

Year	Path A	Path B	Path C	Path D
1963	114	110	109	108
1964	113	111	109	108
1965	112	112	110	108
1966	111	113	110	108
1967	110	112	111	110
1968	110	111	111	111
1969	109	110	111	112
1970	109	110	111	113

Note: Paths A–D are the same as assumed in Table 37.

affected even less, owing to the small elasticity of output with respect to capital for a given labor input. Assuming an elasticity of 0.18 percent, as in Chapter 6, the maximum reduction in potential output in 1970—that which would be realized if path D were followed instead of A—would be 0.5 percent.

A final point of interest concerns the behavior of capacity utilization along each of the alternative growth paths. This is easily studied since each output path implies a corresponding development of capital stock and capacity, from which the implicit utilization rates are readily derived (Table 38).

The abrupt rise to full employment assumed under path A would imply a jump in the utilization rate from 108 percent in 1962 to 114 percent in 1963, after which the rate would fall steadily through the rest of the decade. This steady decline reflects the tendency implied in the investment equation for a gradual approach of capital stock and capacity to a long-term equilibrium relationship with output under steady growth conditions. However, the calculations presented earlier in the chapter indicated that the equilibrium utilization rate for a 3.5 percent growth rate would be 108 percent, so that by 1970 equilibrium would not yet have been reached under the assumed conditions.

Capacity utilization would rise about 1 percent a year along path B until potential output was reached in 1966, by which time it would be well above the equilibrium rate of 108 percent consistent with subsequent growth at 3.5 percent a year. It would therefore decline gradually through the remainder of the decade.

The slow rise of capacity utilization along path C is a reflection of steady growth at an annual rate of 4.3 percent between 1962 and 1970. The rate of 111 percent reached during the late 1960's is the equilibrium value consistent with growth at 4.3 percent, but the rate would necessarily decline after 1970 as the growth rate dropped to its assumed long-term potential of 3.5 percent.

Path D is assumed to parallel potential during 1962–66, and this means that actual output would increase at an annual rate of 3.5 percent during those years. Since the utilization rate was 108 percent in 1962 and since this is the equilibrium value consistent with growth at 3.5 percent a year, there would be no change in utilization through 1966. The utilization rate would increase thereafter, however, as output accelerated to the 1970 potential. Just as in the other examples, a downtrend of utilization would necessarily follow as the actual rate of output growth dropped back to the potential rate after 1970.

Current-Price Estimates

In this section the estimates of real investment demand along the four alternative paths to potential GNP in 1970 are converted to a current-dollar basis. The constant-dollar estimates thus far considered are necessary and sufficient for the study of physical capital requirements corresponding to alternative output assumptions and for the closely related problem of projecting capacity trends. In order to appraise the adequacy of the projected investment demands as offsets to private saving, however, it is necessary to study the ratio of current-dollar investment to current-dollar GNP. The alternative procedure would be to compare deflated saving rates with the real investment shares, but there are serious conceptual difficulties concerning the appropriate deflator for the government surplus or deficit if that approach is used.

As was noted in Chapter 7 in a similar context, the trend of the current-dollar investment shares depends not only on the path of the constant-dollar shares but also on the trend in the ratio of the implicit price indexes for capital goods and GNP. Table 39 shows the consequences of applying three different assumptions about future relative price behavior to the constant-dollar projections for paths A to D. Thus the three current-dollar

TABLE 39. *Alternative Estimates of Current-Dollar Investment Shares Along the Four Paths to Potential GNP in 1970*

(Gross business fixed investment as percent of GNP)

Year	Path A			Path B			Path C			Path D		
	Low	Medium	High	Low	Medium	High	Low	Medium	High	Low	Medium	High
1963	9.3	9.3	9.3	9.0	9.0	9.0	9.0	9.0	9.0	9.0	9.0	9.0
1964	9.8	9.9	10.0	9.2	9.3	9.4	9.0	9.1	9.1	8.9	9.0	9.0
1965	9.5	9.7	9.8	9.3	9.5	9.6	9.0	9.1	9.3	8.7	9.0	9.1
1966	9.3	9.5	9.7	9.3	9.5	9.7	9.0	9.2	9.4	8.7	9.0	9.2
1967	9.1	9.4	9.7	9.3	9.6	9.9	9.0	9.3	9.6	8.6	9.0	9.2
1968	8.9	9.2	9.6	9.1	9.5	9.8	9.0	9.3	9.7	8.7	9.1	9.5
1969	8.7	9.2	9.6	8.9	9.3	9.7	8.9	9.3	9.7	9.0	9.4	9.8
1970	8.5	9.0	9.5	8.6	9.2	9.6	8.8	9.3	9.8	9.0	9.5	10.0

Note: The low projections for each path were made by multiplying the estimated real shares as shown in Table 37 by the constant ratio of the 1963 values of the implicit price indexes for capital goods and GNP. In the medium projections the real shares were multiplied by a relative price ratio which is assumed to increase 0.75 percent a year after 1963, whereas the high projections assume a relative price increase of 1.5 percent a year. Thus the three current-dollar projections for each path assume the same real shares and differ only because of differing assumptions about the behavior of relative prices. The four low (or medium or high) projections, on the other hand, differ only because of the different behavior of the real shares along the four paths and assume the same relative price behavior in each case.

projections for each path are derived from the same real shares for that path as given in Table 37, but the low projection assumes no change in relative prices during 1963–70, whereas the medium and high projections assume annual increases in the relative price ratio of respectively 0.75 and 1.5 percent.

It is evident that the trend of the current-dollar investment share along any real GNP path is quite sensitive to the assumption about relative price changes. Thus in the case of path B, the high projection not only carries the current-dollar investment share to 9.9 percent in 1967, as compared with a maximum of 9.3 percent for the low projection, but also offsets much of the subsequent downtrend in the real share, so that the 1970 value of the high current-dollar projection is a full point above that for the low projection.

In my opinion, the medium projections are the most reasonable of the three alternatives offered for each path in Table 39, and it was on the medium projection for path B that I based my discussion of policy implications in Chapter 1. The low projections seem improbable in view of the long-standing tendency discussed in Chapter 7 for the investment goods implicit price index to rise relative to the GNP deflator. On the other hand, the annual increase of 1.5 percent in the relative price ratio assumed in the high projections also seems improbable. The price ratio did rise at that average rate during 1947–57, but that decade was characterized by exceptional investment demands. The average annual rate of increase for 1929–57 was 1.0 percent and that for 1929–63 was 0.7 percent. The assumption of an annual relative price increase of 0.75 percent underlying the medium projections for 1963–70 is merely one among many reasonable alternatives, of course, but the reader may readily substitute another if he desires, and the resulting current-dollar shares may easily be calculated.[5]

A sizable arbitrary element is admittedly injected into the current-dollar projections because of the necessity of assuming some explicit future trend of relative prices. There is no escaping this dilemma, however, since the constant-dollar projections could not themselves be properly judged in relation to the private saving ratio unless the latter were expressed in real terms, and this last could not be done without making the same sort of explicit assumptions about relative prices (see Appendix A). Under the circumstances, the best that can be done is to investigate the sensitivity of the conclusions to a wide range of alternative price assumptions, as in Table 39. Thus even under what is considered to be an extreme assumption of an annual relative price increase of 1.5 percent, the maximum potential investment share reached along path B in 1967 is only 9.9 percent, as compared with 10.7 percent in 1957, and there is still an implied downtrend in the potential investment ratio of 0.1 percent a year between 1967 and 1970.

[5] The 1963 relative price ratio, which is the starting point for all the alternatives, is given in column 3 of Table 30.

9 / *Is There a Structural Investment Problem?*

A MUCH-DISPUTED policy issue of recent years concerns the relationship between structural unemployment and the over-all unemployment rate. It is sometimes asserted, or implied, that the increased rate of aggregate unemployment since 1957 is due primarily to an increase of structural imbalance—the mismatching of workers with job openings because of race, age, sex, location, education, skills, or other personal characteristics—rather than to a persistent deficiency of aggregate demand. If this were true, it would mean that efforts to reduce aggregate unemployment by aggregative fiscal or monetary policies would be largely self-defeating, tending to raise prices rather than employment and real income. Fortunately a careful examination of the evidence on structural unemployment shows clearly that its over-all incidence has not increased since 1957.[1]

It has recently been suggested, however, that we may be experiencing structural unemployment of capital in the United States.[2] Could this mean that aggregate investment demand is being held down by a mismatching of specific demands with specific capacities instead of by insufficient total demand? In that case, the use of aggregative fiscal or monetary policies to raise the over-all rate of capacity utilization might not induce much additional investment demand, and hence might be considerably less effective than otherwise in raising total demand and output.

It is vital in this connection to distinguish between installed capital and new investment demand. Chronic excess capacity may persist in a depressed industry for many years or even decades, since the process of physical disinvestment can be surprisingly time-consuming even if replacement demand is zero. However, to argue that total investment demand could be depressed

[1] See Chap. 6, note 1.

[2] Benjamin Caplan and Harald Malmgren, "More Than Keynes," *The New Republic* (Dec. 1, 1962), pp. 19–20. The authors do not attribute the recent aggregative investment lag solely to misallocation of capital, however, but cite the secular downtrend in the business capital-output ratio as a primary factor. Their emphasis with regard to structural misallocation of capital appears to be more on its implications for the growth rather than the utilization of potential output.

indefinitely merely by capital misallocation would be to argue that capital funds and capital goods are so specialized that new capital cannot flow into the sectors where it is in short supply even after some years are allowed for adjustment. This is hardly credible.

On the other hand, the idea that a reduction of investment demand in a particular industry can *temporarily* depress the level of aggregate investment demand cannot be lightly dismissed. It implies that new capital is imperfectly mobile, but that is surely a reasonable assumption, given the imperfect foresight and adjustment lags characteristic of an unplanned economy. Moreover, a temporarily uncompensated fall of investment demand in one industry may induce an investment decline in other industries through its feedback effect on national income. But if this last occurs, the other industries are cyclically depressed rather than chronically debilitated, and this in turn implies that a recovery of aggregate demand would induce additional investment demand throughout the system.

Thus there is both a short-run and a long-run aspect to the structural investment problem. The secular aspect would exist even if aggregate investment demand were always sufficient to offset full-employment saving, so that actual GNP always followed the potential path. It would still be true even then that some industries would expand more rapidly than others, for it is an inevitable consequence of economic growth that new products displace the old and new processes alter the relative prices of established products. Possibly the growth rate of potential could be accelerated by fostering a quicker diversion of new capital from the losing to the gaining sectors, and it is certainly conceivable that the composition as well as the growth rate of total output could become an explicit goal of public policy. These purely allocative problems are undeniably important concerns for public policy, but it is crucial that they be clearly distinguished from the short-term or cyclical impact of structural output change on aggregate investment demand. The latter topic will be discussed in this chapter.

To deal adequately with the short-term impact of changes in the industrial composition of investment demand, however, it is necessary to show how individual increases or decreases of investment demand can become generalized through the system. Since I have discussed this topic at length elsewhere,[3] a brief statement of the central points will suffice.

[3] Bert G. Hickman, "Diffusion, Acceleration, and Business Cycles," *American Economic Review* (September 1959), pp. 535–65, and *Growth and Stability of the Postwar Economy* (Brookings Institution, 1960), Chap. 11.

The first point is that a shift in the industrial composition of output can augment or diminish total investment demand at a given level of GNP. This is because either the desired capital-output ratios or adjustment speeds of the gaining and losing industries may be unequal, so that although the output shifts are exactly offsetting, the induced investment changes are not.

Second, if an income-autonomous increase or decrease of aggregate investment demand does occur because of a shift in output composition, the resulting stimulus to national income may react back on all industries and induce a further change of aggregate investment demand in the same direction.

It was shown in Chapter 4 that sizable differences in capital intensities and adjustment speeds do exist among the various industries, so that output shifts may indeed exert a substantial influence over investment demand. A method of measuring the relative importance of the shift factor was developed, and the resulting index was used to investigate the effect of compositional shifts on investment demand during the postwar years in Chapter 7. A brief review of the relevant findings from that chapter will be a useful prelude to further discussion.

First, the postwar downtrend in the aggregate desired capital-output ratio was not due to a decline in the relative importance of industries with high capital-output ratios. To the contrary, unit capital requirements declined in most industrial sectors, but the composition of output shifted in favor of industries with above-average requirements, with the result that aggregate investment demand was augmented, and the aggregate capital-output ratio declined less than it would have with unchanged composition.

Second, the amount by which compositional shifts augmented aggregate gross business fixed investment demand varied considerably during different periods. The maximum stimulus from this source was felt during the first post-Korean business expansion, when the shift index rose to a 1957 peak, indicating a 9 percent investment gain over the amount that would have occurred with an unchanged (1947) output composition. In contrast, the net gain averaged only 3 percent during 1959–62. Thus output shifts, even in recent years, have kept aggregate investment, and hence GNP, higher than it otherwise would be—but by a smaller margin than in the mid-1950's.

But that is not the end of the story. If the outputs of all industries were equally sensitive to changes in national income, the compositional shifts would be determined solely by differential changes in costs or tastes and would therefore be independent of changes in aggregate demand. In fact, however, the observed output shifts are heavily influenced by the differential response of the various industries to changes in the level of aggregate demand. Thus the shift index contains an induced component reflecting the wide swings of product demand in cyclically-sensitive industries as well as an income-autonomous component relating to longer-run changes in output composition. To the extent that the low level of investment demand during recent years reflects the damping effect of inadequate aggregate demand on the cyclically-sensitive industries, an increase of aggregate demand relative to potential would itself tend to augment total investment demand substantially by stimulating these temporarily depressed industries.

There is good reason to believe that this last reading of recent experience is the correct one. The decline in the shift index from the 1957 peak was concentrated in the durable manufactures sector,[4] and the outputs of most durable goods industries are known to be highly elastic to changes in GNP. In contrast, the outputs of most nonmanufacturing industries are rather insensitive to changes in aggregate demand, and the investment gains due to compositional shifts in that sector remained close to the previous level during 1959–62. The implication of these observations is that the decline in the contribution of output shifts to aggregate investment after the 1954–57 expansion was largely the result rather than the cause of the shortfall of aggregate demand at potential output. Some additional evidence on this point is given in the next section.

Induced Output Shifts and Investment Demand

Table 40 presents the results of a rough attempt to isolate the influence of changes in aggregate demand from other determinants of output changes

[4] The shift indexes for gross investment in the three major divisions are as follows:

	1956	1957	1958	1959	1960	1961	1962
Durable manufactures	112	109	88	83	87	86	89
Nondurable manufactures	103	104	101	106	101	102	105
Nonmanufacturing industries	108	111	119	111	108	110	107

For complete industry detail, see Chap. 4, Table 19.

TABLE 40. *Industry Output Regression Results*

Industry or Sector	Regression Coefficients			Standard Errors			$\overline{R}^2$	*SCT*
	GNP-FED (a_2) (1)	FED (a_3) (2)	*T* (a_4) (3)	GNP-FED (a_2) (4)	FED (a_3) (5)	*T* (a_4) (6)	(7)	(8)
Major Sectors								
Manufacturing	1.683**	.1530**	−.0116**	.1901	.0191	.0028	.990	1.752
Railroads	2.325**	.0853	−.0356**	.5330	.0535	.0079	.541	1.470
Nonrail transportation	1.593**	.1330**	−.0088	.4202	.0422	.0062	.957	.837
Public utilities	.9797**	.1237**	.0220**	.2743	.0276	.0041	.996	.784
Communications	.3795	−.0090	.0229**	.2804	.0282	.0042	.993	1.260
Commercial and other	.7804**	.0505**	.0013	.0920	.0092	.0014	.997	1.965
Farming	.3020	.0002	.0020	.3960	.0398	.0059	.768	1.921
Manufacturing Subsectors								
Primary metals	3.966**	.2782**	−.0574**	.3331	.0335	.0049	.928	2.528
Machinery	2.318**	.3010**	−.0226**	.5520	.0554	.0082	.935	.670
Motor vehicles	3.836**	.0821	−.0408*	1.007	.1012	.0150	.784	1.767
Nonautomotive transportation equipment	1.501	1.153**	.0071	1.965	.1973	.0292	.924	.554
Stone, clay, and glass	2.0000**	.1488**	−.0159*	.4028	.0405	.0060	.956	1.355
Other durables	1.401**	.1461**	−.0088	.2882	.0290	.0043	.972	1.766
Food and beverages	.1617	−.0305	.0084**	.1619	.0163	.0024	.982	1.240
Textiles	1.124*	−.0059	−.0102	.4628	.0465	.0069	.676	1.419
Paper	1.497**	.0419	−.0021	.2249	.0226	.0033	.991	2.703
Chemicals	1.601**	.1154**	.0058	.1882	.0189	.0028	.997	1.372
Petroleum and coal	1.347**	.2000**	−.0096*	.2437	.0245	.0036	.979	1.451
Rubber	1.764**	.0508	−.0118	.5340	.0536	.0079	.911	1.000
Other nondurables	.3578	−.0371	.0076	.2324	.0233	.0035	.974	1.185

* Significant at 0.05 level.
** Significant at 0.01 level.
One-tail test for a_2 and two-tail for other coefficients.

in each industry. Regressions of the following form were fitted for each of the 19 industries and for total manufacturing during 1947–62:

$$\log Y = \log a_1 + a_2 \log (\text{GNP-FED}) + a_3 \log \text{FED} + a_4 T, \quad (9.1)$$

where Y is the output of the given industry, GNP and FED are respectively gross national product and federal government expenditures on goods and services in 1954 dollars, and T is a time trend. Except for state and local spending, the variable (GNP-FED) represents privately-purchased GNP, and it will be called private GNP for convenience in the following discussion. Since the regression is fitted in logarithmic form, a_2 and a_3 are estimates respectively of the elasticity of response of industry output to changes in private GNP and federal expenditure, and a_4 is an exponential trend rate.

Although a_2 is an estimate of the percentage change in industry output that accompanies a change of 1 percent in private GNP, it is not an income-elasticity as that concept is usually defined. The output of a particular industry responds to changes in real national income in a proportion that depends not only on the income-elasticity of demand for the final products to which the industry contributes, but also on the elasticity of the derived demands that intervene at each level of production and distribution. Fluctuations in manufacturing production in particular are greatly augmented by induced changes in inventory investment over the course of the business cycle. And induced changes in fixed investment demand tend also to amplify cyclical fluctuations in the durable goods industries.

Thus the a_2 coefficients differ among industries primarily because of technical and economic factors governing the behavior of derived demands rather than because of differences in the income-elasticities of demand for the consumer items and state and local activities ultimately served by the various producing sectors. This proposition emerges rather clearly from a perusal of the first column of Table 40. As expected, the elasticity estimates show that manufacturing production as a whole responds more than proportionally to a change in private GNP. This was true also of the transportation industries, which are heavily engaged, of course, in hauling materials and goods and hence are sensitive to changes in industrial production. In contrast, the public utility, communications, commercial and other, and farm sectors show a less-than-proportional response to private GNP.

The distribution of elasticities among manufacturing industries is also in line with expectations. The largest values by far are found in the durable goods sector, although the elasticities for most nondurable industries are above unity. The exceptions are food and beverages and miscellaneous nondurables, which are quite inelastic to changes in private GNP.

Federal expenditure was included as a separate variable in the regressions because it was a clearly identifiable and quantitatively important source of variation in the composition of total demand during 1947–62. It will be seen from column 2 of Table 40 that large differences exist among the various industries in their sensitivity to changes in federal purchases of goods and services. The wide fluctuations in federal spending since World War II have been due overwhelmingly to changes in expenditures for national defense, and some industries are more heavily dependent on defense business than others. This is true particularly of "other transportation equipment" (aircraft and missiles), but column 2 shows that primary metals, machinery, stone, clay, and glass, "other durables," chemicals, petroleum and coal, nonrail transportation, and public utilities are also stimulated considerably by rising defense expenditures. Conversely, the production of manufactured food and beverages, textiles, "other nondurables," and communications services appears to be depressed when defense expenditures increase, presumably because of the diversion of resources to more essential uses.[5]

Needless to say, the inclusion of total federal spending in the regressions is a crude way to recognize the differential impact of defense spending. But it appears to be a serviceable device that is better than ignoring the problem altogether in the absence of a full-scale investigation of the relations between specific industry outputs and specific items in the final bill of goods.[6]

The time variable is a catch-all term to reflect the net influence of all omitted factors on output change in the particular industry, under the assumption that they operated systematically throughout 1947–62. Whether the industry's output rises or falls relative to GNP over a given time span

[5] These industries would probably not be affected so adversely by an expansion of defense expenditure at a time when unemployed resources were plentiful, but that was not the situation during most of the period for which the regressions were fitted.

[6] It should be noted that the a_3 coefficients relate federal expenditure to the total output of a given industry, rather than to that portion of the industry's production that is directly or indirectly traceable to government demand for final output. That is why the values of a_3 are so much smaller than those of a_2. Unless a very large fraction of the industry's total output is for defense purposes, as in aircraft production, a 1 percent change in federal expenditure cannot be expected to have nearly the same effect on the industry's total output as would a 1 percent change in private GNP.

depends, of course, on the balance between the trend term and the GNP variables. This point is illustrated in Table 41.

The table shows the calculated annual output increase in each industry that would correspond to a 3.5 percent rate of increase of real GNP, assuming that federal spending increased at the same rate as private spending. For each industry, the figure in column 1 is the product of the elasticity coefficient of private GNP and the assumed rate of increase of 3.5

TABLE 41. *Estimated Industry Output Increases Per Annum Assuming a 3.5 Percent Per Annum Increase of GNP*

Industry or Sector	Percentage Increase Attributed to:			
	Private GNP (1)	Federal Spending (2)	Other Factors (3)	All Sources (4)
Major Sectors				
Manufacturing	5.89	.54	−2.67	3.76
Railroads	8.14	.30	−8.20	.24
Nonrail transportation	5.58	.47	−2.03	4.01
Public utilities	3.43	.43	5.06	8.92
Communications	1.33	−.03	5.27	6.60
Commercial and other	2.73	.18	.30	3.21
Farming	1.06	0	.46	1.52
Manufacturing Industries				
Primary metals	13.88	.97	−13.22	1.64
Machinery	8.11	1.05	−5.30	3.87
Motor vehicles	13.43	.29	−9.39	4.32
Nonautomotive transportation equipment	5.25	4.04	1.63	10.92
Stone, clay, and glass	7.00	.52	−3.66	3.86
Other durables	4.90	.51	−2.03	3.38
Food and beverages	0.57	−.11	1.93	2.50
Textiles	3.93	−.02	−2.35	1.58
Paper	5.24	.15	−.48	4.91
Chemicals	5.60	.40	1.34	7.35
Petroleum and coal	4.71	.70	−2.21	3.20
Rubber	6.17	.20	−2.72	3.66
Other nondurables	1.25	−.13	1.75	3.00

Note: The contribution of federal spending was set at zero in computing the total increase from all sources for food and beverages, textiles, other nondurables, and communications, on the assumption that these industries would not be absolutely depressed by an expansion of federal spending when unemployed resources were available. Since the output regressions were fitted in common instead of natural logarithms, the compound interest rate in column 3 of this table is 2.3026 times the trend coefficient shown in column 3 of Table 40.

percent. Column 2 gives the corresponding product for federal spending, and column 3 shows the annual percentage gain or loss of industry output as reflected in the trend term. The net rate of increase of industry output under the assumed conditions is the sum of these three columns and is given in column 4.

The industries with the largest rates of output increase under the assumed conditions include other transportation equipment, chemicals, public utilities, and communications. The rate of increase of other transportation equipment is strongly influenced by federal spending, however, and it would be much lower if the latter were assumed to be constant or to increase considerably less rapidly than GNP. Chemicals output is rather insensitive to federal spending, but it is fairly responsive to changes in the rate of increase of private GNP. In contrast, public utilities and communications have such strong independent growth trends that moderate variations in the rate of increase of aggregate demand would have little effect on them.

With regard to the industries showing the smallest rates of increase, the regressions imply that primary metals and railroads would benefit considerably from an acceleration of aggregate demand, whereas farm and textile production would not.

It is apparent, then, that the various industries would be unevenly affected by a speed-up of aggregate demand in the next few years. This is a relative proposition, however, and it is important to stress that output would rise faster in *all* industries in response to an acceleration of aggregate demand, so that investment demand would be increased everywhere. Furthermore, the calculations shown in Table 42 indicate that the compositional shifts induced by an acceleration of aggregate output would augment the expansion of aggregate investment demand.

The first column of the table shows the estimated output increments for each industry corresponding to a 3.5 percent increase of GNP as derived in Table 41. Column 2 shows similar estimates for a 4.5 percent increase of GNP. The investment factors given in column 3 are the product of the capacity output and the desired long-term marginal capital-output ratio for each industry in 1960.[7] They may be used to estimate the dollar amount

[7] The marginal capital output ratios are from Table 13. The capacity estimates are explained in Chapter 5. Similar investment factors were used as weights for variant III of the aggregative utilization estimates shown in Table 22, except that the weights in that case were averaged for 1950 and 1960.

TABLE 42. *Estimated Investment Effects of Output Shifts for Two Different Rates of Increase of Aggregate Demand*

Industry	Estimated output increases (in percent) for GNP increase of:		Investment factor (in billions of 1954 dollars)	Estimated net investment (in billions of 1954 dollars): With shifts at		Without shifts at		Difference at	
	3.5% (1)	4.5% (2)	(3)	3.5% (4)	4.5% (5)	3.5% (6)	4.5% (7)	3.5% (8)	4.5% (9)
Primary metals	*1.64*	*5.88*	13.55	.22	.80	.47	.61	−.25	.19
Machinery	*3.87*	*6.49*	7.77	.30	.50	.27	.35	.03	.15
Motor vehicles	*4.32*	*8.24*	6.17	.27	.51	.22	.28	.05	.23
Nonautomotive transportation equipment	*10.92*	*13.57*	3.50	.38	.47	.12	.16	.26	.31
Stone, clay, and glass	*3.86*	*6.01*	3.60	.14	.22	.13	.16	.01	.06
Other durables	*3.38*	*4.93*	8.15	.28	.40	.28	.37	0	.03
Food and beverages	*2.50*	*2.66*	6.26	.16	.17	.22	.28	−.06	−.11
Textiles	*1.58*	*2.71*	4.32	.07	.12	.15	.19	−.08	−.07
Paper	*4.91*	*6.45*	4.35	.21	.28	.15	.20	.06	.08
Chemicals	*7.35*	*9.07*	8.96	.66	.81	.31	.40	.35	.41
Petroleum and coal	*3.20*	*4.75*	27.43	.88	1.30	.96	1.23	−.08	.07
Rubber	*3.66*	*5.48*	1.15	.04	.06	.04	.05	0	.01
Other nondurables	*3.00*	*3.36*	3.52	.11	.12	.12	.16	−.01	−.04
Railroads	*0.24*	*2.65*	14.05	.03	.37	.49	.63	.46	−.26
Nonrail transportation	*4.01*	*5.74*	10.25	.41	.59	.36	−.46	.05	.13
Public utilities	*8.92*	*10.02*	34.65	3.09	3.47	1.21	1.56	1.88	1.91
Communications	*6.60*	*6.98*	16.54	1.09	1.15	.58	.74	.51	.41
Commercial and other	*3.21*	*4.04*	92.09	2.96	3.72	3.22	4.14	−.26	−.42
Farming	*1.52*	*1.82*	55.43	.84	1.01	1.94	2.49	−1.10	−1.48
Total				12.14	16.07	11.24	14.46	.90	1.61

Note: See text for methods and assumptions underlying this table.

of net investment corresponding to a given percentage increase of output, on the assumption that the latter is regarded as a permanent increase calling for an equal expansion of capacity. This is in accord with the formula:

$$\Delta K = \left(\frac{\Delta Y}{Y}\right)(Y)\left(\frac{\Delta K}{\Delta Y}\right), \tag{9.2}$$

where the first term on the right hand side is the percentage increase of output or desired capacity and the product of the other terms is the investment factor.

Columns 4 and 5 show the estimated amounts of net investment in each industry corresponding to the output increases in columns 1 and 2. Their sums indicate that net investment would total about $12.1 billion (at 1954 prices) for a GNP increase of 3.5 percent and $16.1 billion for an increase of 4.5 percent, after taking account of the shifts in output composition for either rate of increase. In contrast, columns 6 and 7 show how much each industry would invest if its output increased at the same rate as GNP; that is, at either 3.5 or 4.5 percent. It will be seen that aggregate net investment with unchanged composition is estimated at $11.2 billion for a 3.5 percent increase of GNP, as compared with $12.1 billion when output shifts are included. Similarly compositional shifts are estimated to increase total investment from $14.5 to $16.1 billion for a 4.5 percent rise in GNP. Thus for an over-all output increase of 3.5 percent, compositional shifts would augment net investment by $0.90 billion, or by 8 percent of the $11.2 billion investment which would be forthcoming with unchanged composition. The corresponding figures for an aggregate output increase of 4.5 percent are $1.61 billion and 11 percent.

It is clear from these calculations that output shifts would augment investment demand whether GNP rose 3.5 or 4.5 percent. The calculations also confirm the proposition, however, that an acceleration of aggregate demand would enhance the contribution of output shifts to investment demand by inducing large output increases in the cyclically-sensitive industries. The industrial distribution of the gains and losses of investment demand from output shifts is given for each of the assumed GNP increases in columns 8 and 9. Column 8, for example, shows for each industry the difference between the estimated amount of net investment with and without output shifts (column 4 minus column 6) with a 3.5 percent increase of GNP, and column 9 gives the same information for a 4.5 percent increase. A comparison of the two columns reveals that the largest relative investment gains from an acceleration of GNP would be found in primary metals, motor vehicles, petroleum and coal, and railroads, whereas the largest relative losses would be in the farm and commercial and other sectors.

The preceding results must be qualified in several respects if the reader is to judge them properly. First, as to the output regressions, it has already been emphasized that the estimated elasticities of industry output with respect to aggregate demand have a strong cyclical component. They may provide a reasonable approximation to the sensitivity of industry response to year-to-year variations in aggregate demand on the order of those experienced during 1947–62, but they do not measure the long-term elasticity of industry output under conditions of steady growth of GNP. Moreover, even if the net influence of all variables omitted from an output regression was accurately reflected by the trend term during the period of fit, which is obviously questionable, extrapolation of the trend would imply the unverified assumption that the omitted factors will remain constant or experience only offsetting changes in the future. Furthermore, by no means all of the regression coefficients are statistically significant, as is apparent from Table 40, so that inferences about the relative importance of the independent variables is subject to substantial error in a number of industries. Finally, the regressions are not structural relationships and do not "explain" the behavior of industry output in any fundamental sense. A systematic structural analysis of the factors determining the path of output in each industry would be a formidable research undertaking in itself and cannot be attempted here.

Several features of the method by which the amount of investment demand was inferred for a given output increase also require comment. First, the investment factor was based on the long-term marginal capital-output ratio for each industry and hence refers to the total amount of net investment that would be generated over a long span of years by a permanent output increase. Second, in most industries two or three years would have to pass before the full amount of the output increase is regarded as permanent. As was explained more fully in Chapter 4, for both of these reasons the response of net investment during the first few years following an output increase would be considerably smaller than was indicated in Table 42. Finally, the calculations refer only to net investment, and the relative influence of output shifts on gross investment would be considerably smaller, again as explained in Chapter 4.

These limitations with respect to the investment portion of the analysis could be overcome by using a series of annual output projections for each industry as inputs into the basic investment regressions that were developed in Chapter 3. This is done for major sectors in the next section, but it was decided not to attempt such investment projections for individual manufacturing industries because of the poor forecasting record of several of these equations for 1961–62 (see Chapter 3).

Despite the foregoing qualifications, it is believed that the broad inferences already drawn from the output regressions are valid. That is, the decline in the relative importance of output shifts as a source of investment demand was more a symptom than a cause of the failure of aggregate demand to reach potential output after 1957. An autonomous increase of aggregate demand achieved by fiscal or monetary stimuli would have induced additional investment demand throughout the economy, with especially large increases in some of the very industries where output and investment were lagging the most, including primary metals, petroleum and coal, and railroads (Tables 18 and 19).

Conditional Investment Projections for Major Sectors

Annual projections of the investment response to a specified path of real GNP during 1963–66 are presented below for seven important sectors of the economy. In making the projections, real GNP was assumed to increase at an annual rate of 3.8 percent in 1962–63 and 5.1 percent in 1963–66. These increases would return actual GNP to its potential level in 1966, where potential is based on a 3.5 percent growth rate from the 1955 actual. The assumed path therefore corresponds to the first leg of projection B in Chapter 8, with the minor modification that the actual increase of GNP during 1962–63 is used in the present estimates, so that the average annual increase required during 1963–66 to reach potential in 1966 becomes 5.1 instead of the 4.8 percent that would have sufficed under steady growth from 1962 actual to 1966 potential.

The acceleration of aggregate demand assumed in these projections could be initiated by any income-autonomous increase of expenditure. An example in point is the tax reduction which became effective in March 1964 and which was estimated by the Council of Economic Advisers to produce an initial injection of over $9 billion of consumption expenditure into the income stream.[8] It is impossible to trace the sequential interaction among the induced increases of income, consumption, and investment that will follow on this initial injection without specifying a complete econometric model of the economy. All that can be accomplished here is to estimate the investment response to the specified path of GNP, and even this must be done without explicit attention to the feedbacks between investment demand and GNP. Whether the assumed GNP path is actually achieved, of course, depends not only on the magnitude of the investment response which it would induce but also on the behavior of private saving and the government surplus or deficit (see Chapter 6). This means that the investment extrapolations are necessarily conditional projections rather than forecasts.

Once the path of GNP was specified, the next step was to calculate the corresponding output path in each major sector from the regressions given in Table 40. In making these calculations it was assumed that federal expenditures would increase at the same rate as private GNP. The output projections were then used to extrapolate the actual 1962 outputs through 1966.

Next the extrapolated output variables were used as inputs to the investment equations in order to project the course of net capital stock in each sector during 1963–66. The investment regressions for the nonrail transportation, communications, commercial and other, and farming sectors contain relative price terms, and these were simply held constant during the projection period. Because of the suspicions advanced earlier about the reversal of the curvilinear trend in the commercial and other equation after 1960, the trend terms were suppressed in the projection for that sector.[9]

Finally, replacement investment was estimated as a constant percentage of net capital stock in all years, using the 1962 depreciation rate for each industry.

Table 43 contains the end results of these efforts in the form of output and investment projections for the seven major sectors during 1963–66. The corresponding figures for 1962 are included to serve as benchmarks. Section A shows the actual 1962 output of each industry and the projected

[8] *Economic Report of the President* (January 1964), p. 171.

[9] See the discussion in Chapter 5. If the trend terms were retained in the projection, commercial and other investment would rise more rapidly than is shown in Table 42 and by 1966 would approach $11 billion instead of $10 billion.

TABLE 43. *Conditional Projections of Industry Output, Investment, and Capacity Utilization Under the Assumption of Recovery of GNP to Potential Between 1962 and 1966*

Year	Manu-facturing (1)	Rail-roads (2)	Nonrail trans-portation (3)	Public utilities (4)	Com-munica-tions (5)	Com-mercial and other (6)	Farming (7)	All Indus-tries (8)
				A. Output (in billions of 1954 dollars)				
1962	151.0	8.5	14.5	15.6	10.9	150.1	21.9	372.5
1963	157.3	8.6	15.2	17.1	11.6	155.4	22.3	387.5
1964	168.2	9.0	16.2	19.0	12.5	162.7	22.8	410.4
1965	179.8	9.5	17.4	21.1	13.5	170.5	23.2	435.0
1966	192.1	9.9	18.6	23.4	14.6	178.5	23.7	460.8
Percentage increase 1962–66	*27*	*16*	*28*	*50*	*34*	*19*	*8*	*24*
				B. Gross Investment Expenditure (in billions of 1954 dollars)				
1962	12.10	.83	1.92	4.51	3.19	7.90	3.86	34.31
1963	13.04	.86	1.96	4.71	3.70	8.28	3.98	36.53
1964	13.28	.91	2.03	5.03	3.81	8.90	4.15	38.11
1965	14.09	1.06	2.12	5.66	4.18	9.46	4.31	40.88
1966	14.65	1.12	2.20	6.28	4.55	10.00	4.48	43.28
Percentage increase 1962–66	*21*	*35*	*15*	*39*	*43*	*27*	*16*	*26*
				C. Capacity Utilization (percent)				
1962	*107*	*91*	*113*	*116*	*113*	*115*	*106*	*108*
1963	*106*	*91*	*113*	*119*	*113*	*115*	*107*	*110*
1964	*108*	*94*	*114*	*122*	*113*	*116*	*108*	*112*
1965	*109*	*98*	*115*	*125*	*114*	*118*	*109*	*113*
1966	*109*	*100*	*115*	*127*	*114*	*119*	*110*	*114*
Percentage increase 1962–66	*2*	*10*	*2*	*10*	*1*	*3*	*4*	*6*

outputs for 1963–66. The projections of gross investment expenditures are given in Section B, whereas Section C contains the projected capacity utilization rates. The figures for aggregate activity shown in the last column of the table are summations of the industry projections.

The projected output increases between 1962 and 1966 range from 8 percent in farming to 50 percent for public utilities. The increase for all industries together is 24 percent, with below-average gains projected for farming, railroads, and commercial and other enterprises and above-average increases for manufacturing, nonrail transportation, public utilities, and communications.

As for gross investment, the largest projected percentage increases are found in public utilities, communications, and railroads, whereas the smallest are in manufacturing, nonrail transportation, and farming. The percentage increase for the commercial and other sector is about equal to the average for all industries.

The above-average investment increases for public utilities and communications parallel their above-average output gains and hence reflect the powerful independent growth trends in those industries. The sizable investment gain for railroads, however, would be achieved despite a below-average output gain. The reason is that the high cyclical response of railroad output to the aggregate demand increase would slow the long-term relative output decline of the industry and substantially diminish its rate of net disinvestment.

Capacity utilization would increase universally under the postulated conditions, but again at an uneven rate among industries. The largest utilization increases would be in railroads and public utilities, and the smallest would be found in communications, manufacturing, and nonrail transportation.

The projected utilization trends are affected both by the degree of acceleration of output growth as compared with recent years and by the speed of adjustment of capacity to the new output trend. The substantial rise in railroad utilization is due primarily to the fact that the projected output increase represents an actual reversal of the recent downtrend in railroad output. In contrast, the pronounced rise in the utilization rate for public utilities is influenced by the slow response of expected output to actual output increases in that industry as well as by the considerable acceleration of growth of output in response to the postulated acceleration of aggregate demand. Communications is an example of an industry in which little output growth acceleration would be forthcoming from the acceleration of aggregate demand (Table 40). Consequently, even though the projected rate of increase of communications output is next to the highest in the group, capacity would continue to adjust quickly to the rise in output, and the operating rates would remain approximately constant.

Let us turn for a moment to the aggregative implications of these industry projections. If the individual investment projections are summed as in column 8 of Table 43, they indicate a total gross investment of $34.3 billion in 1962. But actual aggregate investment amounted to only $32.9 billion in 1962 (Table B-1). The consensus of the industry investment projections exceeds this figure by about $1.4 billion because of the general tendency for the equations to overpredict realized investment in 1962 (Chapter 3). It appears likely that the projected investment aggregates for 1963–66 shown in Table 43 are also overstated by about the same amount.

This judgment is based on a comparison of the investment totals in column 8 with corresponding projections derived from the aggregative investment equation under the same assumption about the behavior of aggregate output. That is, the *output* sums shown in column 8 of Table 43 were used as inputs in the aggregative equation to project aggregate investment. These projected values compare as follows with those based on the industry consensus (in billions of 1954 dollars):

Source	1962	1963	1964	1965	1966
Industry consensus	34.3	36.5	38.1	40.9	43.3
Aggregate equation	32.0	34.0	36.0	38.7	41.1
Difference	2.3	2.5	2.1	2.2	2.2

Notice that the projection by consensus is higher in every year, but by an approximately constant amount. At the very least this means that the predictive bias of the set of major equations relative to the aggregative equation is constant over the observed range of extrapolation. It seems reasonable to assume that the bias would also be constant relative to the investment that would actually be realized along the postulated GNP path.

The conclusion reached from all this is that the trend of aggregate investment as shown in column 8 is projected with reasonable accuracy even though its level is overestimated in every year. Because of the possibility of offsetting errors, it does not necessarily follow that the individual industry trends are projected with comparable accuracy, however. All that is certain is that the known degree of overstatement of gross investment in 1962 varied considerably from industry to industry (in billions of 1954 dollars):

Industry	Predicted Investment (Table 43) (1)	Realized Investment (Table B-1) (2)	(1)–(2) (3)
Manufacturing	12.10	12.20	–.10
Railroads	.83	.70	.13
Nonrail transportation	1.92	1.69	.23
Public utilities	4.51	4.20	.31
Communications	3.19	2.82	.37
Commercial and other	7.90	7.52	.38
Farming	3.86	3.72	.14

Manufacturing investment was underestimated, whereas the degree of overestimation was relatively largest for railroads and absolutely largest for the commercial and other sector. Provided the individual trends are accurately estimated, approximately the same absolute differences between the projected and realized values of investment would be expected in the various industries during 1963–66.

It may be concluded from the foregoing analysis that the sectoral investment projections make aggregative sense after allowing for the difference in level between the predictions by aggregative equation and industry consensus. It is also found that the projection of aggregate capacity utilization rates (in percent) derived from the industry consensus is similar to that based on the aggregate equation:

Source	1962	1963	1964	1965	1966
Industry consensus	108	110	112	113	114
Aggregate equation	108	109	111	113	114

Thus the industry projections form a satisfactory set insofar as their own internal consistency is concerned.[10]

Conclusions

According to projection B of the preceding chapter, the constant-dollar share of business fixed investment in GNP would increase from 8.6 percent in 1962 to 8.9 percent in 1966 if aggregate output recovered to its estimated potential by the latter year. Neither the conditional investment projections for major sectors nor the analysis of the causes and implications of recent output shifts in the present chapter has suggested that the earlier aggregative projection was unduly optimistic. Although it is true that the parameters of the aggregate equation implicitly reflect the favorable influence of compositional shifts on the aggregate investment-output relation-

[10] The reader may recall that the aggregate equation yielded a slightly different projection of capacity utilization along path B in the preceding chapter (see Table 38). The discrepancy is due to the fact that the aggregate output of the covered sectors was assumed to rise less rapidly in the former projection than is shown by the consensus of industry outputs in Table 43.

ship during the postwar period (see Chapter 7), a direct examination of the industry detail for recent years has uncovered no evidence that such shifts have lost their potency as an independent investment stimulus. Instead, the post-1957 decline in the relative contribution of output shifts to investment demand appears to have been induced largely by the failure of aggregate demand to return to potential after the 1958 recession.

Unfortunately it cannot be concluded that income-autonomous compositional shifts must always favor investment demand as much as they did in 1949–62—or even that they must continue to do so in the near future. This question was actually begged in the sectoral investment projections for 1963–66, since the underlying output extrapolations were based on the assumption that the independent growth trends in the output regressions for 1949–62 would continue at undiminished rates during 1963–66. If instead the strong growth trend in a key investment sector such as public utilities or communications should weaken substantially, much of the independent support for aggregate investment demand at a given level or growth rate of GNP would be lost unless or until some other fast-growing and capital-intensive sector took its place. The reverse might also occur, of course, but in either event the resulting change in the aggregate investment-GNP relationship could be offset by appropriate fiscal or monetary actions and would pose no insuperable barrier to the achievement of full employment without inflation. In this sense, the cyclical or demand aspect of the structural investment problem is simply an additional complication to the process of determining the appropriate size and timing of policy measures to maintain full employment in future years.

APPENDIXES

APPENDIX A / *How Critical Are the Assumptions?*

THE PRINCIPAL FINDING of Chapters 6 and 7 was that the failure of aggregate effective demand to grow along a full-employment path since the mid-fifties is traceable largely to a downtrend in the implicit share of business fixed investment demand at potential GNP, together with the failure to offset that downtrend by expansionary fiscal or monetary policies. The principal implication of Chapter 8 is that the same problem will face us in future years unless the downtrend in the business fixed investment share at potential output is somehow reversed or offset by policy actions or some independent change in saving rates or other investment demands. These conclusions hinge on the twofold assumption that the downtrend in the desired capital-output ratio has been correctly measured and is likely to continue at the same rate as in the recent past. The purpose of this appendix is to examine the validity of this crucial assumption from several viewpoints.

The Secular Downtrend in the Capital-Output Ratio

The investment regressions used in this study were fitted only to the postwar data. The question immediately arises as to whether the postwar decline in the desired capital-output ratio is a prolongation of a past trend or a new departure. One can have more confidence in projecting a long-term trend into the future than would be true of a tendency which had been manifest for a mere 10 or 15 years.

The ratio of the net stock of business plant and equipment to the gross private domestic product is plotted annually for 1890–1960 in the upper panel of Chart A-I. Both stock and output are measured in 1929 prices. The data are taken from John W. Kendrick's productivity study, and Kendrick in turn leaned heavily on the work of Raymond Goldsmith for the stock estimates and Simon Kuznets and the Department of Commerce for the GNP estimates.[1] Capital stock is esti-

[1] John W. Kendrick, *Productivity Trends in the United States* (Princeton Univ. Press, 1961). The net stock figures are the sum of equipment stocks and nonresidential structures for the private domestic economy as given in Kendrick's Table A-XVI, except that

CHART A-I. *Ratios of Business Fixed Investment and Capital to Gross Private Domestic Product, 1890–1960*

(In billions of 1929 dollars)

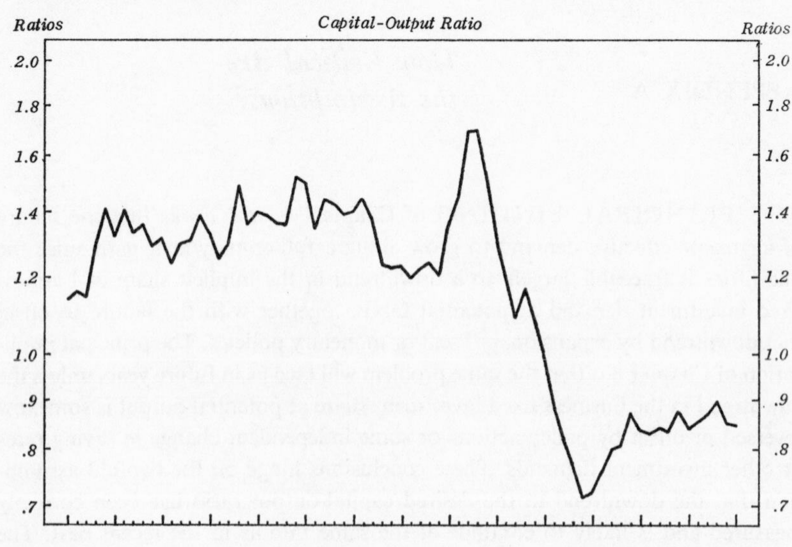

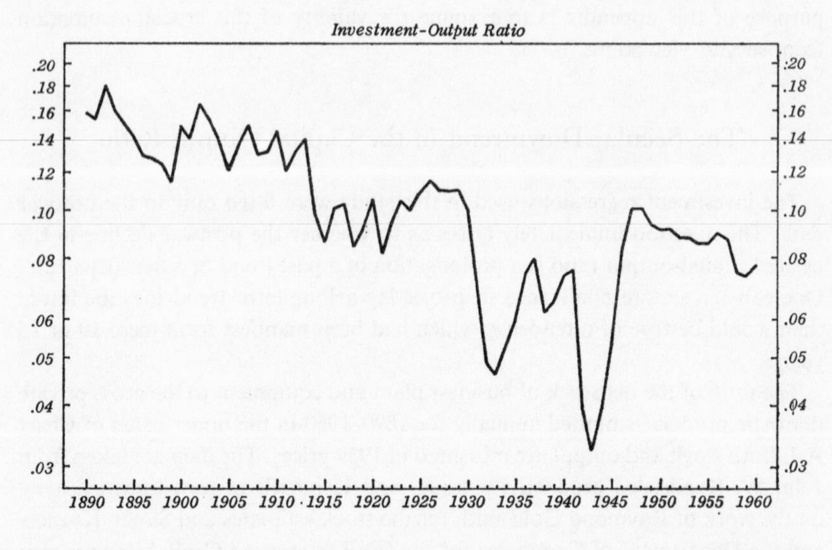

See text footnote [1] for source.

mated by the perpetual inventory method. Depreciation is estimated according to the straight-line formula and is based on useful lives approximating those of *Bulletin F* of the United States Treasury Department. Capital stock is measured exclusive of inventories, government capital, and residential structures. Privately-produced GNP excludes the product of general government employees. The estimates of stock and output are therefore reasonably close to the concepts used in the present study.

The capital-output ratio followed an ascending path from the early 1890's until World War I and a descending course thereafter. This secular rise and fall in unit fixed capital requirements stands out clearly despite the marked fluctuations occasioned by cyclical swings in output, including especially the grossly abnormal spurt in the ratio during the Great Depression. The same pattern of secular increase until about World War I and of secular decline thereafter appears in Daniel Creamer's estimates of the manufacturing capital-output ratio, though not in Melville Ulmer's estimates for the regulated industries.[2]

---

the estimates for structures were adjusted to exclude the real value of land, which Kendrick had estimated by applying a constant land-structure ratio to the real value of structures (p. 276). After 1953 the Kendrick series was extrapolated by the OBE estimates of net capital stock shown in column 3 of Table A-1. For 1890–1928 gross private business fixed investment is from Kendrick's Table A-IIa, column 7, minus estimates of residential construction from Leo Grebler, David M. Blank, and Louis Winnick, *Capital Formation in Residential Real Estate* (National Bureau of Economic Research, 1956), Table B-6. In 1929 and later years the investment data are the sum of producers' durable equipment and other new construction as given in the U. S. Department of Commerce GNP accounts, but converted to 1929 prices. Gross private domestic product for 1890–1944 is from Kendrick's Table A-III and is equal to GNP minus net factor income from abroad and government product. The estimates were extended through 1960 by the most recent revision of the Commerce GNP accounts.

[2] Daniel Creamer, *Capital and Output Trends in Manufacturing Industries, 1880–1948*, Occasional Paper 41 (National Bureau of Economic Research, 1954) Chap. 3; and Melville Ulmer, *Capital in Transportation, Communications, and Public Utilities: Its Formation and Financing* (National Bureau of Economic Research, 1960), Chap. 4. Paul S. Anderson has questioned at least the amplitude of the secular rise and fall of the manufacturing capital-output ratio as estimated by Creamer from data of the U. S. Bureau of the Census on the grounds that "The rise after 1879 appears to have resulted from more complete reporting of capital assets in successive censuses. The fall after 1919 seems to be explained largely by the bookkeeping procedure of subtracting annual depreciation from the cost prices of capital assets which began on a wide scale with the imposition of the federal corporate income tax." ("The Apparent Decline in Capital-Output Ratios," *Quarterly Journal of Economics* [November 1961], pp. 615–34.) Estimates of net business fixed capital (Goldsmith-Kendrick) and aggregate gross or net physical capital including business fixed capital, residences, inventories, and government capital (Simon Kuznets, *Capital in the American Economy* [National Bureau of Economic Research, 1961], Chapter 3) also show a secular rise and fall in the capital-output ratio, however. So the Creamer estimates for manufacturing are consistent in direction with the aggregates of which they are a major component, even if they exaggerate the amplitude of the secular swing.

The constant-dollar ratio of gross business fixed investment to privately-produced GNP is also pictured in Chart A-I. Unlike the capital-output ratio, the investment-output ratio shows a steady downtrend from the 1890's on, although with a suggestion of some deceleration in the decline between the 1920's and the 1950's. A falling gross investment share was compatible with a rising net capital-output ratio until World War I because depreciation was a small share of gross investment in those early years when the capital stock was still comparatively small.

It appears, then, that both a falling investment share and a falling net capital-output ratio were to be expected during the postwar years unless there was a reversal of long-standing trends in the behavior of gross business fixed investment. A close inspection of Chart A-I shows a slight *uptrend* in the capital-output ratio during the 1950's, however, although the expected decline in the investment share is clearly evident. It will be shown later that the slight postwar uptrend in the realized capital-output ratio is due to the fact that the actual ratio was below the desired ratio at the end of World War II. This is not incompatible with the previous trend toward declining unit capital requirements.

Current or Constant Dollars?

Another issue is whether the investment-output and capital-output ratios should be measured in current or in constant dollars. That this choice can imply a significant difference in the observed trends of the two ratios is readily apparent from a comparison of Charts A-I and A-II. The only difference between the charts is that the variables are measured in current prices in Chart A-II. With regard to the capital-output ratio, it will be seen that the current-dollar estimates decline less between the 1920's and 1950's and display a sharper uptrend during the 1950's than do the constant-dollar ratios. Similarly the investment share in current dollars was about the same instead of lower in the 1950's than in the 1920's and declined less sharply in the postwar period than did the constant-dollar share. Evidently it is important to decide whether the analysis should be done in current or constant dollars, although it will be shown that the choice is not nearly as crucial as might be expected.

Since capital goods are demanded because of the services they contribute to the production process, it is the physical unit of capital that is basic to investment analysis. This is not to deny, of course, that capital goods prices may affect the demand for real capital in conjunction with interest rates and other relevant prices. The basic point is simply that it is real rather than money capital that enters the production function along with labor and other inputs and that the role of relative prices is to determine the level of production and optimum combination of resources from among the physical production possibilities.

Given the fact that the real quantity of capital is the basic unit for analysis, it

CHART A-II. *Ratios of Business Fixed Investment and Capital to Gross Private Domestic Product, 1890–1960*

(In billions of current dollars)

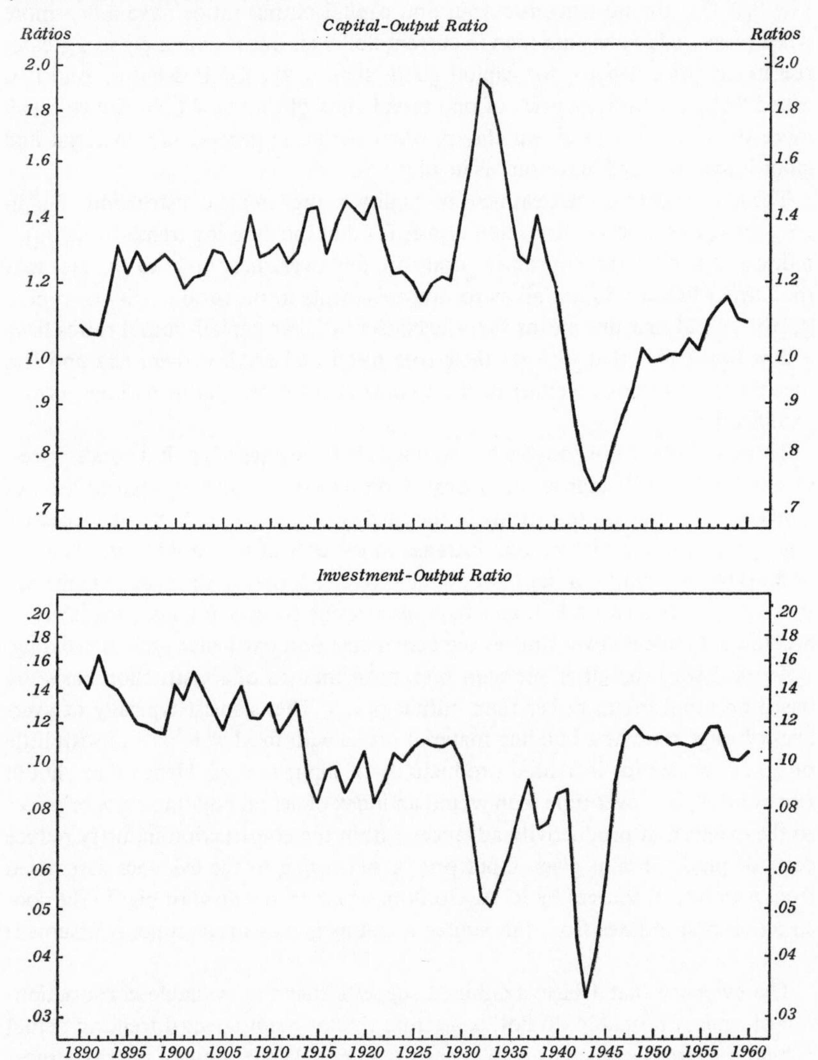

See text footnote [1] for source.

may still be questioned whether the available data on real capital formation and capital stock are accurate empirical estimates of the desired theoretical quantities. It has been argued by Paul S. Anderson, for example, that the secular downtrend of the aggregate real capital-output ratio as conventionally measured is seriously exaggerated by a faulty correction for the trend of capital goods prices. The fact that the investment-output and capital-output ratios have fallen more when measured in constant than in current dollars is due proximately to a greater rise in the price deflator for capital goods than in the GNP deflator. And it is asked "why the average price of one broad class of output should rise so much more than the average of all classes when the same general raw material and labor inputs are used in the one as in all?"[3]

The issue concerns the treatment of quality change in the construction of capital goods price indexes. Anderson argues (1) that the differing trends in the price indexes of capital and consumer goods are due overwhelmingly to the fact that the former indexes do not allow for improvements in the productivity of capital goods and (2) that this means that the constant-dollar capital-output ratios have a downward bias that distorts their true trend and renders them less and less meaningful over time. Neither of these conclusions is acceptable without serious qualification.

There are two major sources of possible bias in indexes of capital goods prices. One is the fact that indexes of prices of producers' durable equipment are not adjusted for those improvements in the quality or the productivity of successive vintages that occur without any increase in the cost of the equipment.[4] The second, to which Anderson does not allude directly, is that in the case of construction cost indexes, an additional bias may result from a failure adequately to account for changes over time in the actual cost of a particular type of building.

To deal with the latter problem first, most indexes of construction costs are based on input prices rather than output prices. They consist typically of averages of wage rates and building material prices with fixed weights and with little or no allowance for increased productivity of input factors. Hence they should rise more rapidly over time than would an index of actual building costs or prices to the extent that productivity advances within the construction industry reduce costs of production at given input prices. According to the evidence assembled from a variety of sources by R. A. Gordon, however, the upward bias in the construction cost indexes from this source is not as great as is commonly assumed:

> The evidence that I have examined suggests that the available construction-cost indices probably do not exaggerate the long-run upward trend in actual building costs as much as is frequently assumed. While some of the rise almost certainly has to be discounted, there are substantial reasons for believing that,

[3] Anderson, *op. cit.*, p. 617

[4] Such adjustments are not made in indexes of consumer goods prices either, but the bias may be larger on the average for capital goods.

> over the last half century or more, actual costs of construction have risen more than the prices of, for example, consumers' goods.[5]

The relative rise of construction costs is primarily attributable to a below-average rate of productivity advance in construction work.

It appears, then, that some, but not all, of the differential rise of capital goods prices is due to the use of construction cost indexes based on input prices. In addition, neither construction cost indexes nor indexes of prices of producers' durable equipment are adjusted for "costless" improvements in the quality or productivity of successive vintages of capital goods. The bias due to the use of input prices as a substitute for output prices is to be regretted and avoided as much as possible, but the (virtually unavoidable) neglect of quality improvements in capital goods gives little cause for concern.

Whereas it is true, as Anderson says, that this neglect implies that output per dollar of new capital measured at constant cost will be greater than that per dollar of old capital, there is no difficulty in accepting that implication, just as there is no difficulty in accepting the fact that the quality of an hour of labor input can increase as education and skill levels rise with successive generations. What is important is simply to recognize the implications of measuring capital in constant-cost rather than constant-quality units, including the proposition that vintage weighting to allow for differences in the efficiency of capital goods of different ages can be accomplished by measuring capital at its depreciated cost value, as is discussed in Chapter 2 above. Contrary to Anderson's argument, the neglect of quality change in capital goods price indexes does not impart a downward bias to the constant-dollar capital-output ratio in the sense of producing a misleading trend, provided the implications of the treatment of quality change are properly understood.

These implications extend beyond those already mentioned. Granted that the differential trends of capital and consumers' goods prices as conventionally measured are to be accepted as meaningful, except for some exaggeration from the use of input prices in the construction cost indexes, it is still necessary to allow for the effects of the differential price changes on saving-investment relationships.[6]

The saving-investment condition for aggregative equilibrium can be stated in either real or money terms. If one chooses to work in money terms while comparing potential investment demand with potential saving and the implicit full-employment surplus, all that is necessary is to convert the constant-dollar estimates of the potential investment share to a current-price basis by making appropriate assumptions about price relationships at full employment. This was the procedure followed in earlier chapters whenever the topic under discussion was the adequacy of private investment demand to offset *ex ante* saving at full

[5] "Differential Changes in the Prices of Consumers' and Capital Goods," *American Economic Review* (December 1961), p. 942.

[6] See *ibid.*, for an illuminating discussion of these effects.

employment. It will be recalled that the projected current-dollar investment shares were higher and declined less rapidly than the constant-dollar shares. These differences are due, of course, to the projected differential price trends that are under discussion.

The fact that the gross business fixed investment share is larger in current than in 1954 dollars may at first appear to imply that the constant-dollar projections for 1956 and later years are misleadingly low.[7] After all, the larger is investment demand at potential GNP, the more likely that it will be sufficient to offset full-employment saving and permit the potential to be realized. Hence a 9.8 percent (current dollar) investment share of potential GNP in 1962 appears to promise higher production and employment than does an 8.9 percent (1954 dollar) share. In fact, however, the production and employment levels implied by the two investment ratios are identical.

The reason is simply that the saving-investment equilibrium condition may be stated in either current or constant dollars, as already noted. When investment is measured in constant dollars, so also must be saving. To say that investment goods prices have risen relatively to consumers' goods prices since the base year is to say that consumption expenditure is a larger share of GNP when measured in constant than in current dollars. Put the other way around, it means that the purchasing power of a dollar of money saving in terms of investment goods has fallen relative to that of a dollar spent on consumer goods, so that real saving is a smaller share of real GNP than is money saving of money GNP. Hence to the extent that the constant-dollar investment share is smaller because of relative price increases for investment goods, so also is the constant-dollar saving ratio, and in the same proportion. Thus a given volume of investment expenditure will offset the same proportion of the saving ratio whether the comparison is made in real or money terms. The only essential condition for avoiding misleading implications is that both investment and saving, or alternatively, both investment and consumption, be included in the analysis of the determinants of aggregate demand and that all comparisons be made in either real or money terms, and not in a mixture of the two.[8] The comparison in money terms is to be preferred when the government sector is included in the analysis, however, because private saving is not unambiguously devoted to investment expenditure in that case, and it makes little sense to deflate the government surplus or deficit by an investment goods price index.

Although the foregoing discussion was directed to the discrepancy in level

[7] On this reasoning, of course, the pre-1954 constant-dollar shares would be considered to be misleadingly high, since the level of the capital goods price index was lower than that of the GNP deflator before 1954 when both indexes are on a 1954 base (see Chart XI).

[8] The interested reader is referred to Gordon, *loc. cit.*, for a discussion of the implications of the differential price changes for multiplier and growth-equilibrium analysis.

between the current- and constant-dollar investment shares for a given year, the same reasoning applies to the differential trends in the two investment ratios over time. The fact that the real share has decreased faster than the current-dollar share over the long run, and is projected to continue to do so in future years, does not mean that the downtrend in the real share is misleadingly rapid—unless, of course, the real share is mistakenly compared with a current-dollar saving ratio instead of a real saving ratio which is adjusted for the relative downtrend in the purchasing power of money saving in terms of investment goods. Proper deflation of the saving ratio to make it comparable with the real investment share would produce the same relative trend between the real saving and investment ratios as exists between their current-dollar counterparts. It is a separate issue, of course, whether an appropriate allowance is made for future relative price trends in any particular forward projection of current-dollar investment demand intended for comparison with projections of *ex ante* money saving, but this same issue would also arise if the alternative comparison were attempted between projections of real investment and real saving.

Alternate Concepts of Capital Stock

The next question to be faced is: to what extent would the results of the analysis be changed if a different measure of capital stock were substituted for the present estimates? The rationale of the decision to measure capital stock net of depreciation as calculated on a declining-balance formula is discussed in Chapter 2 and Appendix B. The reader may or may not agree fully with that decision, but in either event he is entitled to know how much the choice affects the final results. He is also entitled to know whether the conclusions would be substantially altered by the substitution of capital stock estimates prepared by other investigators using different data sources and assumptions about depreciation rates.

As a first step in investigating these questions, some alternative estimates of the aggregate stock of fixed business capital as listed in Table A-1 and pictured in Chart A-III will be examined. Seven series are presented in all. Six of them were prepared in the Office of Business Economics of the United States Department of Commerce, whereas the seventh is the series which I developed and which is used throughout the earlier portions of this study.

The six OBE series illustrate the effects of varying the assumptions about useful lives and depreciation formulas.[9] All six variants were derived by the perpetual inventory method from the same underlying estimates of gross business fixed

[9] For a complete description of the estimates, see George Jaszi, Robert C. Wasson, and Lawrence Grose, "Expansion of Fixed Business Capital in the United States," *Survey of Current Business* (November 1962), pp. 9–18 and 28.

TABLE A-1. *Six Variants of the Stock of Fixed Business Capital as Estimated by the Office of Business Economics,*[a] *1948–61*

(In billions of 1954 dollars)

Year	I	II	III	IV	V	VI
1948	444.4	371.0	235.0	191.4	189.9	154.2
1949	459.2	386.5	246.3	200.6	199.6	161.7
1950	476.8	402.3	258.8	210.9	210.4	170.2
1951	498.6	417.6	272.2	221.8	222.0	179.5
1952	517.6	434.7	283.9	231.2	231.9	187.2
1953	536.6	452.4	296.2	241.2	241.9	195.4
1954	555.1	467.5	306.2	249.0	249.3	201.1
1955	581.4	483.6	318.5	259.2	258.8	209.2
1956	609.7	498.3	331.9	270.7	269.9	218.7
1957	635.5	508.9	343.9	280.7	280.1	227.2
1958	650.2	511.3	348.1	283.2	283.3	228.7
1959	662.8	516.6	353.4	287.1	288.1	232.1
1960	672.0	524.2	360.6	293.0	295.1	237.7
1961	678.8	532.1	366.4	297.4	300.7	241.9

[a] Of the U. S. Department of Commerce.

Notes on variants:

I—Gross stock, useful lives according to *Bulletin F* of the U. S. Treasury Department.

II—Gross stock, useful lives 20 percent shorter than in *Bulletin F.*

III—Net stock, straight-line depreciation, *Bulletin F* lives.

IV—Net stock, double-rate declining-balance depreciation, *Bulletin F* lives.

V—Net stock, straight-line depreciation, lives 20 percent shorter than *Bulletin F.*

VI—Net stock, double-rate declining balance depreciation, lives 20 percent shorter than *Bulletin F.*

investment. Variants I and II are both gross of depreciation, but they differ because assets were assigned useful lives according to *Bulletin F* of the United States Treasury in the first variant, whereas the lives were shortened by 20 percent in the second. Variants III and IV are estimates of net depreciated stock based on *Bulletin F* lives, but III assumes straight-line depreciation, and IV assumes double-rate declining-balance depreciation. Variants V and VI are also estimates of net stock based respectively on straight-line and double-rate declining-balance depreciation, but with lives 20 percent shorter than quoted in *Bulletin F.*

It will be seen from Chart A-III that varying the assumptions about depreciation formulas and useful lives markedly affects the level of the resulting OBE stock estimates during 1948–61. Of the three variants based on *Bulletin F* lives, the gross stock series (I) is considerably higher than the net stock based on straight-line depreciation (III), which in turn lies above that based on declining-balance depreciation (V). The same relationship holds among the three variants based on lives 20 percent shorter than in *Bulletin F*, of course, so that variants II, IV, and VI all lie below their respective counterparts. Quite by accident the

CHART A-III. *Capital Stock and Capital-Output Ratios, Seven Variants, 1948–61*

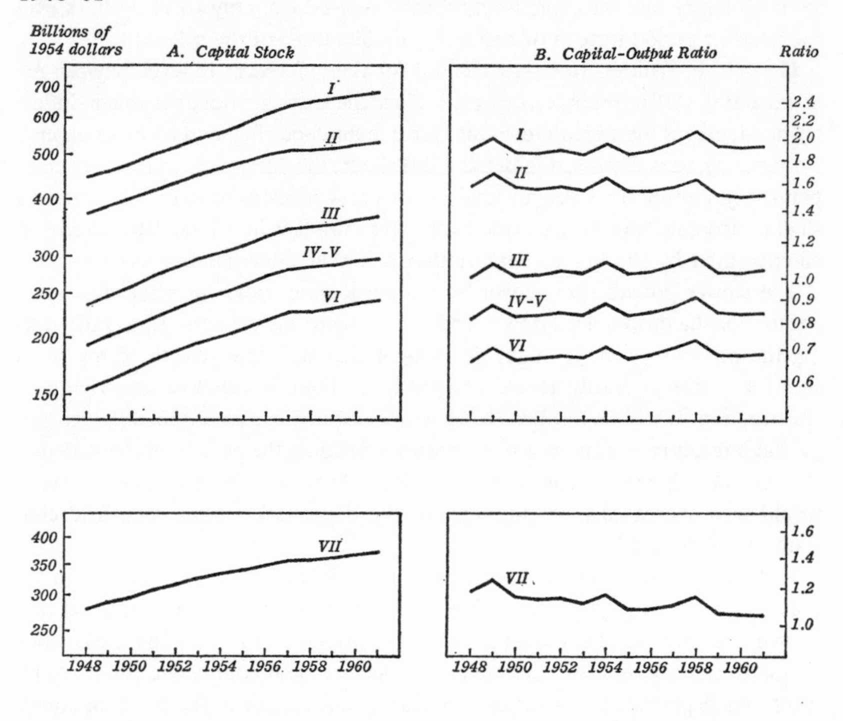

See text for explanatory remarks.

shorter lives embodied in the straight-line variant (V) are almost exactly offset by the faster depreciation method underlying the double-rate declining-balance estimates based on longer lives (IV), so that these two series are virtually identical and are plotted as a single line in the chart.

The various OBE stock series also differ in slope, particularly after 1957. On the whole, however, their slopes or growth rates are more nearly alike than their levels. This is significant, since it implies rather similar trends in the capital-output ratios based on the various stock concepts. That implication is confirmed when the capital-output ratios are plotted as in section B of Chart A-III, especially as regards the virtually common trend of the four variants of depreciated stock (III–VI). The denominator of each of these ratios is the same output series as was used in the regression analysis.

Chart A-III also shows how the capital stock series used in this study, labeled variant VII, compares with the OBE estimates. With regard to level, the estimates developed herein are higher than any of the net stock variants prepared by OBE but lower than their gross stock series. As for trend, it is much flatter for my series than for any of the OBE variants, especially during 1948–57. Indeed, it is so much flatter that the capital-output ratio derived from my series declines over the postwar period instead of rising slightly like most of the others!

It would be fruitless to try to account for the differences in level between my series and the OBE estimates, especially since the latter are not available in industry detail except for a breakdown into farm, manufacturing, and all other capital. Fortunately, as is discussed in detail a little later, the differences in level are comparatively unimportant for an analysis of gross investment demand, since the smaller absolute rate of net capital formation implicit in a lower stock series is compensated by the higher depreciation rate that underlies the series.

The slower growth rate shown by my stock series deserves more discussion because of the pronounced downtrend it imparts to the capital-output ratio during the postwar years. It might be thought that the slow growth of my stock series was due primarily to the assumptions about useful lives underlying its construction. It will be recalled that postwar acquisitions were generally depreciated at a faster rate than prewar purchases, providing the pattern of rising depreciation rates shown in Appendix Table B-8. Obviously the net stock estimates would have increased more rapidly had the depreciation rates been held constant at the prewar level.

It should not be assumed, however, that the depreciation rates implicit in the OBE stock estimates are entirely free of such a rising trend, despite the fact that prewar and postwar lives are the same for any given variant. The OBE stock estimates were developed separately for structures and equipment. Since equipment was depreciated at a faster rate than plant, and since the stock of equipment increased more rapidly than that of structures, the composite depreciation rate exhibits a rising trend for each OBE variant of net capital stock between 1948 and 1957. During that span, the depreciation rates for variants III–VI increased respectively 7, 3, 4, and 1 percent, as compared with 12 percent for my series. All the rates stabilized or declined thereafter.

It is also worth noting that the growth rates of all four OBE variants of net stock were virtually the same during 1948–61, despite the substantial differences among them in the trend of depreciation rates. Hence it seems reasonable to infer that the uptrend in depreciation rates underlying my stock series is not the primary explanation of its relatively low growth rate. That inference is confirmed by the evidence in Chart A-IV, which shows that the slow growth of my net stock series is largely the result of a lower gross investment series than was used in the OBE estimates.

Two series of annual estimates of net capital stock for the period 1948–61 are shown in the middle section of the chart. They are designated respectively as variants VII and VIII. Variant VII is the stock series used throughout the present study. Variant VIII is new, however, and it was derived by combining the depreciation rates underlying variant VII with the gross investment estimates

CHART A-IV. *Alternative Estimates of Gross Investment and Net Capital Stock, Variants VII and VIII, 1948–61*

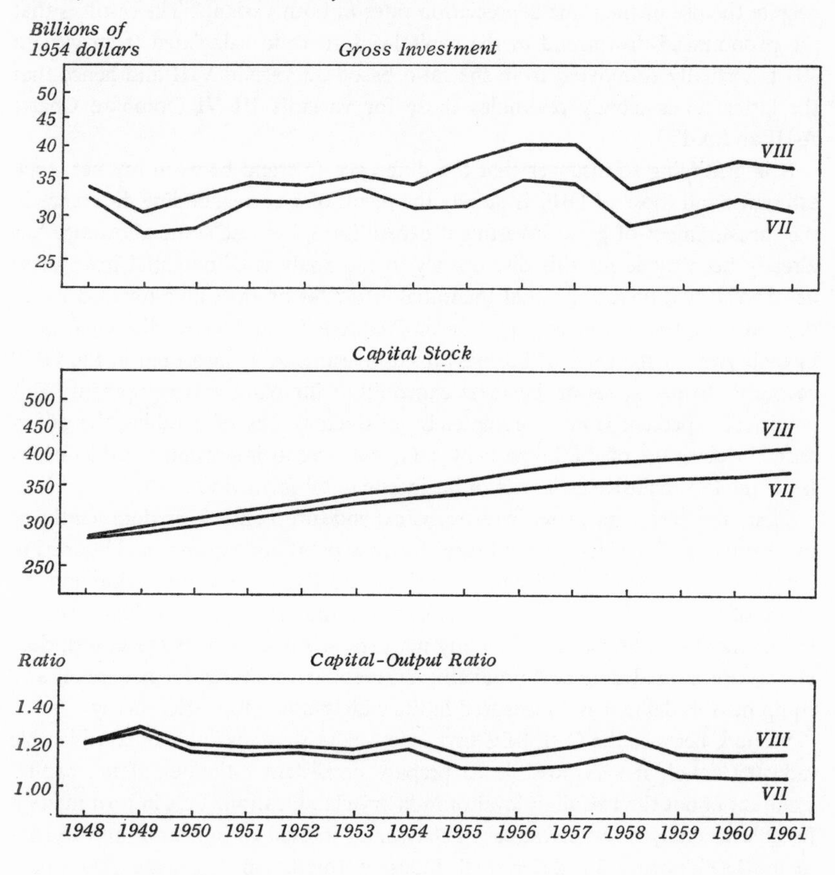

See text for explanatory remarks.

used to prepare the OBE series.[10] Apart from a minor adjustment for construction of farm residences, the OBE investment series is the same as business fixed investment in the GNP accounts.

As may be seen from the upper portion of the chart, the OBE investment series, labeled VIII for convenience even though it also underlies variants I to VI, is considerably higher in level and has a more pronounced uptrend than my

[10] This was done as follows: The initial (1947) capital stock estimate is the same in both variants. Variant VIII was then carried forward by the usual method and with the same depreciation rates as in variant VII (Table B-8), but using the OBE estimates of gross investment.

series on aggregate plant and equipment expenditure. These differences produce a large and growing discrepancy between the corresponding stock estimates, despite the use of the same depreciation rates in both variants. The result is that the pronounced downtrend in the capital-output ratio calculated from variant VII is virtually eliminated from the ratio based on variant VIII and hence that the latter series closely resembles those for variants III–VI (compare Charts A-III and A-IV).

It is gratifying to discover that the difference in trend between my net stock estimates and those of OBE is largely the result of a corresponding difference in the measurement of gross investment expenditure, because some allowance has already been made for this discrepancy in the analysis of potential investment demand. It will be recalled that the initial estimates of gross investment demand derived from the regression equation in Chapters 7 and 8 were adjusted upward in each year by the ratio of business fixed investment, as measured in the GNP accounts, to my series on business expenditure for plant and equipment. This empirical expedient is not a completely satisfactory way of handling the differences in coverage of the investment data, but several important considerations favor the less inclusive estimates of business capital formation.

First, my series on gross investment expenditure consists predominantly of the estimates of business expenditures for new plant and equipment obtained in the joint survey conducted by the Securities and Exchange Commission and the Office of Business Economics, supplemented in the farm sector by data from the Department of Agriculture. Thus my net capital stock series is the appropriate one to use in analyzing and predicting business expenditures for new plant and equipment as defined and measured in the widely-used OBE-SEC survey.

Second, because the OBE-SEC investment data were available in considerable industry detail, it was possible to prepare consistent estimates of net capital stock on about the two-digit level of industry classification. This in turn made it feasible to analyze the investment behavior of individual industries and to estimate the influence of differential industry trends on aggregate investment demand. In contrast, no industrial breakdown is as yet published for the GNP estimates of business fixed investment.

Third, with regard to the discrepancy between the OBE-SEC investment data and the investment estimates included in GNP, "The main difference lies in the inclusion in the gross national product of investment by farmers, professionals, institutions, real estate firms, and of certain outlays charged to current account."[11] My series does include investment by farmers, but it excludes the other items accounting for the difference between the OBE-SEC and GNP estimates. Since the omitted items consist largely of estimates of institutional investment and business purchases of passenger automobiles, neither of which represents the sort of production-related investment decision underlying most plant and equip-

[11] *Economic Report of the President* (January 1964), note to Table C-35.

ment expenditures, the OBE-SEC series is conceptually better for empirical implementation of the model used here. Since the OBE-SEC series does account for the bulk of business fixed investment in the GNP accounts, moreover, a better projection of the latter may be obtained through my approach of estimating the former and then adding a coverage adjustment than by directly applying my model to the conceptually less suitable GNP investment data.

A Regression Experiment

In order to study further the influence of alternative stock concepts on the analysis of business fixed investment demand, it was decided to run new regressions using the six OBE variants. The new equations are shown in Table A-2, together with the original regression for aggregate investment based on my own capital stock estimates. Apart from the different stock measures, the new regressions are exactly comparable to the original one. That is, they were fitted to the same output data and for the same time span (1949–60) as before, and a value of unity was again imposed on the elasticity of capital stock with respect to output.

The coefficient of multiple determination, as corrected for degrees of freedom, is given for each regression in column 9 of Table A-2. Judged by goodness of fit, the original equation (variant VII) is the best of all, with an $\bar{R}^2$ of .969.

The value of $\bar{R}^2$ for the six OBE variants ranges from .487 to .948. The lowest values were obtained from variants I and II, based on a gross stock concept. This finding is consistent with the a priori expectation expressed in Chapter 2 that net capital stock is the better concept to employ in a stock-adjustment model of investment decisions, since depreciation accounting provides an implicit vintage-adjustment for quality change.

The original equation also has the most "significant" regression coefficients of any in the group. All four of its coefficients are statistically significant by a t-test at the 1 percent level. However, all coefficients of variants III and VI are significant at the 5 percent level. Again, the gross stock variants I and II are the poorest in the group, lacking one or more significant slope coefficients. Finally, it is only for the original regression that the hypothesis of positive serial correlation in the residuals can be rejected, since the Durbin-Watson statistic (column 10) falls in the inconclusive range for all six OBE variants.

Let us now examine the influence of alternative stock concepts on the regression coefficients by comparing the six OBE variants. The constant term is shown in the first column, and it will be seen that it becomes progressively smaller as one moves from variant I to variant VI. This is because of the differences in level of the various capital stock series pictured earlier in Chart A-III.

There is also a tendency for the coefficients of the modified output terms to increase as one moves down the table, except in the case of variants I and II. This implies a corresponding increase in the speed of adjustment of actual to

TABLE A-2. *Regression Results for Variants I–VII*

	Regression coefficients:				Standard errors:					
	Constant terms (1)	$\log Y_t - \log K_{t-1}$ (2)	$\log Y_{t-1} - \log K_{t-1}$ (3)	T (4)	Constant terms (5)	$\log Y_t - \log K_{t-1}$ (6)	$\log Y_{t-1} - \log K_{t-1}$ (7)	T (8)	$\bar{R}^2$ (9)	*SCT* (10)
I Gross stock (F)	.0800**	.1342*	.0954	−.0002	.0238	.0611	.0709	.0003	.487	.738
II Gross stock (F-20)	.0586**	.1263*	.0621	−.0015**	.0151	.0453	.0511	.0002	.859	.726
III Net stock (S.L., F)	.0235**	.1605**	.0954*	−.0008**	.0011	.0359	.0418	.0002	.910	.823
IV Net stock (D.B., F)	−.0026	.1840**	.1095*	−.0008**	.0065	.0425	.0508	.0002	.883	.815
V Net stock (S.L., F-20)	−.0038	.1908**	.1167**	−.0007**	.0045	.0288	.0336	.0002	.948	1.256
VI Net stock (D.B., F-20)	−.0412**	.2205**	.1351*	−.0006*	.0120	.0386	.0473	.0002	.909	1.120
VII Net stock (Hickman)	.0337**	.1236**	.1141**	−.0018**	.0018	.0142	.0157	.0001	.969	2.484

Note: All regressions are of the same form, with a value of unity imposed on the elasticity of capital stock with respect to output, as explained in Chapter 3. The same output data are used for all. However, each regression was fitted to a different series on capital stock.

* Coefficient significant at .05 level.

** Coefficient significant at .01 level.

One-tail test for modified output coefficients and two-tail test for other coefficients.

desired stock, since the adjustment speed is found by summing the modified output coefficients. The range of adjustment speeds for the OBE net stock variants is from 26 to 36 percent of the relative gap between desired and actual stock.

Finally, it will be observed that the trend coefficients carry a negative sign in all variants, indicating a downtrend in the desired capital-output ratio no matter which concept of capital is employed. These downtrends are illustrated in Chart A-V. The left-hand portion of the chart shows the actual capital-output ratio for each variant, whereas the ratio of desired stock to normal output is shown on the right side. Both desired stock and normal output are derived from the regressions in the usual way, of course.

CHART A-V. *Actual and Desired Capital-Output Ratios, Seven Variants, 1948–61*

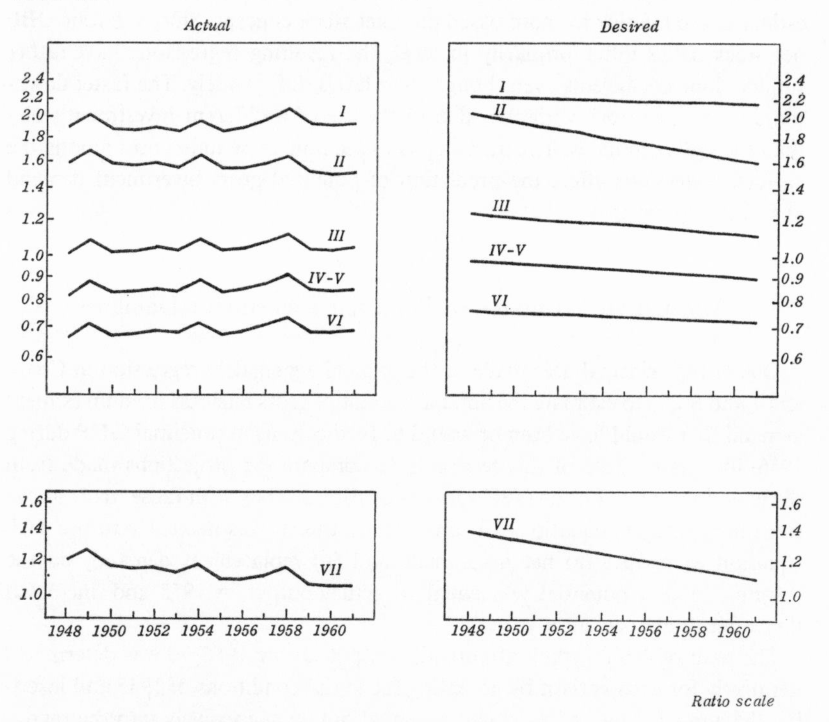

See text for explanatory remarks.

It is clear from the chart that a downtrend in the desired capital-output ratio is consistent with the slight uptrend which appears in the actual ratios for all but one of the variants. This is the proof for the statement made earlier in this appendix that the slight uptrend in the realized net capital-output ratio based on the GNP concept of business fixed investment is due to the fact that the actual ratio was below the desired ratio at the end of World War II. Hence the actual ratio rose slightly in the catching-up process despite the gradual decline in the desired ratio.

The rate of decline of the desired ratio is not the same for all variants, of course. In particular, the downtrend is much steeper for the original version (VII) than for any of the OBE net stock variants (III–VI), all of which have roughly equal trends. As was explained above, the faster downtrend of my actual stock series, and hence of the desired capital-output ratio inferred from it, is due primarily to the use of a different underlying gross investment series than in the OBE estimates.

To sum up, aggregative regressions of the same form as that used throughout the study, but based on variant stock concepts, differ somewhat in the quality and magnitude of the estimated parameters. The regressions fitted to gross stock estimates are inferior to those based on a net stock concept. Since the four OBE net stock series differ primarily in level, the resulting regressions have rather similar slope coefficients even though their levels differ widely. The faster downtrend of my net stock variant is due to the use of a different investment series than the OBE estimates. The next step is to see how these differences among the various regressions affect the prediction of potential gross investment demand at full employment.

Alternative Estimates of Potential Investment Demand

One of the principal uses made of the original aggregative regression in Chapters 7 and 8 was to estimate the annual amount of gross business fixed investment demand that would have been or would be forthcoming at potential GNP during 1956–70. The purpose of this section is to compare the projections made from the equations based on the OBE variants of capital stock with those made above from the aggregate equations. In order to do this, it was necessary to use each equation to predict (a) net investment and (b) replacement demand, on the assumption that potential was equal to actual output in 1955 and increased thereafter at 3.5 percent a year.

The path of capital stock at potential output during 1956–70 was determined iteratively for each variant by accepting the initial conditions of 1955 and inserting the annual values of estimated potential output successively into the regression equation. The potential stock estimates were then first-differenced to yield the annual estimates of potential net investment in 1954 dollars.

The procedure for estimating potential replacement demand—and indeed, the very meaning of "replacement"—differs between the gross and net stock variants. Under the gross stock concept, and neglecting the dispersion of individual retirements about the average life, replacement during year t is equal to gross investment expenditure in year $t-n$, where n is the useful life of the capital goods in question. Thus an asset is considered to be replaced only when it is completely retired from service, so no allowance is made for effective retirement through functional downgrading or partial utilization of old assets. The actual annual amounts of replacement demand underlying the OBE gross stock variants could readily be determined for 1956–61 by subtracting the reported change in the capital stock each year from the reported amount of gross investment expenditure in the same year. It was then assumed that the same actual annual series of replacement investments would have been forthcoming even at potential output during 1956–61. This is because the useful lives underlying the stock estimates are much longer than six years, so that replacement demand as estimated for gross stock (that is, replacement to offset permanent retirements) is completely independent of the path of net investment (that is, gross investment minus permanent retirements) during that short a period.

The calculation of potential replacement demand was slightly more complicated for the net stock variants. The first step was to determine the depreciation stream underlying each actual OBE net stock variant during 1956–61 by subtracting the actual annual change in capital stock from the actual gross investment of the same year. The depreciation of each year was then related to the capital stock of the preceding year-end to derive an annual series of actual depreciation rates for 1956–61. The same rates were then applied to the potential stock estimates for 1956–61 to yield estimated potential replacement demand annually in 1954 dollars. The appropriate replacement concept when stock is measured net of accumulated depreciation (including obsolescence) includes, of course, an allowance for effective retirement of old assets through partial utilization and functional downgrading as well as for the permanent withdrawal of old assets from the gross stock. Correspondingly, net investment is defined as gross investment minus depreciation instead of gross investment minus permanent retirements.

An unchanged depreciation rate was assumed for years after 1961 in order to extend the estimates of potential replacement demand through 1970 for each net stock variant. A similar extrapolation beyond 1961 was not made for the gross stock variants, since replacement demand is not functionally related to current capital stock under the gross concept and I did not know the history of past acquisitions. Indeed, there is some error involved in the procedure for estimating replacement even under the net stock variants III and V, since straight-line depreciation is properly a function of gross rather than net stock.

Finally, the annual estimates of net investment and replacement demand at potential output were summed to derive potential gross investment demand as shown for each OBE variant in Table A-3. The gross investment shares of potential GNP are also given in the table.

To begin the comparisons among the OBE series, it will be observed that the gross stock variants I and II behave quite differently from the net stock variants and from each other. Variant I shows a sharp rise in the gross investment share of potential GNP during 1956–61, in marked contrast to all other variants. This

TABLE A-3. *Alternative Estimates of Real Gross Business Fixed Investment Demand at Potential GNP, 1956–70*[a]

Year	Business Fixed Investment in Billions of 1954 Dollars, Variant:							Investment as a Percentage of Potential GNP in 1954 Dollars, Variant:						
	I	II	III	IV	V	VI	VII	I	II	III	IV	V	VI	VII
1956	36.4	39.3	39.1	39.1	40.0	39.7	40.8	9.0	9.7	9.6	9.6	9.8	9.8	10.0
1957	38.6	42.6	40.2	40.0	40.5	40.2	41.3	9.2	10.1	9.6	9.5	9.6	9.5	9.8
1958	42.8	43.4	41.2	40.9	40.6	40.5	41.6	9.8	10.0	9.4	9.4	9.3	9.3	9.6
1959	46.9	41.9	42.2	41.8	41.4	41.1	41.8	10.4	9.3	9.4	9.3	9.2	9.1	9.3
1960	52.8	41.5	43.1	42.6	41.9	41.9	42.4	11.3	8.9	9.2	9.1	9.0	9.0	9.1
1961	54.6	39.7	43.6	43.5	42.5	42.5	43.0	11.3	8.2	9.0	9.0	8.8	8.8	8.9
1962	n.a.	n.a.	44.8	44.6	43.6	43.7	43.7	n.a.	n.a.	9.0	8.9	8.7	8.8	8.8
1963	n.a.	n.a.	45.9	45.8	44.8	45.0	44.5	n.a.	n.a.	8.9	8.9	8.7	8.7	8.6
1964	n.a.	n.a.	47.0	47.2	46.1	46.3	45.6	n.a.	n.a.	8.8	8.8	8.6	8.6	8.5
1965	n.a.	n.a.	48.2	48.4	47.4	47.8	46.6	n.a.	n.a.	8.7	8.7	8.6	8.6	8.4
1966	n.a.	n.a.	49.5	49.7	48.7	49.2	47.6	n.a.	n.a.	8.6	8.7	8.5	8.6	8.3
1967	n.a.	n.a.	50.7	51.1	50.2	50.6	48.7	n.a.	n.a.	8.6	8.6	8.5	8.5	8.2
1968	n.a.	n.a.	52.1	52.6	51.6	52.2	49.9	n.a.	n.a.	8.5	8.6	8.4	8.5	8.1
1969	n.a.	n.a.	53.6	54.0	53.2	53.9	51.0	n.a.	n.a.	8.4	8.5	8.4	8.5	8.0
1970	n.a.	n.a.	54.9	55.5	54.6	55.5	52.0	n.a.	n.a.	8.4	8.4	8.3	8.4	7.9

n.a. not available.

[a] Potential GNP is assumed to equal actual GNP in 1955 and to grow at 3.5 percent a year thereafter.

Note: The investment shares for variant VII are slightly lower than those reported in Table 35, col. 5. This is because investment in farm residences has been excluded from the gross business fixed investment concept underlying the OBE capital stock estimates, and hence it was excluded from the adjustment ratio used to raise the variant VII potential investment estimates to a level comparable to those for the OBE variants in this table.

result should be completely discounted. The regression equation for variant I was much the poorest of the lot, and the predicted potential investment values in Table A-3 range from less than the actual gross investment of 1956–57 to 50 percent more than the actual in 1961. The rapid uptrend of predicted potential investment demand under variant I is the result solely of a 250 percent rise in predicted replacement demand between 1956 and 1961, which in turn is largely an echo of the sharp recovery of gross equipment expenditures from the World War II nadir of 1943, to judge from the equipment service lives underlying variant I.[12]

The gross stock variant II goes in the opposite direction, showing the greatest decline in the estimated potential investment share of any of the variants between 1956 and 1961. Since the useful equipment lives underlying variant II are 20 percent shorter than in variant I, the annual replacement estimates for the former series reflect the relatively stable investment expenditures of the early postwar years instead of the sharp rise which preceded them. The combination of relatively stable replacement estimates and the pronounced negative trend in the net investment regression for variant II is responsible for the sharp drop in the investment share between 1956 and 1961, whereas its intermediate fluctuations are due to the moderate year-to-year fluctuations appearing in the replacement estimates.

With regard to the four OBE net stock variants, the estimated potential business fixed investment shares are remarkably similar in both level and trend during 1956–70. Variants V and VI start from a slightly higher level and drop a little faster than III and IV, but all four variants imply a substantial secular decline in the potential investment share.

Thus, varying the assumptions about depreciation methods and useful lives over a substantial range has produced little difference in the predictions of potential gross investment demand at full employment. This is because altering the depreciation assumptions affected mainly the level of net stock and not its growth rate. Similar growth rates mean similar net investment regressions for the several variants. Although it is true that the same net stock growth rate implies a smaller absolute amount of net investment the lower is the level of the stock series, this difference is compensated by the higher depreciation rate underlying the lower stock estimate. After all, the stock estimate was lower in the first place precisely because a faster depreciation method or rate was applied to the same gross investment stream. Hence the principal result of varying the depreciation assumptions is to produce a different division of predicted gross investment demand between net investment and replacement expenditure without substantially altering the growth rates of either. As long as the analysis is focused on gross rather than net investment, similar results will be obtained from any of the OBE net stock variants.

Finally, it will be noted that there is a growing discrepancy between the potential investment shares as projected by the OBE net stock variants and my own

[12] Jaszi, *et al.*, *op. cit.*, Table 7.

TABLE A-4. *Alternative Estimates of Capacity and Capacity Utilization, All Covered Sectors, 1948–61*

Variant	1948	1949	1950	1951	1952	1953	1954	1955	1956	1957	1958	1959	1960	1961
A. Capacity Output (in billions of 1954 dollars)														
I	195	203	211	220	230	239	248	259	272	285	295	302	308	313
II	176	189	200	212	221	238	252	265	279	292	301	309	319	330
III	184	196	208	220	232	244	255	266	280	293	302	309	317	325
IV	188	201	213	225	237	249	260	271	284	298	307	312	320	327
V	188	201	213	226	239	250	261	271	284	297	306	312	320	329
VI	193	207	218	231	244	255	266	276	289	302	310	315	323	331
VII	197	208	218	229	241	253	264	274	285	297	307	315	325	335
B. Actual Utilization Rates (in percent)														
I	*121*	*113*	*121*	*121*	*119*	*121*	*114*	*120*	*118*	*113*	*105*	*112*	*113*	*113*
II	*134*	*121*	*127*	*126*	*124*	*121*	*112*	*117*	*115*	*111*	*103*	*110*	*109*	*107*
III	*128*	*117*	*123*	*122*	*118*	*118*	*111*	*117*	*115*	*110*	*103*	*110*	*110*	*108*
IV	*125*	*114*	*120*	*119*	*116*	*116*	*109*	*115*	*113*	*108*	*101*	*109*	*109*	*108*
V	*125*	*114*	*120*	*118*	*115*	*115*	*108*	*115*	*113*	*109*	*102*	*109*	*109*	*107*
VI	*122*	*110*	*117*	*116*	*113*	*113*	*106*	*113*	*111*	*107*	*100*	*108*	*108*	*106*
VII	*120*	*110*	*117*	*117*	*114*	*114*	*107*	*114*	*113*	*108*	*101*	*108*	*107*	*105*
C. Normal Utilization Rates (in percent)														
I	*119*	*114*	*116*	*119*	*118*	*118*	*115*	*115*	*116*	*113*	*107*	*108*	*112*	*112*
II	*132*	*122*	*123*	*124*	*123*	*119*	*113*	*114*	*114*	*110*	*105*	*107*	*108*	*106*
III	*126*	*118*	*118*	*119*	*117*	*116*	*112*	*113*	*114*	*110*	*104*	*107*	*109*	*108*
IV	*123*	*115*	*115*	*117*	*114*	*114*	*110*	*111*	*112*	*108*	*103*	*105*	*108*	*107*
V	*123*	*115*	*115*	*116*	*114*	*113*	*109*	*110*	*112*	*108*	*103*	*105*	*108*	*107*
VI	*120*	*112*	*112*	*114*	*111*	*111*	*107*	*109*	*110*	*106*	*102*	*104*	*107*	*106*
VII	*117*	*111*	*111*	*114*	*112*	*111*	*108*	*109*	*111*	*108*	*103*	*103*	*106*	*105*

CHART A-VI. *Actual and Normal Capacity Utilization Rates, Seven Variants, 1948–61*

(In percent)

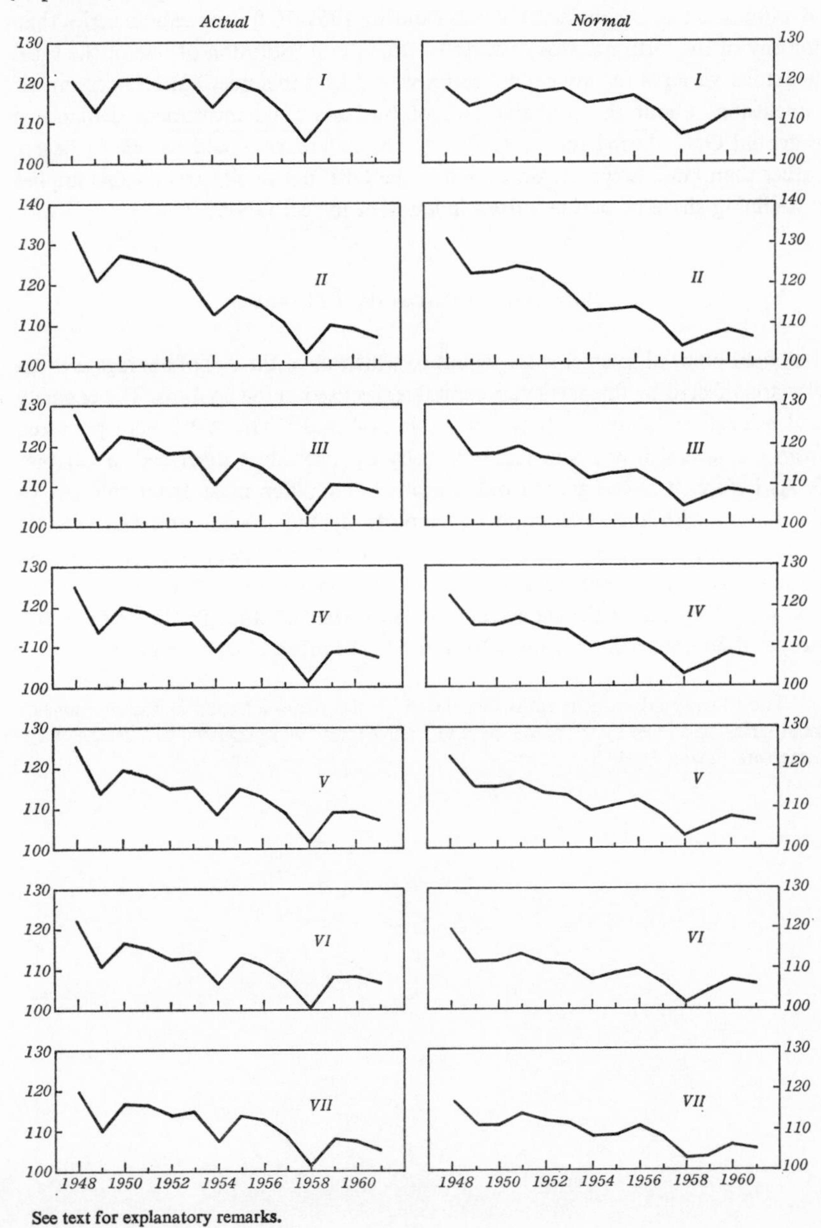

See text for explanatory remarks.

variant VII, especially after 1964. This occurs despite the fact that the original projections from variant VII were adjusted upward by an increasing percentage each year to allow for the higher level and faster growth of gross investment as measured in the OBE estimates.[13] Despite this adjustment, the projected gross investment share is considerably lower during 1965–70 for my capital series than for any of the OBE net stock variants. Thus the substitution of one of the OBE net stock variants for my capital series would lead to somewhat less pessimistic conclusions about the probable size of business fixed investment demand at potential GNP during the years ahead. The difference would be one of degree rather than kind, however, since each of the OBE net stock variants also implies a declining share of business fixed investment in real GNP.

Alternative Capacity Estimates

A final point of interest is the extent to which the estimates of aggregate capacity are affected by the particular capital series used in the analysis. The capacity and utilization estimates shown in Table A-4 and Chart A-VI were prepared from the several investment regressions by the procedure described in Chapter 5. As before, it is the gross stock variants that differ most from the rest of the group, with I and II implying respectively the slowest and fastest rates of capacity growth, and hence the mildest and sharpest downtrends in utilization during 1948–61. The net stock variants differ primarily in level. Thus the utilization rates have about the same trend for all variants, although III is noticeably steeper than the others. Variants VI and VII are much alike even in level.

[13] The moving adjustment ratio was based on the relative trends in the two investment series, as shown by the actual data in 1956–61, and was projected to increase at the same rate during 1961–70.

APPENDIX B / *The Capital Stock Estimates*

IN ORDER TO ACCOMPLISH the objectives of the present study, it was necessary to obtain consistent estimates of annual gross and net investment and net capital stock in considerable industry detail for the postwar period. The purpose of this appendix is to describe the sources and characteristics of these estimates and to make them available for use by other investigators.

General Characteristics of the Estimates

The capital stock estimates were derived by cumulating annual estimates of net investment. The basic data required were annual estimates of gross investment and depreciation. Net investment for a particular year was derived by subtracting depreciation from gross investment; net capital stock at the end of the year was obtained by adding net investment to the value of net capital stock at the beginning of the year. Since the estimates of gross investment used in the cumulation were in constant (1954) dollars, the derived estimates of depreciation, net investment and net capital stock are also in constant dollars. If desired, the entire set of estimates may easily be converted to current dollars or replacement cost by multiplying the constant-dollar estimates for each year by the capital goods price index of the same year.

In deriving the estimates it was assumed that depreciation occurs at a constant percentage rate for groups of assets having a given average useful life. This assumption of exponential or declining-balance depreciation can be supported on both theoretical and empirical grounds. The incidence of obsolescence is presumably random over time, since there is no reason to believe that it is more likely to occur at one stage of service life than another.[1] On the average, therefore, obsolescence may be expected to occur at a uniform rate. Probability considerations also suggest that, on the average, physical deterioration and accidental damage will be a constant fraction of capital stock for populations of assets with

[1] George Terborgh, *Realistic Depreciation Policy* (Machinery and Allied Products Institute, 1954), Chaps. 4–5.

TABLE B-1. *Gross Expenditures on Plant and Equipment, All Industries, 1946–62*

(In billions of 1954 dollars)

Industry or Sector	1946	1947	1948	1949	1950	1951
All Industries	28.07	32.50	32.24	27.84	28.70	31.94
Manufacturing and petroleum extraction	12.47	12.56	12.18	9.29	9.30	12.39
Durable goods industries	5.52	4.76	4.44	3.14	3.66	5.61
Primary metals	1.41	1.18	1.26	.91	.86	1.62
Electrical machinery and equipment	.49	.41	.37	.26	.28	.40
Machinery, except electrical	.83	.72	.66	.46	.48	.72
Motor vehicles and parts	.95	.70	.61	.42	.59	.90
Nonautomotive transportation equipment	.20	.15	.14	.12	.10	.34
Stone, clay, and glass	.39	.45	.34	.22	.32	.42
Other durable goods	1.26	1.16	1.06	.76	1.02	1.21
Nondurable goods industries	6.95	7.80	7.74	6.14	5.64	6.78
Food and beverage	1.07	1.30	1.31	1.05	.88	.91
Textile	.54	.70	.77	.56	.52	.56
Paper	.37	.51	.48	.36	.38	.44
Chemical	2.02	1.46	1.19	.80	.90	1.32
Petroleum and coal (including petroleum extraction)	2.07	2.92	3.30	2.83	2.42	2.98
Rubber	.24	.20	.13	.10	.12	.16
Other nondurable goods	.65	.73	.56	.44	.42	.40
Railroads	.82	1.14	1.54	1.57	1.26	1.58
Nonrail transportation	1.97	2.30	1.77	1.03	1.38	1.56
Electric utilities	.94	1.56	2.61	2.84	2.60	2.49
Gas utilities	.47	1.02	.92	1.13	1.33	1.44
Telephone communication	1.00	1.49	1.83	1.32	1.03	1.17
Commercial and other	7.22	8.12	6.27	5.47	6.53	6.28
Farming	3.17	4.31	5.12	5.19	5.27	5.04

fixed age distribution.[2] These theoretical considerations are supported by such limited empirical evidence as exists on the decline of capital value with age. Studies of prices of used equipment in second hand markets reveal a consistent pattern of market depreciation closely approximating an exponential decline.[3] Unfortunately, similar data are lacking for industrial or commercial plant.

Depreciation rates were based on estimates of the average useful life of assets in each industrial sector. The reciprocal of the average useful life is the straight-line rate of depreciation. A multiple of the straight-line rate was used for the declining-balance depreciation estimates presented here. In the case of manufacturing industries, the declining-balance rate was set at twice the straight-line

[2] See Dale W. Jorgenson, "Business Fixed Investment," unpublished report to the Social Science Research Council Conference on an Econometric Model of the United States (Aug. 26, 1961), Part 4.

[3] Terborgh, *loc. cit.*; Zvi Griliches, "The Demand for a Durable Input: Farm Tractors in the United States, 1921–57," in Arnold Harberger, ed., *The Demand for Durable Goods* (Univ. of Chicago Press, 1960).

Table B-1 (continued)

1952	1953	1954	1955	1956	1957	1958	1959	1960	1961	1962
31.83	33.42	31.06	31.35	34.81	34.60	28.88	30.07	32.11	30.80	32.86
13.09	13.39	12.88	12.06	14.18	14.36	10.10	10.44	12.26	11.47	12.20
6.08	6.33	6.24	5.64	6.85	6.84	4.55	4.68	5.75	5.00	5.54
2.11	1.64	1.00	1.04	1.51	2.17	1.36	1.10	1.53	1.11	1.11
.40	.48	.44	.42	.54	.51	.38	.42	.54	.55	.54
.73	.81	.69	.78	.97	1.09	.76	.74	.88	.88	1.00
.89	1.00	1.30	1.09	1.51	.89	.46	.52	.71	.60	.65
.48	.79	1.34	.65	.40	.47	.31	.32	.34	.30	.37
.34	.35	.36	.48	.62	.49	.33	.43	.50	.41	.46
1.15	1.26	1.11	1.17	1.30	1.22	.94	1.17	1.12	1.16	1.41
7.01	7.06	6.64	6.42	7.34	7.52	5.55	5.75	6.51	6.48	6.66
.80	.82	.76	.69	.72	.72	.62	.67	.74	.78	.78
.45	.38	.33	.35	.42	.34	.24	.33	.42	.40	.48
.38	.41	.46	.50	.72	.69	.48	.51	.60	.54	.57
1.44	1.45	1.14	1.00	1.30	1.46	1.10	1.00	1.28	1.29	1.23
3.40	3.42	3.38	3.30	3.58	3.72	2.62	2.68	2.78	2.78	2.90
.16	.16	.13	.14	.18	.17	.11	.15	.18	.17	.18
.39	.41	.45	.42	.43	.42	.39	.41	.51	.52	.52
1.45	1.32	.85	.90	1.11	1.21	.63	.76	.85	.55	.70
1.54	1.58	1.51	1.56	1.56	1.53	1.26	1.67	1.59	1.52	1.69
2.84	3.21	2.64	2.42	2.97	3.58	3.52	3.14	3.18	3.18	3.16
1.00	1.20	.90	1.11	1.16	1.18	1.06	1.09	1.22	1.06	1.04
1.41	1.52	1.52	1.84	2.42	2.69	2.22	2.25	2.62	2.61	2.82
5.77	6.43	6.51	7.29	7.72	6.48	6.16	6.84	6.93	6.81	7.52
4.72	4.77	4.23	4.18	3.67	3.56	3.93	3.89	3.46	3.60	3.72

rate. A double rate declining-balance formula depreciates about two-thirds of the value of an asset in the first half of its life, in accordance with the empirical evidence on market depreciation of industrial assets cited in the footnote on page 223. It is unrealistically fast for long-lived assets, however, and slower rates were used for most of the nonmanufacturing industries.

The estimates of gross investment, depreciation, net investment, and net capital stock are shown for 21 industries in Tables B-1 through B-4. (The two machinery groups and the two utility groups were each combined into one industrial grouping for the regression analysis, which provides only a 19-industry breakdown.) Details of the estimating procedure are given in the following notes.

Gross Expenditures on Plant and Equipment

The data on gross fixed investment in current dollars are presented in Table B-5. They consist predominantly of the estimates of business expenditures for

TABLE B-2. *Depreciation on Plant and Equipment, All Industries, 1946–62*

(In billions of 1954 dollars)

Industry or Sector	1946	1947	1948	1949	1950	1951
All Industries	13.86	16.09	18.12	19.46	20.42	21.45
Manufacturing and petroleum extraction	5.00	6.01	6.84	7.37	7.67	8.11
Durable goods industries	2.01	2.47	2.79	2.97	3.07	3.30
Primary metals	.45	.52	.59	.63	.66	.71
Electrical machinery and equipment	.14	.20	.24	.26	.26	.28
Machinery, except electrical	.28	.36	.42	.45	.46	.49
Motor vehicles and parts	.26	.34	.39	.41	.43	.48
Nonautomotive transportation equipment	.14	.15	.16	.16	.16	.17
Stone, clay, and glass	.20	.23	.26	.27	.28	.29
Other durable goods	.53	.65	.74	.79	.82	.88
Nondurable goods industries	2.99	3.54	4.05	4.40	4.60	4.81
Food and beverage	.51	.61	.71	.78	.82	.84
Textile	.29	.34	.39	.42	.44	.46
Paper	.16	.19	.22	.24	.26	.28
Chemical	.54	.71	.80	.84	.85	.89
Petroleum and coal (including petroleum extraction)	1.13	1.27	1.45	1.16	1.70	1.80
Rubber	.08	.10	.11	.11	.12	.12
Other nondurable goods	.26	.33	.37	.40	.41	.41
Railroads	1.06	1.06	1.08	1.09	1.13	1.16
Nonrail transportation	.86	1.14	1.34	1.40	1.41	1.46
Electric utilities	.84	.86	.93	1.02	1.11	1.19
Gas utilities	.27	.29	.31	.33	.36	.40
Telephone communication	.43	.50	.59	.66	.68	.71
Commercial and other	3.61	4.26	4.75	4.92	5.08	5.27
Farming	1.78	1.98	2.29	2.66	2.98	3.16

new plant and equipment prepared jointly by the United States Department of Commerce, Office of Business Economics and the Securities and Exchange Commission and published periodically in the *Survey of Current Business*. The OBE-SEC series have been supplemented from a variety of sources, however, as is explained in the notes on individual sectors.

Manufacturing and Petroleum Extraction

The data on manufacturing investment are taken directly from the OBE-SEC estimates except for the following modifications:

1. The company rather than the establishment is the reporting unit in the OBE-SEC survey of business capital expenditures. One result of this is that the entire investment expenditure of a given company is classified in the industry that accounts for the major portion of its business, even though a substantial amount of expenditure may be for facilities in another industrial classification. This problem is particularly acute in the petroleum industry, where the large

Table B-2 (continued)

1952	1953	1954	1955	1956	1957	1958	1959	1960	1961	1962
22.50	23.53	24.34	24.93	25.54	26.35	26.59	26.52	26.69	26.95	27.13
8.69	9.25	9.76	10.12	10.50	10.95	11.11	11.04	11.11	11.23	11.36
3.63	3.96	4.28	4.53	4.77	5.04	5.12	5.08	5.12	5.18	5.21
.81	.90	.94	.95	.98	1.06	1.12	1.13	1.15	1.16	1.16
.30	.33	.36	.37	.40	.42	.43	.42	.44	.46	.47
.53	.57	.60	.63	.67	.72	.76	.76	.77	.79	.81
.54	.59	.67	.74	.81	.87	.85	.80	.78	.77	.76
.20	.25	.35	.43	.44	.44	.44	.43	.42	.41	.40
.31	.32	.33	.34	.37	.40	.40	.40	.41	.42	.42
.94	.99	1.03	1.06	1.10	1.13	1.14	1.14	1.15	1.17	1.19
5.06	5.29	5.47	5.59	5.73	5.92	5.98	5.96	5.99	6.06	6.14
.85	.85	.85	.84	.83	.82	.81	.80	.79	.79	.79
.47	.47	.47	.46	.46	.45	.44	.43	.43	.43	.44
.29	.30	.32	.34	.37	.40	.42	.43	.44	.46	.47
.96	1.03	1.07	1.08	1.09	1.13	1.16	1.15	1.15	1.17	1.19
1.94	2.08	2.20	2.31	2.41	2.52	2.58	2.58	2.60	2.61	2.63
.12	.13	.14	.14	.14	.14	.14	.14	.15	.15	.16
.42	.42	.43	.43	.44	.44	.44	.43	.44	.45	.46
1.20	1.21	1.22	1.21	1.22	1.26	1.27	1.26	1.26	1.26	1.24
1.52	1.56	1.60	1.61	1.63	1.64	1.62	1.62	1.64	1.64	1.65
1.25	1.38	1.45	1.51	1.57	1.66	1.76	1.85	1.92	1.99	2.05
.44	.49	.54	.55	.57	.61	.63	.65	.67	.69	.70
.74	.79	.84	.91	1.02	1.34	1.44	1.53	1.63	1.74	1.84
5.40	5.49	5.54	5.57	5.60	5.55	5.40	5.27	5.19	5.07	4.99
3.27	3.36	3.41	3.45	3.42	3.33	3.35	3.31	3.29	3.32	3.30

integrated companies engage in extensive mining operations. Thus the OBE-SEC figures on investment in petroleum refining, a manufacturing activity, include a large but unknown amount of mining investment. For this reason the OBE-SEC estimates of investment by companies classified under petroleum refining have been combined with those of companies classified under mining operations. The small amount of investment in the remainder of the mining classification has been ignored.

2. Estimates of the value of plant and equipment acquired from war surplus disposal have been added to the OBE-SEC figures, which cover only new plant and equipment. The estimates of surplus disposal were compiled from records of the War Assets Administration and the General Services Administration. The assets were included at disposal price rather than original acquisition cost on the assumption that the former valuation gave the best approximation to the present value of the remaining production services at the time of disposal. When assets were first leased and later purchased for private use, the investment was entered at the time of lease, at a value determined by its eventual disposal price and an estimate of its rate of depreciation during the lease period. The estimates

TABLE B-3. *Net Expenditures on Plant and Equipment, All Industries, 1946–62*

(In billions of 1954 dollars)

Industry or Sector	1946	1947	1948	1949	1950	1951
All Industries	14.21	16.41	14.12	8.38	8.28	10.48
Manufacturing and petroleum extraction	7.47	6.55	5.34	1.91	1.63	4.28
Durable goods industries	3.51	2.29	1.65	.18	.59	2.30
Primary metals	.96	.65	.67	.28	.20	.90
Electrical machinery and equipment	.35	.21	.13	.01	.02	.12
Machinery except electrical	.55	.35	.24	.01	.02	.23
Motor vehicles and parts	.68	.35	.22	0	.16	.42
Nonautomotive transportation equipment	.06	0	−.02	−.04	−.06	.17
Stone, clay, and glass	.18	.21	.08	−.05	.05	.13
Other durable goods	.73	.50	.32	−.03	.20	.33
Nondurable goods industries	3.96	4.26	3.69	1.74	1.04	1.98
Food and beverage	.55	.69	.60	.27	.07	.07
Textile	.25	.36	.38	.14	.08	.10
Paper	.21	.32	.25	.11	.12	.17
Chemical	1.47	.75	.40	−.03	.05	.43
Petroleum and coal (including petroleum extraction)	.94	1.65	1.85	1.22	.72	1.18
Rubber	.15	.09	.02	−.02	0	.04
Other nondurable goods	.38	.40	.19	.05	.01	−.01
Railroads	−.24	.07	.46	.48	.14	.42
Nonrail transportation	1.11	1.16	.43	−.37	−.03	.09
Electric utilities	.09	.69	1.68	1.81	1.48	1.30
Gas utilities	.20	.74	.61	.80	.97	1.04
Telephone communication	.57	1.00	1.24	.66	.36	.46
Commercial and other	3.62	3.87	1.52	.55	1.45	1.01
Farming	1.39	2.33	2.84	2.53	2.29	1.88

of surplus sales are included in the investment totals of Table B-5 and are shown separately in Table B-6.

3. During the Korean War a considerable volume of production facilities was added to the capital stock of the aircraft industry at government expense. Crude estimates of the annual gross investment in such facilities were constructed from data furnished by the Department of Defense on scheduled completions of programmed expansions. The estimates, included in the relevant totals of Table B-5, are as follows (in billions of current dollars):

1951	.10
1952	.25
1953	.60
1954	1.15
1955	.40

Table B-3 (continued)

1952	1953	1954	1955	1956	1957	1958	1959	1960	1961	1962
9.33	9.90	6.72	6.43	9.27	8.25	2.29	3.55	5.42	3.85	5.73
4.40	4.14	3.13	1.95	3.68	3.41	−1.01	− .60	1.15	.24	.84
2.45	2.36	1.96	1.11	2.08	1.80	− .58	− .39	.63	− .17	.31
1.30	.74	.06	.09	.53	1.11	.24	− .03	.38	− .05	− .05
.10	.15	.08	.05	.15	.09	− .04	0	.11	.09	.04
.19	.24	.09	.15	.30	.36	0	− .02	.11	.09	.19
.35	.41	.63	.35	.70	.03	− .39	− .29	− .07	− .18	− .10
.28	.54	.99	.22	− .05	.02	− .13	− .11	− .08	− .10	− .03
.03	.03	.03	.14	.25	.09	− .07	.03	.08	− .01	.04
.20	.26	.08	.11	.20	.09	− .19	.03	.10	− .01	.22
1.95	1.77	1.17	.83	1.60	1.61	− .43	− .21	.52	.42	.53
− .05	− .03	− .09	− .15	− .12	− .10	− .19	− .13	− .05	0	− .01
− .02	− .09	− .14	− .10	− .04	− .11	− .20	− .10	0	− .03	.04
.08	.11	.14	.16	.35	.29	.06	.08	.16	.08	.10
.47	.42	.07	− .07	.21	.33	− .06	− .15	.13	.12	.04
1.46	1.34	1.17	1.00	1.17	1.20	.05	.09	.18	.17	.27
.03	.03	0	.01	.04	.02	− .04	.01	.04	.02	.03
− .03	− .01	.02	− .01	− .01	− .02	− .04	− .02	.07	.07	.06
.25	.11	− .37	− .31	− .11	− .05	− .64	− .50	− .41	− .71	− .54
.03	.02	− .08	− .05	− .06	− .11	− .36	.05	− .04	− .12	.04
1.59	1.83	1.20	.91	1.40	1.92	1.76	1.29	1.27	1.19	1.11
.56	.71	.36	.56	.58	.57	.43	.44	.55	.37	.34
.68	.72	.68	.92	1.40	1.35	.77	.72	.99	.87	.98
.37	.94	.97	1.72	2.12	.93	.76	1.57	1.74	1.73	2.53
1.45	1.42	.82	.73	.26	.24	.58	.57	.17	.27	.43

Transportation

The OBE-SEC estimates were used for both railroad and nonrail transportation. See Table B-6 for estimates of surplus disposal of ships and airplanes included under nonrail transportation in Table B-5.

Electric and Gas Utilities

The data for electric utilities are from OBE-SEC. Those for gas utilities are from *Gas Facts*, published annually by the American Gas Association. Natural gas production facilities are excluded, since this is a mining operation classified under the petroleum and coal industry in the present estimates.

TABLE B-4. *Net Depreciated Value of Stock of Plant and Equipment, All Industries, 1945–62*[a]

(In billions of dollars)

Industry or Sector	1945	1946	1947	1948	1949	1950
All Industries	234.79	249.00	265.41	279.52	287.90	296.18
Manufacturing and petroleum extraction	51.88	59.35	65.90	71.23	73.15	74.78
Durable goods industries	21.10	24.62	26.90	28.55	28.73	29.31
Primary metals	5.66	6.62	7.27	7.94	8.22	8.42
Electrical machinery and equipment	1.07	1.42	1.64	1.77	1.78	1.80
Machinery, except electrical	2.46	3.01	3.36	3.60	3.62	3.64
Motor vehicles and parts	2.56	3.25	3.60	3.82	3.82	3.98
Nonautomotive transportation equipment	1.66	1.72	1.72	1.70	1.66	1.60
Stone, clay, and glass	2.42	2.61	2.82	2.90	2.85	2.90
Other durable goods	5.26	5.99	6.49	6.82	6.79	6.98
Nondurable goods industries	30.77	34.73	39.00	42.68	44.42	45.46
Food and beverage	4.90	5.45	6.14	6.74	7.01	7.07
Textile	3.82	4.07	4.43	4.81	4.95	5.03
Paper	1.82	2.03	2.35	2.60	2.71	2.83
Chemical	4.61	6.08	6.83	7.23	7.20	7.25
Petroleum and coal (including petroleum extraction)	12.32	13.25	14.91	16.76	17.98	18.69
Rubber	.74	.89	.98	.99	.98	.98
Other nondurable goods	2.58	2.96	3.36	3.56	3.60	3.61
Railroads	41.26	41.03	41.10	41.56	42.04	42.18
Nonrail transportation	8.44	9.54	10.71	11.14	10.77	10.74
Electric utilities	14.87	14.96	15.66	17.34	19.15	20.63
Gas utilities	8.00	8.20	8.93	9.54	10.34	11.30
Telephone communication	4.51	5.08	6.08	7.33	7.99	8.34
Commercial and other	69.81	73.43	77.29	78.82	79.37	80.82
Farming	36.02	37.41	39.74	42.58	45.10	47.39

[a] End of year.

Telephone

The estimates for the telephone industry were prepared by the American Telephone and Telegraph Company. The figures through 1949 were published in Melville J. Ulmer, *Capital in Transportation, Communications and Public Utilities* (Princeton Univ. Press, 1960), Table E-2. Later estimates (through 1960) were obtained by letter from the American Telephone and Telegraph Company and were extrapolated by OBE-SEC data for 1961–62. The OBE-SEC data for the communications industry include telegraph, radio, and television expenditures in addition to capital formation in telephones. Telegraph, radio, and TV expenditures averaged only 8.5 percent of total communications expenditures in 1946–60, however, and were negelected in the present estimates as quantitatively unimportant.

Table B-4 (continued)

1951	1952	1953	1954	1955	1956	1957	1958	1959	1960	1961	1962
306.67	315.99	325.89	332.60	339.03	348.30	356.55	358.84	362.39	367.81	371.66	377.39
79.06	83.46	87.60	90.72	92.67	96.35	99.76	98.75	98.15	99.30	99.54	100.38
31.62	34.07	36.43	38.39	39.50	41.58	43.38	42.80	42.41	43.04	42.87	43.18
9.32	10.62	11.36	11.41	11.50	12.03	13.14	13.38	13.35	13.73	13.68	13.63
1.91	2.00	2.15	2.24	2.28	2.43	2.52	2.48	2.48	2.58	2.68	2.72
3.87	4.06	4.30	4.39	4.54	4.84	5.21	5.21	5.19	5.30	5.39	5.58
4.41	4.76	5.17	5.80	6.15	6.85	6.87	6.49	6.20	6.13	5.95	5.85
1.77	2.05	2.59	3.58	3.80	3.76	3.78	3.65	3.54	3.46	3.36	3.33
3.02	3.06	3.09	3.12	3.26	3.51	3.60	3.53	3.56	3.65	3.63	3.67
7.31	7.52	7.78	7.85	7.96	8.17	8.26	8.06	8.10	8.19	8.18	8.40
47.44	49.39	51.16	52.33	53.16	54.77	56.38	55.94	55.74	56.26	56.68	57.20
7.14	7.09	7.06	6.97	6.82	6.71	6.60	6.41	6.28	6.23	6.23	6.22
5.13	5.10	5.01	4.88	4.77	4.73	4.62	4.42	4.32	4.32	4.29	4.33
3.00	3.08	3.19	3.33	3.49	3.84	4.13	4.19	4.27	4.42	4.50	4.60
7.68	8.15	8.57	8.64	8.56	8.77	9.10	9.04	8.90	9.02	9.14	9.19
19.87	21.33	22.68	23.85	24.84	26.01	27.21	27.25	27.34	27.53	27.70	27.96
1.02	1.06	1.09	1.08	1.09	1.13	1.16	1.12	1.13	1.17	1.19	1.22
3.60	3.58	3.56	3.59	3.58	3.57	3.55	3.51	3.49	3.56	3.62	3.68
42.60	42.85	42.96	42.59	42.28	42.17	42.12	41.47	40.98	40.57	39.86	39.32
10.83	10.86	10.88	10.80	10.76	10.69	10.58	10.23	10.28	10.23	10.11	10.15
21.93	23.52	25.35	26.54	27.45	28.86	30.77	32.53	33.82	35.09	36.28	37.39
12.35	12.91	13.62	13.98	14.54	15.12	15.69	16.12	16.56	17.11	17.48	17.82
8.80	9.48	10.20	10.89	11.81	13.21	14.56	15.33	16.05	17.04	17.90	18.88
18.84	82.21	83.15	84.12	85.84	87.96	88.89	89.65	91.22	92.96	94.70	97.23
49.27	50.72	52.14	52.96	53.69	53.94	54.18	54.76	55.34	55.51	55.78	56.21

Commercial and Other

This heterogeneous sector covers trade, services, finance, and contract construction. The estimates are from OBE-SEC.

Farming

The data are from the United States Department of Agriculture, *Farm Income Situation* (July 1961), Table 17-H, and subsequent issues. Included are gross expenditures on tractors, trucks, automobiles for business use, other machinery and equipment, farm dwellings, and service buildings.

TABLE B-5. *Gross Expenditures on Plant and Equipment, All Industries, 1946–62*

(In billions of dollars)

Industry or Sector	1946	1947	1948	1949	1950	1951
All Industries	17.87	24.15	26.19	23.30	24.64	29.93
Manufacturing and petroleum extraction	7.91	9.19	9.79	7.69	7.93	11.57
Durable goods industries	3.47	3.47	3.57	2.63	3.13	5.28
Primary metals	.88	.86	1.01	.76	.74	1.52
Electrical machinery and equipment	.31	.30	.30	.22	.24	.37
Machinery, except electrical	.52	.52	.53	.39	.41	.68
Motor vehicles and parts	.60	.51	.49	.35	.51	.85
Nonautomotive transportation equipment	.13	.11	.11	.10	.08	.32
Stone, clay, and glass	.24	.33	.27	.18	.28	.40
Other durable goods	.79	.84	.86	.63	.87	1.14
Nondurable goods industries	4.43	5.72	6.22	5.06	4.78	6.29
Food and beverage	.67	.95	1.05	.88	.76	.85
Textile	.34	.51	.62	.47	.45	.53
Paper	.23	.37	.38	.30	.33	.42
Chemical	1.27	1.06	.96	.67	.77	1.25
Petroleum and coal (including petroleum extraction)	1.36	2.16	2.66	2.30	2.00	2.71
Rubber	.15	.14	.10	.08	.10	.15
Other nondurable goods	.41	.53	.45	.37	.36	.38
Railroads	.58	.89	1.32	1.35	1.11	1.47
Nonrail Transportation	1.30	1.75	1.47	.89	1.21	1.49
Electric utilities	.53	1.03	1.90	2.18	2.10	2.24
Gas utilities	.27	.69	.69	.89	1.09	1.28
Telephone communication	.73	1.26	1.55	1.15	.94	1.13
Commercial and other	4.52	6.09	5.15	4.66	5.67	5.92
Farming	2.04	3.24	4.32	4.49	4.59	4.82

Price Deflators

Annual indexes of prices of new plant and equipment are shown for each industry in Table B-7. For the most part these are implicit indexes derived by dividing total gross capital expenditures in current dollars by the sum of separately deflated series on plant expenditure and equipment expenditure in constant dollars. The indexes may be used to convert the estimates of depreciation, net investment, and net stock to a current-dollar or replacement cost basis by multiplying the constant-dollar values of each year by the price index of the same year.

Table B-5 (continued)

1952	1953	1954	1955	1956	1957	1958	1959	1960	1961	1962
30.60	32.90	31.06	32.25	38.08	39.79	34.06	36.44	39.38	38.11	41.24
12.56	13.19	12.88	12.50	15.71	16.68	12.01	12.71	15.13	14.29	15.36
5.88	6.26	6.24	5.84	7.63	8.03	5.48	5.78	7.18	6.27	7.03
2.03	1.62	1.00	1.08	1.68	2.54	1.63	1.35	1.91	1.39	1.41
.39	.48	.44	.44	.60	.60	.46	.52	.68	.69	.68
.70	.80	.69	.81	1.08	1.28	.92	.91	1.10	1.10	1.27
.86	.99	1.30	1.13	1.69	1.06	.56	.64	.89	.75	.83
.46	.78	1.34	.67	.44	.54	.37	.39	.42	.38	.47
.33	.35	.36	.50	.69	.57	.40	.53	.62	.51	.58
1.11	1.24	1.11	1.21	1.45	1.44	1.14	1.44	1.56	1.45	1.79
6.69	6.94	6.64	6.66	8.08	8.66	6.54	6.94	7.95	8.02	8.33
.77	.81	.76	.72	.80	.85	.74	.82	.92	.98	.99
.43	.38	.33	.37	.46	.41	.29	.41	.53	.50	.61
.36	.41	.46	.52	.80	.81	.58	.63	.75	.68	.72
1.39	1.43	1.14	1.04	1.46	1.72	1.32	1.24	1.60	1.62	1.56
3.20	3.34	3.38	3.44	3.89	4.17	3.01	3.14	3.28	3.37	3.56
.15	.16	.13	.15	.20	.20	.13	.19	.23	.22	.23
.38	.40	.45	.44	.48	.49	.47	.51	.64	.65	.66
1.40	1.31	.85	.92	1.23	1.40	.75	.92	1.03	.67	.85
1.50	1.56	1.51	1.60	1.71	1.77	1.50	2.02	1.94	1.85	2.07
2.63	3.12	2.64	2.49	3.32	4.25	4.30	3.90	3.95	3.90	3.90
.91	1.13	.90	1.16	1.32	1.43	1.33	1.42	1.63	1.44	1.43
1.35	1.49	1.52	1.86	2.56	2.94	2.53	2.63	3.11	3.20	3.61
5.56	6.31	6.51	7.49	8.36	7.37	7.20	8.21	8.44	8.46	9.52
4.70	4.78	4.23	4.23	3.86	3.96	4.44	4.63	4.15	4.30	4.50

Manufacturing and Petroleum Extraction

The same deflation procedure was followed for all manufacturing industries except petroleum and coal, which will be discussed later.

The plant and equipment components of fixed investment were separately deflated. The price index used to deflate plant expenditures was the same for all manufacturing industries, as was the case for the equipment price index. The breakdown of expenditures in current dollars between plant and equipment, however, was determined independently for each industry.

Plant expenditures and equipment expenditures are reported separately for the manufacturing *establishments* in each industry in the *Annual Survey of*

TABLE B-6. *Estimated Value of Production Facilities Acquired Through War Surplus Disposal, 1946–58*

(In millions of dollars)

Industry or Sector	1946	1947	1948
All Industries	786	596	287
Manufacturing and petroleum extraction	414	141	104
Durable goods industries			
Primary metals	290	43	45
Electrical machinery and equipment	26		6
Machinery, except electrical	12	2	3
Motor vehicles and parts	7	4	17
Nonautomotive transportation equipment	20	17	2
Stone, clay, and glass	2		4
Other durable goods	7		2
Nondurable goods industries			
Chemical	28	1	18
Petroleum and coal (including petroleum extraction)	11	73	6
Rubber	10		
Nonrail transportation	372	455	183

Manufactures of the United States Bureau of the Census. These data were used to calculate the ratio of plant expenditure to total capital expenditure in each postwar year for each industry. These ratios were then applied to the OBE-SEC investment data based on *company* reports, on the assumption that the same proportions would hold under either basis of classification. The final result was a breakdown of the OBE-SEC data into separate plant and equipment series in current dollars for each industry. The estimates of plant expenditure were deflated by the Boeckh Construction Cost Index for Commercial and Factory Buildings in the United States Bureau of the Census, *Historical Statistics of the United States* (1960), page 385, shifted to the base 1954 = 100. Equipment expenditures were deflated by the United States Bureau of Labor Statistics Wholesale Price Index for Producer Finished Goods for Manufacturing Industries.

The petroleum industry required special treatment because of its combination of manufacturing and mining activities. A weighted index of prices of capital goods for mining and refining operations was calculated for each year. For 1946–54, the index was based on three components. The price indexes for oil and gas drilling and for oil field machinery are those implicit in the estimates of those components in the national income accounts. The implicit price index for all manufacturing investment from the same source was used to deflate refining expenditures. The price indexes were weighted each year by the corresponding estimates of real investment expenditure in each category. The procedure was similar for 1955–62, except that data were lacking on the price and quantity of expenditures on oil field machinery, so that it was necessary to use crude extrapolation procedures for this component of the index.

Table B-6 (continued)

1949	1950	1951	1952	1953	1954	1955	1956	1957	1958
33	19	12	16	1	5	25	4	1	3
33	19	12	16	1	5	25	4	1	3
12	6	12	11			4			3
4									
4	7			1					
							3		
10	2							1	
1									
1	3		5		5	21			
	1								

Railroads

The deflator was the United States Interstate Commerce Commission Index of the Cost of Road and Equipment, taken from the *Schedule of Annual Indices for Carriers by Railroad* (mimeographed). The index comprises 77 asset categories.

Nonrail Transportation

A breakdown of total investment between plant and equipment is available in the OBE-SEC data for 1958, which indicates that plant accounted for 25 percent of investment in that year. The same percentage was applied to the investment data for all years to estimate the plant component for purposes of deflation. The series of estimated plant expenditure was deflated by the implicit price index for nonresidential construction in the national income accounts. The equipment component was deflated by the implicit price index for producers' durable equipment from the same source.

Electric and Gas Utilities

The Handy Indexes of Construction Costs of Electric Light and Power and of Gas Plants were used to deflate capital expenditures in the two industries. See *Historical Statistics of the United States* (1960), page 386.

TABLE B-7. *Indexes of Prices of New Plant and Equipment, All Industries, 1946–62*

(1954=100)

Industry or Sector	1946	1947	1948	1949	1950	1951
All Industries	63.6	74.3	81.2	83.7	85.9	93.7
Manufacturing and petroleum extraction	63.4	73.2	80.4	82.8	85.3	93.4
Durable goods industries	62.7	72.9	80.4	83.8	85.5	94.1
Primary metals	62.8	72.9	80.3	83.5	86.1	94.1
Electrical machinery and equipment	63.1	73.1	80.3	83.4	86.3	94.0
Machinery, except electrical	63.0	72.9	80.3	83.4	86.2	94.2
Motor vehicles and parts	63.1	72.9	80.2	83.7	86.1	94.3
Nonautomotive transportation equipment	63.0	73.1	80.3	83.7	86.3	94.0
Stone, clay, and glass	62.8	72.8	82.8	83.4	86.2	94.3
Other durable goods	63.0	72.9	80.3	83.5	86.1	94.2
Nondurable goods industries	63.8	73.3	80.4	82.5	84.8	92.8
Food and beverage	62.9	72.9	80.2	83.3	86.1	94.1
Textile	63.0	73.0	80.2	83.6	86.2	94.5
Paper	63.0	73.0	80.2	83.6	86.2	94.5
Chemical	62.8	72.9	80.4	83.4	86.1	94.3
Petroleum and coal (including petroleum extraction)	65.7	73.9	80.6	81.3	82.9	90.7
Rubber	63.2	73.0	80.3	83.5	85.7	94.3
Other nondurable goods	63.0	72.9	80.4	83.6	86.1	94.3
Railroads	70.7	78.3	85.7	86.0	87.8	93.3
Nonrail transportation	65.6	76.3	83.1	85.9	88.0	95.8
Electric utilities	56.9	66.1	72.8	77.0	80.7	90.2
Gas utilities	57.4	67.6	75.0	78.8	82.0	88.9
Telephone communication	73.1	84.3	84.7	86.9	91.6	96.7
Commercial and other	62.6	75.0	82.1	85.2	86.8	94.3
Farming	64.2	75.2	84.2	86.6	87.2	95.8

Telephone

The index is a weighted average of indexes of costs of telephone apparatus, commercial buildings, telephone poles in place, and wages in building trades. See Ulmer, *op. cit.*, pages 370–71 for a complete description. I have extended the index to 1960, using Ulmer's sources and methods. For 1961–62, the index was extrapolated by the Fuller Construction Cost Index for commercial buildings, reported regularly in the *Construction Review.*

Commercial and Other

The Department of Commerce estimates of the volume of commercial building construction, as published regularly in *Construction Review*, provided the

Table B-7 (continued)

1952	1953	1954	1955	1956	1957	1958	1959	1960	1961	1962
96.1	98.4	100.0	102.9	109.4	115.0	118.0	121.2	122.6	123.7	125.5
95.9	98.5	100.0	103.6	110.7	116.2	118.9	121.8	123.4	124.5	125.9
96.7	98.9	100.0	103.5	111.4	117.4	120.4	123.5	124.9	125.5	126.8
96.6	98.7	100.0	103.5	111.3	117.1	120.1	123.1	124.8	125.3	126.7
96.5	98.8	100.0	103.6	111.3	117.0	120.2	123.3	124.8	125.4	126.9
96.6	98.8	100.0	103.6	111.4	117.1	120.4	123.3	125.0	125.6	126.9
96.5	98.7	100.0	103.5	111.8	118.6	121.3	124.0	125.5	126.0	127.3
96.3	98.9	100.0	103.4	110.8	116.5	119.4	122.6	124.3	125.0	126.3
96.8	98.6	100.0	103.5	111.2	117.2	120.2	123.0	124.7	125.3	126.6
96.6	98.7	100.0	103.5	111.2	117.6	120.2	123.2	124.8	125.4	126.8
95.4	98.3	100.0	103.7	110.2	115.1	117.8	120.6	122.2	123.8	125.2
96.6	98.7	100.0	103.4	111.4	117.6	120.4	123.3	125.0	125.6	126.9
96.7	98.7	100.0	103.4	111.8	118.3	121.0	123.7	125.3	125.9	127.1
96.8	98.7	100.0	103.5	111.6	117.9	120.8	123.7	125.3	125.9	127.0
96.9	98.7	100.0	103.5	111.7	117.9	120.5	123.5	125.1	125.7	126.9
94.1	97.7	100.0	104.0	108.7	112.2	114.6	117.2	118.0	121.1	122.8
96.9	98.8	100.0	103.4	111.7	118.3	121.8	124.2	125.7	126.4	127.1
96.7	98.8	100.0	103.6	111.2	118.0	120.5	123.4	125.2	125.7	126.9
96.0	99.4	100.0	102.4	110.4	116.1	118.9	121.4	121.6	121.0	120.7
97.2	99.0	100.0	102.7	109.4	115.7	118.6	121.4	121.8	122.0	122.2
92.4	97.2	100.0	103.0	111.7	118.8	122.0	124.2	124.0	122.6	123.1
91.0	94.2	100.0	104.5	113.8	121.2	125.5	130.3	133.6	135.2	137.5
95.4	98.2	100.0	101.3	105.7	109.1	114.4	116.9	118.8	122.7	128.2
96.4	98.1	100.0	102.7	108.3	113.7	116.8	120.0	121.8	124.3	126.6
99.6	100.2	100.0	101.3	105.2	110.9	113.1	119.0	119.7	119.4	120.8

basis for the breakdown of the OBE-SEC investment data between plant and equipment for purposes of deflation. For this purpose, "commercial construction" was defined to include stores, restaurants, and garages; office buildings and warehouses; social and recreational buildings; and nonhousekeeping residential units. (See Frederick C. Schadrack, "Capital Formation in Commercial Real Estate" [Ph.D. dissertation, Univ. of California, 1960], Chap. 1, for the rationale for including social and recreational and nonhousekeeping residential buildings in the definition of commercial real estate.) The Commerce deflators were accepted for these components of plant investment. Next the estimates of commercial building in current dollars were subtracted from the OBE-SEC estimates of plant and equipment expenditure in the commercial and other sector to yield residual estimates of equipment expenditure in current dollars. The latter were deflated by the BLS Wholesale Price Index of Producer Finished Goods for Nonmanufacturing Industries.

Farming

Price indexes provided by the Department of Agriculture were used to deflate the various components of farm investment already described.

Depreciation

Annual estimates of depreciation were derived from the following formula:

$$D = dK + \frac{d}{2} I,$$

where D is depreciation, K is the net value of the stock of plant and equipment at the beginning of the year, d is the depreciation rate for the year, and I is gross investment during the year. Since capital stock is measured net of accumulated depreciation, the application of a proportional depreciation rate implies a declining-balance depreciation model. A charge of a half year's depreciation is made against current investment according to the standard convention.

In order to apply the formula to a given period, it is necessary to have annual estimates of gross investment and depreciation rates (which may or may not be constant), plus a benchmark estimate of net capital stock for some year during the period. Given the benchmark stock, one may cumulate the estimates of capital stock either forward or backward in time by estimating depreciation each year and subtracting it from gross investment to derive the net change in capital stock during the year. The derivation of the estimates of depreciation rates and benchmark stocks will be described in that order.

Useful Lives and Depreciation Rates

The information on useful lives and depreciation rates is drawn from several sources, depending on the nature of the available data for the various industrial sectors.

Manufacturing and Petroleum Extraction

The estimates of average useful lives were developed from the corporate income tax records published by the United States Internal Revenue Service in *Statistics of Income*. These records include data on annual depreciation charges and gross depreciable assets, from which implied composite straight-line depreciation rates may be derived. Assuming that a certain type of asset is depreciated at a constant rate, the gross stock of that asset type will be the sum of the gross investment expenditures undertaken in all previous years of its useful life span. Each year's gross investment will be depreciated at an annual rate determined by the reciprocal of the useful life of the asset type. Total depreciation for the year will therefore equal the product of the depreciation rate and the gross stock. Thus one may solve for the depreciation rate, or the reciprocal of the useful life, by dividing the annual depreciation charge by the gross stock. In symbols:

$$d = \frac{\frac{1}{a} \sum_{n=t-a}^{t} I_n}{\sum_{n=t-a}^{t} I_n}, \tag{B.1}$$

where d is the depreciation rate, a the useful life, and I_n the gross investment of year n.

If two or more assets groups with different average lives are being depreciated, the calculated depreciation rate will be a weighted average of the separate rates. In the case of two asset groups, the average composite depreciation rate will be:

$$d = \frac{\frac{1}{a'} \sum_{n=t-a'}^{t} I'_n + \frac{1}{a''} \sum_{n=t-a''}^{t} I''_n}{\sum_{n=t-a'}^{t} I'_n + \sum_{n=t-a''}^{t} I''_n}, \tag{B.2}$$

where the primes identify the two asset groups. This is the rate which, if applied to the gross stock of all assets, would yield the same annual depreciation charge as is found by adding the depreciation streams from the separate stocks. The reciprocal of the average depreciation rate is the average composite life of the assets.

Patrick Huntley has shown that a progressive decline occurred during the postwar years in the average composite life of assets in each (two-digit) manufacturing industry, as measured from the corporate income tax records using the above procedure.[4] I have assumed, as did Huntley, that this postwar downtrend of average useful lives resulted from a growing proportion of shorter-lived assets purchased in postwar years as compared with longer-lived prewar assets, and I have accordingly depreciated postwar acquisitions at a higher rate than is applicable to prewar assets. Thus the gradual rise of the implicit depreciation rates on the total stock of assets shown in Table B-8 reflects a gradual increase in the relative importance of postwar acquisitions to the stock.

One important reason for the shorter average life of postwar acquisitions is the rise in the ratio of equipment to plant expenditures, as compared with prewar

[4] See his "State Distribution of Manufacturers' Plant and Equipment in Place, 1954–56" (Ph.D. dissertation, Univ. of North Carolina).

TABLE B-8. *Annual Declining-Balance Depreciation Rates, All Industries, 1946–62*

(In percent)

Industry or Sector	1946	1947	1948	1949	1950	1951
All Industries	5.57	6.07	6.44	6.63	6.75	6.87
Manufacturing and petroleum extraction	8.60	9.16	9.50	9.72	9.86	10.02
Durable goods industries	8.42	9.15	9.59	9.85	10.05	10.29
Primary metals	7.06	7.27	7.43	7.55	7.62	7.71
Electrical machinery and equipment	10.54	12.15	12.92	13.43	13.82	14.14
Machinery, except electrical	9.83	10.83	11.40	11.76	12.03	12.28
Motor vehicles and parts	8.69	9.56	10.00	10.27	10.48	10.78
Nonautomotive transportation equipment	8.23	8.57	8.78	9.00	9.15	9.45
Stone, clay, and glass	7.72	8.25	8.72	8.97	9.16	9.46
Other durable goods	8.97	9.91	10.53	10.92	11.24	11.61
Nondurable goods industries	8.73	9.16	9.45	9.62	9.73	9.84
Food and beverage	9.43	10.00	10.47	10.77	10.97	11.12
Textile	7.14	7.61	8.02	8.32	8.52	8.72
Paper	7.89	8.28	8.62	8.81	8.96	9.10
Chemical	9.70	10.39	10.73	10.95	11.09	11.27
Petroleum and coal (including petroleum extraction)	8.49	8.61	8.74	8.84	8.88	8.94
Rubber	9.96	10.47	10.74	10.94	11.09	11.21
Other nondurable goods	9.12	9.82	10.23	10.53	10.74	10.85
Railroads	2.55	2.56	2.57	2.58	2.64	2.70
Nonrail transportation	9.17	10.61	11.56	12.01	12.32	12.70
Electric utilities	5.37	5.48	5.48	5.46	5.45	5.44
Gas utilities	3.30	3.30	3.30	3.30	3.30	3.30
Telephone communication	8.50	8.52	8.40	8.28	7.96	7.92
Commercial and other	4.92	5.49	5.91	6.04	6.14	6.27
Farming	4.74	5.01	5.40	5.89	6.24	6.32

years.[5] Rough experimental calculations suggest, however, that this factor fails to explain all of the observed decline of average useful lives. That is, a weighted average postwar life derived by applying rough estimates respectively of the stock of plant and that of equipment in 1954 to estimates of the prewar useful lives of the two asset types, indicates a decline in the composite life from the prewar level. But it is a considerably smaller decline in most industries than is shown by the income tax data on depreciation and gross fixed assets.

Another factor which may have substantially affected the trend of average composite life in some of the less homogeneous manufacturing groups is shifts in the relative importance of sub-industries having assets with differing average lives.

[5] *Ibid.*, pp. 141–43 and pp. 174–76; Donald G. Wooden and Robert C. Wasson, "Manufacturing Investment Since 1929," *Survey of Current Business* (November 1956), pp. 8–20.

Table B-8 (continued)

1952	1953	1954	1955	1956	1957	1958	1959	1960	1961	1962
6.98	7.07	7.13	7.16	7.16	7.21	7.17	7.09	7.06	7.03	6.99
10.15	10.26	10.37	10.45	10.53	10.58	10.60	10.62	10.66	10.70	10.76
10.48	10.65	10.83	10.98	11.11	11.20	11.22	11.25	11.30	11.36	11.47
7.82	7.90	7.94	7.96	8.01	8.04	8.09	8.10	8.12	8.14	8.14
14.45	14.78	15.08	15.25	15.46	15.60	15.73	15.77	15.87	15.98	16.06
12.57	12.82	13.02	13.14	13.29	13.46	13.53	13.60	13.68	13.74	13.80
11.05	11.27	11.47	11.64	11.76	11.87	11.91	11.90	11.94	11.98	12.03
9.85	10.30	10.77	11.01	11.08	11.16	11.16	11.21	11.24	11.26	11.31
9.67	9.86	10.00	10.19	10.36	10.55	10.64	10.73	10.82	10.91	10.95
11.94	12.20	12.40	12.59	12.77	12.91	13.01	13.12	13.22	13.32	13.41
9.93	9.99	10.04	10.06	10.09	10.11	10.12	10.13	10.16	10.18	10.21
11.25	11.34	11.46	11.53	11.61	11.67	11.70	11.78	11.84	11.87	11.95
8.85	8.95	9.02	9.08	9.18	9.24	9.28	9.35	9.41	9.49	9.63
9.19	9.27	9.36	9.42	9.51	9.58	9.64	9.64	9.72	9.74	9.75
11.46	11.58	11.70	11.78	11.84	11.92	11.98	12.01	12.06	12.10	12.15
8.99	9.02	9.04	9.05	9.05	9.05	9.04	9.03	9.04	9.03	9.02
11.35	11.52	11.70	11.67	11.82	11.82	11.94	12.00	12.00	12.18	12.10
10.98	11.14	11.24	11.34	11.47	11.56	11.61	11.68	11.76	11.82	11.89
2.78	2.78	2.82	2.82	2.86	2.94	3.00	3.00	3.03	3.09	3.09
13.06	13.38	13.71	13.88	14.20	14.31	14.47	14.61	14.78	14.94	15.08
5.36	5.51	5.43	5.43	5.43	5.43	5.42	5.42	5.41	5.41	5.42
3.40	3.60	3.80	3.80	3.80	3.90	3.90	3.90	3.90	3.90	3.90
7.78	7.74	7.68	7.74	7.84	9.22	9.22	9.32	9.42	9.50	9.50
6.37	6.42	6.41	6.34	6.24	6.09	5.87	5.66	5.48	5.26	5.07
6.34	6.32	6.28	6.26	6.15	5.97	5.96	5.84	5.76	5.80	5.72

Thus compositional shifts may account for much of the observed decline in average lives of assets used in manufacturing. It appears, nevertheless, that a general reduction of expected lives of many types of plant and equipment also occurred. *Bulletin F*, the United States Treasury manual which is the primary source of information on prewar useful lives, reflects the average experience of the 1930's with its low standards of obsolescence. Although used until quite recently as a guideline for fixing expected lives when the taxpayer's own records were inadequate to establish probable service lives, *Bulletin F* has never been binding, and it is clear that many companies have been able to demonstrate to the satisfaction of Treasury officials that their own retirement experience calls for shorter lives.

The prewar and postwar lives used to estimate depreciation allowances in the various manufacturing industries are listed in Table B-9. The prewar lives were taken from Huntley's study. I have computed the postwar lives on the basis of the corporate income tax records for 1954 and 1955. By 1954–55 the influence of prewar acquisitions on depreciation charges and the value of gross fixed assets

TABLE B-9. *Estimated Useful Lives of Prewar and Postwar Acquisitions in Manufacturing Industries and Nonrail Transportation*

(In years)

Industry	Prewar	Postwar
Durable goods industries		
Primary metals	29	24
Electrical machinery and equipment	22	12
Machinery, except electrical	22	14
Motor vehicles and parts	25	16
Nonautomotive transportation equipment	25	17
Stone, clay, and glass	27	17
Other durable goods	24	14
Nondurable goods industries		
Food and beverage	22	16
Textile	29	19
Paper	26	20
Chemical	22	16
Petroleum and coal (including petroleum extraction by integrated producers)	27	24
Rubber	21	16
Other nondurable goods	23	16
Nonrail transportation	24	12

was minor, so the calculated implicit lives largely reflect postwar acquisitions. These were also the latest years in which reported depreciation allowances were largely free from the effects of the adoption of curvilinear depreciation methods under the Internal Revenue Code of 1954 and could therefore be used to infer the composite useful life under a straight-line formula.

The postwar life in each industry was estimated by the ratio of the 1955 values of gross depreciable assets and depreciation charges. The 1955 value of gross assets was taken as the average of the asset values at the end of 1954 and 1955. Accelerated (five-year) amortization on defense facilities was excluded from both depreciation charges and the value of depreciable assets to avoid distortion of normal expected lives from that source. Amortization allowances were published separately from normal depreciation charges in 1955, but it was necessary to estimate amortization for 1954 by linear interpolation between the 1953 and 1955 values. The stock of amortized facilities at the end of 1954 and 1955 was then estimated as five times the corresponding amortization allowances and was deducted from the value of depreciable assets to arrive at the stock of fixed assets excluding amortized facilities.

The reciprocals of the useful lives listed in Table B-9 are composite straight-line depreciation rates. Since the capital stock estimates used in this study are based on a declining-balance depreciation model, the straight-line rates were doubled to arrive at the final depreciation rates underlying the stock estimates. Assets acquired before 1946 were depreciated at the prewar rate and subsequent acquisitions at the postwar rate. The implicit average declining-balance depreciation rate on the total net stock of assets in each postwar year is shown by industry in Table B-8. The implicit rate was obtained by dividing the sum of estimated depreciation on the prewar and postwar acquisitions by the sum of the net depreciated values of the corresponding stocks.

Railroads

I have extended to 1961 Ulmer's series of annual depreciation rates during 1870–1949 (*op. cit.*, pp. 224–25 and Table C-12), and the 1961 rate was held constant in 1962. Ulmer's series is based on unpublished data of the United States Interstate Commerce Commission for the years 1917 and 1949, with the 1917 rate applied to all prior years and with the rates for the years between 1917 and 1949 determined by linear interpolation. The series of annual rates for 1950–61 was compiled from *Annual Reports on Transport Statistics* of the ICC. The rate on equipment is from Table 96. The rate on plant was found by dividing depreciation of way and structures (Table 90) by the value of investment in road property (Table 138). The rates on road and equipment were combined with weights based on the relative importance of the two stocks as shown in Table 138. The declining-balance rate was set at one and one-half times the computed straight-line rate in view of the long life of railroad assets.

Nonrail Transportation

As in the case of manufacturing, prewar and postwar acquisitions were depreciated at different rates. Both the prewar and postwar rates are based on the Internal Revenue Service data on depreciation and fixed assets. The prewar useful life of 24 years is an average for 1939–41, and the postwar life of 12 years is based on 1954 data. The declining-balance rate is set at twice the straight-line rate. In the case of this heterogeneous group, the primary explanation for the pronounced decline in average composite lives was the striking growth in the relative importance of transport by aircraft and motor vehicle. The average useful life of assets in these industries is much shorter than in the rapidly declining street railway industry or the relatively stable pipeline and water transportation industries.

Electric Utilities

Ulmer gives an average life of 37 years for assets installed after 1920 (*op. cit.*, pp. 310–11). This rate agrees closely with the income tax data for 1954 and was used throughout the postwar period. The rate was doubled for our declining-balance estimates.

Gas Utilities

The annual series of depreciation rates for 1946–60 was computed from data on depreciation and the value of utility plant in *Historical Statistics of the Gas Industry* (Tables 191 and 197) and in *Gas Facts* (1960 edition, Tables 176 and 181), both published by the American Gas Association. The 1960 rate was held constant in 1961–62. The implied useful lives vary from about 45 years in the late 1940's to less than 40 years in the late 1950's. Prior to 1946 a constant life of 47 years was assumed on the basis of the estimate of average composite life given in *Bulletin F.* A declining-balance rate of one and one-half times the straight-line rate was assumed for all years.

Telephone

The prewar depreciation rates are from Ulmer, *op. cit.*, page 380. "For 1880, the rate is based on information provided by A.T. & T. whose records indicate that in 1884 the comptroller of the American Bell Telephone Company had suggested that a depreciation rate of 10 percent was applicable to the original cost of plant and equipment." Ulmer interpolated linearly between the 1880 estimate and an estimate for 1950 based on rates prescribed by the Federal Communications Commission for various kinds of plant and equipment. I compiled the depreciation rates for postwar years shown in Table B-8 from reports of 22 Bell Telephone companies in the "Form M Annual Report" to the FCC. The straight-line rates for prewar and postwar years were doubled to provide the declining-balance estimates.

Commercial and Other

The annual depreciation rates shown in Table B-8 are those implicit in the final estimates of depreciation and net stock. The data on depreciation and net stock of commercial buildings were prepared by Frederick Schadrack, *op. cit.* He assumed constant declining-balance depreciation rates of 2.6 percent for stores, restaurants, garages, office buildings, and warehouses; 3.1 percent for social and recreational buildings; and 3.5 percent for nonhousekeeping residential structures. I used a constant depreciation rate of 16.7 percent in preparing the estimates of equipment depreciation. This is twice the straight-line rate based on an average life of 12 years. Twelve years is an average of the lives of office equipment, store equipment, construction equipment, business motor vehicles, and equipment used in hotels, laundries, barber and beauty shops, restaurants, and gasoline filling stations, as given in *Bulletin F.*

Farming

The estimates of depreciation are from the United States Department of Agriculture. The Department uses the following declining-balance depreciation rates: operators' dwellings, 2.0 percent; other structures, 2.7 percent; automobiles 22.0 percent; motor trucks, 21.0 percent; tractors, 18.5 percent; and other machinery and equipment, 14.0 percent. The composite rates shown in Table B-8 are those implicit in the estimates of total depreciation and capital stock.

Benchmark Estimates of Capital Stock

Manufacturing and Petroleum Extraction

The benchmark estimates are for December 31, 1945. They were derived by cumulating estimates of net investment expenditure over the prewar lives of manufacturing assets in each industry as given in Table B-9. The procedure required annual estimates of gross investment in constant dollars going back to the early 1920's.

The estimates of prewar expenditures on plant and equipment in current dollars were prepared in the following way. The OBE-SEC data include estimates for 1939. The 1939 estimates were extrapolated backward by the use of annual data on investment in manufacturing industries prepared by Lowell J. Chawner for the interwar years.[6] Direct estimates of expenditures for plant and equipment in primary metals, motor vehicles, stone, clay, and glass, food and beverages, textiles, paper, lumber, printing and publishing, petroleum refining, rubber, and leather were available from Chawner for the 1920's and 1930's. His estimates of total manufacturing investment were used as an extrapolator for the remaining industries. The investment estimates for all industries were split between plant and equipment for purposes of deflation. The split was the same for all

[6] See the series of articles by Chawner in the *Survey of Current Business* (March 1941, December 1941, May 1942).

industries and was based on the annual breakdown of plant and equipment for total manufacturing provided by Chawner.

It was necessary also to extrapolate the 1939 estimates through 1944. Two extrapolators were used: one for war industries (all durable goods except stone, clay, and glass; chemicals; petroleum and coal; and rubber) and the other for nonwar industries (food and beverages, textiles, paper, other nondurable goods, and stone, clay, and glass). The extrapolating indexes were based on estimates of wartime private capital formation in manufacturing industries prepared by D. Stevens Wilson.[7] For purposes of deflation, the annual estimates of wartime expenditures in each industry were divided between plant and equipment by a linear interpolation of the proportions reported for each industry in the *Census of Manufactures* for 1939 and for 1947.

The series on gross expenditures for plant and for equipment during the 1920's and 1930's were deflated by the price indexes implicit in Chawner's estimates of plant investment and equipment investment for total manufacturing in current and constant dollars. The same deflators were used for all manufacturing industries. The Boeckh Construction Cost Index for Commercial and Factory Buildings was used as the wartime deflator for plant expenditures. Wartime equipment expenditures were deflated by the implicit price index for producers' durable equipment from the national income accounts.

Given the estimates of gross expenditures for plant and equipment in constant dollars, the perpetual inventory method was used to prepare the 1945 benchmark estimates of net capital stock in each industry. The procedure was to cumulate annual estimates of net investment before 1945 over the prewar useful lives shown in Table B-9. That is, the depreciation for each year was estimated as a given percentage of the net stock at the beginning of the year and of investment outlays during the year and was subtracted from gross investment to determine the net change in capital stock during the year. The depreciation rate was twice the straight-line rate implicit in the prewar useful life for each industry. The cumulation was performed as if there had been no capital stock in existence prior to the year during the early 1920's in which the cumulation was begun. The error introduced by this assumption is minor, since only a small fraction of the net stock in existence before the cumulation period would survive until 1945 even under declining-balance depreciation.

Railroads

Ulmer has prepared annual estimates of gross and net capital formation and net capital stock on a straight-line depreciation basis for the period 1870–1950.[8]

[7] See U. S. Department of Commerce, *Survey of Current Business* (June 1945), Chart 3; and (July 1945), Table 4.

[8] *Op. cit.*, Appendix C.

His estimate of net capital stock in 1869 was converted to 1954 dollars and served as the initial benchmark from which I cumulated the net stock, using declining-balance depreciation. The declining-balance rate for each year was set at one and one-half the straight-line rate given by Ulmer.

Nonrail Transportation

The estimate of 1945 capital stock was developed from annual estimates of gross investment for the period 1919–44, using the perpetual inventory method. The estimates of depreciation were based on the prewar useful life shown in Table B-9, using twice the straight-line rate. The estimates of gross investment for 1939–44 are from Ulmer, *op. cit.*, Table B-2. For earlier years, I summed Ulmer's estimates of gross investment for motor transportation (Table B-3), street and electric railways (Table F-1), local bus lines (Table G-1), and miscellaneous industries (Table B-3, column 4 times 3 percent), and added the estimates of construction of petroleum pipelines given in "Construction Volume and Costs, 1915–56," supplement *Construction Review* (U. S. Departments of Commerce and Labor, 1958), p. 4.

Electric Utilities

The benchmark stock estimate for 1945 was derived by the perpetual inventory method from Ulmer's data on gross investment and useful lives covering the period 1881–1945. Capital stock was negligible (less than $100,000) prior to 1881. The gross investment expenditures for 1881–99 were depreciated at a rate based on a useful life of 17 years, and useful lives of 19, 24, 29, 34, and 37 years, respectively, were used for assets acquired in 1900–04, 1905–09, 1910–14, 1915–19, and 1920–45. The useful lives for 1881–99 and 1920–45 were taken directly from Ulmer, *op. cit.*, Table D-21, whereas the lives for the intervening periods are five-year averages of his annual figures. The declining-balance rates are double the implicit straight-line rates.

Gas Utilities

The perpetual inventory method was applied to gross investment estimates for the period 1890–1945. The estimates of investment in natural and manufactured gas are from John W. Kendrick, *Productivity Trends in the United States* (National Bureau of Economic Research and Princeton Univ. Press, 1961), Appendix H, except that this series for natural gas was reduced 15 percent to exclude expenditures for facilities used in the production (mining) of natural gas. The reduction ratio is an average of the ratios for 1945–53 given in *Historical Statistics of the Gas Industry*, Table 213. The price deflator for gross investment is described in Kendrick, *op. cit.*, page 571. The depreciation rate was discussed in the preceding section of this appendix.

Telephone

Perpetual inventory estimates were prepared from Ulmer's data for the period 1880–1945. The data on gross investment and depreciation rates were described in previous sections of this appendix.

Commercial and Other

The derivation of the estimates of the net stock of structures is fully described in Schadrack, *op. cit.* The basic procedure was to derive a benchmark estimate of the value of commercial real estate from the *Census of Governments* (1957) and to carry it forward and backward by use of the annual estimates of commercial construction from the Department of Commerce and the depreciation rates discussed in the previous section of this appendix.

The estimate of equipment stock in 1945 I prepared by using the perpetual inventory method. Annual equipment expenditures for 1929–45 were estimated from data on 21 categories of producers' durable equipment as given in the national income accounts, using constant allocation percentages derived from an unpublished OBE study for 1954. The derivation of the average depreciation rate for equipment used in the sector was described above.

Farming

The estimates of net capital stock are those underlying the published estimates of depreciation of the Department of Agriculture. See *United States Department of Agriculture Handbook No. 118*, pages 17–18, for a description of data and methods.

* * *

This completes the description of the derivation of the set of estimates presented in Tables B-1 through B-4. The depreciation estimate for a given year as shown in Table B-2 is equal to the product of the depreciation rate in Table B-8 and the sum of net stock at the end of the previous year from Table B-4 and one-half the gross investment of the current year from Table B-1. Net investment in any year (Table B-3) is equal to gross investment (Table B-1) *minus* depreciation (Table B-2). Net capital stock at the end of any year (Table B-4) is equal to net stock at the end of the preceding year *plus* net investment for the same year (Table B-3).

APPENDIX C / *Data Used as Independent Variables*

THE PURPOSE OF this appendix is to reproduce the data used as independent variables in the investment regressions. A brief description of the data included in each table is given below.

TABLE C-1. *Gross Output in 1954 Dollars*

The data refer to real gross product originating in each industry. Gross product originating is measured net of the value of materials and services purchased from other industries but gross of depreciation and indirect business taxes in the given industry. The data for nonmanufacturing industries are from Martin L. Marimont, "GNP by Major Industries," *Survey of Current Business* (October 1962), pp. 6–18. The estimates for manufacturing industries were prepared by Charles Schultze and Joseph Tryon and are described in *Prices and Costs in Manufacturing Industries*, Study Paper No. 17, U. S. Congress, Joint Economic Committee Study of Employment, Growth, and Price Levels, 86 Cong. 2 sess. (Jan. 25, 1960). Crude oil and natural gas mining are combined with petroleum manufacturing in all tables in Appendixes B and C.

TABLE C-2. *Price of Output*

Implicit price indexes obtained as ratio of estimates of gross product originating in current and constant dollars. Current dollar estimates for nonmanufacturing industries are published in Marimont, *op. cit.* The current dollar estimates for manufacturing industries were obtained from Schultze and Tryon.

TABLE C-3. *Long-Term Interest Rate*

Moody's bond yields as given in United States Department of Commerce, *Business Statistics* (1961 ed.), Supplement to the *Survey of Current Business*, p. 100, were used for all sectors except farming. The average industrial yield was used for all manufacturing industries and the average yield for public utilities was used for that industry and also for communications. The average corporate bond yield was used in the nonrail transportation and commercial and other sectors. The farm mortgage interest rate is from United States Department of Agriculture, *Agricultural Finance Review* (September 1960), p. 132. The interest rate for the over-all aggregate is an average of the individual industry rates, weighted by gross investment in 1954 dollars from Table B-1.

TABLE C-4. *Money Wage Rate*

The estimates for each industry were obtained by dividing employee compensation by man-hours of production and nonproduction workers. Employee compensation by industry is taken from the official GNP statistics. The man-hour estimates were obtained from Schultze and Tryon, *op. cit.*

TABLE C-5. *Real Price of Capital*

The formula for this variable is $P_k(d+r)/P$. The price of capital goods P_k is from Table B-7. The depreciation rate d is from Table B-8. Product price P and interest rate r are shown in Tables C-2 and C-3. Since d and r were scaled as decimal fractions instead of percentages, the entire compound variable was scaled as a decimal fraction in the regressions.

TABLE C-6. *Ratio of Money Wage and Money Price of Capital*

The formula for this variable is $w/P_k(d+r)$. The money wage w is from Table C-4. Sources of the other variables and an explanation of the scaling of the compound variable are given in the paragraph above.

TABLE C-1. *Gross Output, 1947–60*

(In billions of 1954 dollars)

Industry or Sector	1947	1948	1949	1950	1951	1952	1953	1954	1955	1956	1957	1958	1959	1960
All industries	225.7	235.3	228.7	254.9	267.2	274.1	288.7	282.8	311.2	321.1	322.5	311.1	340.0	348.7
Manufacturing and petroleum extraction	88.24	91.60	86.65	99.16	106.49	109.91	119.58	111.98	126.32	129.46	129.68	119.74	135.86	139.40
Primary metals	8.45	8.78	7.39	9.36	10.26	9.28	10.67	8.70	11.25	11.09	10.67	8.32	9.60	9.60
Machinery industries	13.82	13.96	12.21	14.30	16.83	18.72	20.03	17.58	19.13	21.30	20.61	17.61	21.17	21.87
Motor vehicles and parts	6.25	6.78	6.95	8.94	8.18	7.02	8.90	8.03	11.48	9.22	9.73	7.44	9.73	11.19
Nonautomotive transportation equipment	1.67	1.71	1.61	1.49	2.94	5.22	6.50	6.00	6.10	7.06	7.96	7.24	7.66	7.21
Stone, clay, and glass	2.58	3.00	2.80	3.37	3.72	3.54	3.63	3.52	4.00	4.18	4.12	3.91	4.53	4.53
Other durable goods	13.07	13.51	12.93	14.74	15.39	16.01	17.80	16.56	18.21	18.33	18.16	17.17	19.70	20.07
Food and beverages	10.67	10.46	10.57	10.88	11.10	11.41	11.52	11.73	12.26	12.68	12.68	12.92	13.44	13.82
Textiles	4.14	4.39	4.01	4.56	4.43	4.39	4.56	4.18	4.60	4.64	4.43	4.34	5.01	4.83
Paper	2.86	2.92	2.80	3.37	3.57	3.40	3.72	3.77	4.26	4.46	4.43	4.47	4.91	4.96
Chemicals	4.63	4.97	4.87	5.98	6.71	6.95	7.43	7.38	8.59	9.22	9.61	9.61	10.95	11.62
Petroleum and coal (including petroleum extraction)	7.63	8.31	7.87	8.67	9.76	9.97	10.48	10.35	11.14	11.64	11.62	11.08	11.70	11.71
Rubber	1.45	1.38	1.26	1.50	1.57	1.58	1.70	1.60	1.86	1.78	1.78	1.70	2.04	2.05
Other nondurable goods	11.03	11.42	11.40	12.00	12.05	12.42	12.65	12.58	13.46	13.87	13.87	13.92	15.42	15.94
Railroads	9.7	9.4	7.4	8.7	9.6	9.0	8.8	8.1	9.3	9.7	9.1	8.3	8.6	8.6
Nonrail transportation	7.6	7.7	8.1	9.3	10.6	10.1	10.2	9.9	11.0	11.3	11.6	11.0	12.5	12.8
Public utilities	4.2	4.7	5.0	5.8	6.6	7.1	7.7	8.3	9.4	10.4	11.1	11.6	12.9	13.8
Telephone communication	4.2	4.7	4.8	5.0	5.4	5.8	6.0	6.5	7.3	7.9	8.4	8.6	9.2	9.8
Commercial and other	94.9	97.9	98.5	107.6	110.4	113.4	116.9	117.7	126.5	131.4	132.0	131.0	140.1	142.5
Farming	16.9	19.3	18.3	19.3	18.1	18.8	19.5	20.3	21.4	20.9	20.6	20.9	20.8	21.8

TABLE C-2. *Price of Output, 1947–60*

(1954 = 100)

Industry or Sector	1947	1948	1949	1950	1951	1952	1953	1954	1955	1956	1957	1958	1959	1960
All industries	83.2	89.7	89.7	89.4	98.0	99.4	99.6	100.0	100.0	102.4	106.6	109.4	109.9	110.7
Manufacturing and petroleum extraction	78.5	86.6	87.8	89.9	98.4	98.5	98.6	100.0	101.2	103.8	107.3	109.1	109.4	109.1
Primary metals	62.8	68.7	76.4	79.1	92.4	90.7	96.8	100.0	100.4	108.3	117.5	122.7	121.4	123.6
Machinery industries	73.5	81.3	86.2	89.2	98.4	98.5	96.9	100.0	98.4	101.9	111.0	117.8	116.3	115.9
Motor vehicles and parts	65.6	69.3	80.6	84.9	89.5	106.3	103.2	100.0	101.0	99.9	101.0	97.4	104.8	97.0
Nonautomotive transportation equipment	95.2	114.0	124.8	143.6	118.4	96.9	91.7	100.0	98.8	95.5	100.0	103.2	97.8	99.3
Stone, clay, and glass	77.1	76.7	81.1	84.9	87.9	87.8	95.6	100.0	105.8	105.0	106.8	112.5	113.2	113.2
Other durable goods	79.9	87.9	84.2	92.1	103.6	101.5	98.8	100.0	101.4	106.2	108.2	111.0	109.5	108.9
Food and beverages	78.4	91.3	89.5	91.4	93.4	99.1	102.7	100.0	104.2	103.6	104.5	107.2	109.6	109.5
Textiles	118.1	123.7	110.0	106.8	125.1	112.3	104.6	100.0	103.3	104.3	104.5	102.3	101.6	105.6
Paper	83.9	87.3	85.0	87.5	103.4	101.5	98.9	100.0	99.3	106.7	104.7	103.6	106.1	108.1
Chemicals	86.2	94.6	98.4	95.0	101.9	96.6	96.9	100.0	101.8	98.4	99.4	98.5	99.4	94.5
Petroleum and coal (including petroleum extraction)	69.1	91.0	87.0	88.1	92.0	91.3	94.7	100.0	103.6	108.2	110.5	109.6	114.3	118.1
Rubber	88.3	88.4	88.1	87.3	114.6	119.0	112.9	100.0	103.8	123.0	127.0	127.1	125.1	127.8
Other nondurable goods	85.9	88.7	88.5	86.9	95.4	97.5	100.5	100.0	100.1	103.5	106.4	106.8	104.4	105.9
Railroads	76.3	86.2	100.0	93.1	94.8	104.4	106.8	100.0	95.7	95.9	102.2	102.4	98.8	97.7
Nonrail transportation	84.2	88.3	86.4	82.8	84.0	92.1	98.0	100.0	99.1	101.8	107.8	112.7	107.2	109.4
Public utilities	95.2	93.6	102.0	94.8	97.0	97.2	98.7	100.0	95.7	93.3	94.6	95.7	93.8	94.2
Telephone communication	78.6	78.7	83.3	90.0	94.4	98.3	105.0	100.0	95.9	96.2	98.8	102.3	105.4	105.1
Commercial and other	81.0	86.7	87.7	86.0	94.3	97.1	98.6	100.0	101.1	104.3	109.6	112.5	115.1	117.3
Farming	122.5	123.3	105.5	106.2	130.4	121.3	107.2	100.0	91.6	92.3	94.2	101.9	96.2	95.9

TABLE C-3. *Long-Term Interest Rate, 1947–60*

(In percent)

Industry	1947	1948	1949	1950	1951	1952	1953	1954	1955	1956	1957	1958	1959	1960
All Industries	3.00	3.23	3.18	3.10	3.26	3.32	3.55	3.33	3.41	3.66	4.22	4.17	4.65	4.70
Manufacturing industries	2.67	2.87	2.74	2.67	2.89	3.00	3.30	3.09	3.19	3.50	4.12	3.98	4.53	4.59
Railroads	3.11	3.34	3.24	3.10	3.26	3.36	3.35	3.25	3.34	3.65	4.32	4.39	4.73	4.92
Nonrail transportation	2.86	3.08	2.96	2.86	3.08	3.19	3.43	3.16	3.25	3.57	4.21	4.16	4.65	4.73
Public utilities	2.78	3.03	2.90	2.82	3.09	3.20	3.45	3.15	3.22	3.54	4.18	4.10	4.70	4.69
Telephone communication	2.78	3.03	2.90	2.82	3.09	3.20	3.45	3.15	3.22	3.54	4.18	4.10	4.70	4.69
Commercial and other	2.86	3.08	2.96	2.86	3.08	3.19	3.43	3.16	3.25	3.57	4.21	4.16	4.65	4.73
Farming	4.50	4.50	4.50	4.50	4.60	4.60	4.60	4.70	4.70	4.70	4.70	4.80	4.90	5.00

TABLE C-4. *Money Wage Rate, 1947–60*

(In dollars per hour)

Industry or Sector	1947	1948	1949	1950	1951	1952	1953	1954	1955	1956	1957	1958	1959	1960
All industries	1.19	1.29	1.34	1.42	1.56	1.65	1.75	1.81	1.89	2.02	2.14	2.21	2.32	2.43
Manufacturing and petroleum extraction	1.40	1.53	1.60	1.68	1.84	1.95	2.07	2.15	2.23	2.37	2.52	2.63	2.74	2.86
Primary metals	1.60	1.71	1.80	1.93	2.12	2.30	2.43	2.52	2.68	2.85	3.08	3.29	3.42	3.53
Machinery industries	1.49	1.66	1.74	1.79	1.97	2.11	2.22	2.32	2.39	2.54	2.68	2.84	2.96	3.07
Motor vehicles and parts	1.59	1.75	1.84	2.04	2.26	2.42	2.55	2.67	2.76	2.97	3.14	3.45	3.50	3.61
Nonautomotive transportation equipment	1.65	1.81	1.82	1.88	2.07	2.18	2.35	2.44	2.60	2.72	2.87	3.09	3.29	3.45
Stone, clay, and glass	1.28	1.43	1.51	1.60	1.77	1.84	1.98	2.07	2.18	2.30	2.44	2.55	2.68	2.78
Other durable goods	1.25	1.38	1.45	1.52	1.67	1.78	1.89	1.98	2.04	2.16	2.30	2.41	2.50	2.62
Food and beverages	1.28	1.38	1.43	1.51	1.62	1.71	1.83	1.91	2.00	2.11	2.23	2.32	2.43	2.53
Textiles	1.17	1.31	1.36	1.41	1.51	1.54	1.56	1.59	1.61	1.68	1.75	1.79	1.86	1.95
Paper	1.38	1.51	1.57	1.65	1.80	1.92	2.02	2.10	2.20	2.32	2.45	2.56	2.67	2.78
Chemicals	1.58	1.69	1.79	1.90	2.08	2.20	2.33	2.46	2.57	2.75	2.92	3.09	3.22	3.36
Petroleum and coal (including petroleum extraction)	1.83	2.03	2.14	2.17	2.39	2.56	2.72	2.81	2.87	3.04	3.26	3.41	3.59	3.65
Rubber	1.61	1.62	1.66	1.77	1.95	2.11	2.19	2.25	2.37	2.51	2.70	2.80	2.86	3.02
Other nondurable goods	1.34	1.45	1.49	1.55	1.63	1.68	1.77	1.85	1.88	2.00	2.08	2.17	2.23	2.33
Railroads	1.46	1.61	1.76	1.91	2.10	2.21	2.25	2.31	2.34	2.56	2.74	2.96	3.10	3.19
Nonrail transportation	1.53	1.64	1.70	1.82	1.93	2.04	2.21	2.26	2.38	2.48	2.61	2.70	2.86	2.97
Public utilities	1.48	1.58	1.68	1.78	1.93	2.07	2.22	2.34	2.44	2.56	2.73	2.91	3.05	3.24
Telephone communication	1.50	1.52	1.65	1.71	1.82	1.96	2.07	2.16	2.22	2.36	2.44	2.59	2.77	2.88
Commercial and other	1.30	1.41	1.45	1.52	1.61	1.69	1.79	1.88	1.94	2.05	2.17	2.23	2.32	2.43
Farming	.47	.50	.50	.51	.55	.58	.56	.56	.58	.59	.62	.63	.66	.68

TABLE C-5. *Real Price of Capital, 1947–60*

(In percent)

Industry or Sector	1947	1948	1949	1950	1951	1952	1953	1954	1955	1956	1957	1958	1959	1960
All industries	.080	.084	.090	.093	.096	.099	.105	.105	.108	.115	.123	.122	.129	.129
Manufacturing and petroleum extraction	.110	.115	.118	.119	.122	.128	.135	.135	.140	.150	.159	.159	.169	.172
Primary metals	.115	.120	.112	.112	.108	.115	.114	.110	.115	.118	.121	.118	.128	.128
Machinery industries	.140	.146	.146	.148	.151	.159	.171	.168	.179	.191	.193	.186	.200	.205
Motor vehicles and parts	.136	.149	.135	.133	.144	.128	.139	.146	.152	.171	.188	.198	.194	.214
Nonautomotive transportation equipment	.086	.082	.079	.071	.098	.128	.147	.139	.148	.169	.178	.175	.197	.198
Stone, clay, and glass	.103	.125	.120	.120	.132	.140	.136	.131	.131	.147	.161	.156	.166	.170
Other durable goods	.115	.122	.136	.130	.132	.142	.155	.155	.161	.170	.185	.184	.198	.204
Food and beverages	.118	.117	.126	.128	.141	.139	.141	.146	.146	.162	.178	.176	.184	.188
Textiles	.064	.071	.084	.090	.088	.102	.116	.121	.123	.136	.151	.157	.169	.166
Paper	.095	.106	.114	.115	.110	.116	.126	.124	.131	.136	.154	.159	.165	.166
Chemicals	.110	.116	.116	.125	.131	.145	.152	.148	.152	.174	.190	.195	.206	.220
Petroleum and coal (including petroleum extraction)	.121	.103	.108	.109	.117	.124	.127	.121	.123	.126	.134	.136	.139	.136
Rubber	.109	.124	.130	.135	.116	.117	.130	.148	.148	.139	.148	.153	.164	.163
Other nondurable goods	.106	.119	.125	.133	.136	.139	.142	.143	.150	.161	.174	.176	.192	.193
Railroads	.058	.059	.050	.054	.059	.056	.059	.061	.066	.075	.082	.086	.095	.099
Nonrail transportation	.122	.138	.149	.161	.180	.172	.170	.169	.178	.191	.199	.196	.218	.217
Public utilities	.052	.061	.058	.064	.072	.074	.081	.080	.088	.101	.115	.116	.129	.129
Telephone communication	.121	.123	.117	.110	.113	.106	.105	.108	.116	.125	.148	.149	.156	.160
Commercial and other	.077	.085	.087	.091	.094	.095	.098	.096	.097	.102	.107	.104	.108	.106
Farming	.058	.068	.085	.088	.080	.090	.102	.110	.121	.124	.126	.119	.133	.134

TABLE C-6. *Ratio of Money Wage and Money Price of Capital, 1947–60*

Industry or Sector	1947	1948	1949	1950	1951	1952	1953	1954	1955	1956	1957	1958	1959	1960
All industries	.177	.165	.163	.168	.164	.167	.168	.173	.174	.170	.163	.166	.163	.168
Manufacturing and petroleum extraction	.161	.154	.155	.157	.152	.154	.155	.160	.158	.152	.147	.152	.148	.152
Primary metals	.221	.207	.210	.218	.213	.220	.220	.229	.232	.223	.217	.227	.220	.223
Machinery industries	.145	.140	.139	.136	.133	.135	.134	.138	.136	.130	.125	.129	.127	.130
Motor vehicles and parts	.179	.169	.169	.180	.175	.178	.177	.184	.180	.174	.166	.179	.172	.174
Nonautomotive transportation equipment	.201	.193	.185	.184	.178	.176	.175	.176	.177	.168	.161	.171	.170	.175
Stone, clay, and glass	.162	.149	.155	.157	.152	.150	.153	.158	.157	.149	.142	.145	.143	.144
Other durable goods	.136	.129	.127	.127	.122	.124	.124	.128	.125	.120	.115	.118	.115	.118
Food and beverages	.138	.129	.127	.129	.123	.124	.127	.131	.131	.125	.120	.123	.121	.123
Textiles	.156	.150	.147	.146	.138	.134	.129	.131	.127	.119	.111	.112	.108	.111
Paper	.173	.164	.163	.164	.159	.163	.163	.169	.168	.160	.152	.156	.152	.155
Chemicals	.165	.154	.156	.160	.155	.157	.158	.166	.166	.160	.154	.160	.158	.161
Petroleum and coal (including petroleum extraction)	.219	.217	.227	.227	.222	.228	.226	.232	.226	.223	.221	.228	.226	.227
Rubber	.168	.148	.145	.150	.146	.151	.149	.152	.154	.147	.143	.145	.139	.145
Other nondurable goods	.148	.138	.134	.134	.126	.125	.124	.129	.125	.120	.113	.116	.112	.114
Railroads	.330	.319	.352	.380	.377	.376	.358	.381	.371	.356	.325	.336	.330	.330
Nonrail transportation	.149	.135	.132	.136	.127	.129	.133	.134	.135	.128	.122	.122	.125	.125
Public utilities	.297	.279	.284	.293	.276	.286	.277	.291	.291	.271	.251	.262	.252	.266
Telephone communication	.157	.157	.169	.173	.170	.187	.189	.200	.200	.196	.167	.170	.169	.172
Commercial and other	.208	.190	.189	.195	.183	.184	.186	.196	.197	.193	.185	.191	.187	.193
Farming	.066	.060	.055	.054	.053	.053	.052	.051	.052	.052	.053	.052	.052	.052

Index